BY JAMES F. SIMON

The Judge

In His Own Image: The Supreme Court
in Richard Nixon's America

Independent Journey: The Life of
William O. Douglas

JAMES F. SIMON

THE ANTAGONISTS

Hugo Black, Felix Frankfurter
and Civil Liberties in
Modern America

SIMON AND SCHUSTER

NEW YORK   LONDON   TORONTO   SYDNEY   TOKYO

Simon and Schuster
Simon & Schuster Building
Rockefeller Center
1230 Avenue of the Americas
New York, New York 10020

Designed by Sheree L. Goodman
Manufactured in the United States of America

10   9   8   7   6   5   4   3   2   1

Library of Congress Cataloging in Publication Data

Simon, James F.
    The antagonists : Hugo Black, Felix Frankfurter and civil liberties in modern
America / James F. Simon.
        p.   cm.
    Bibliography: p.
    Includes index.
    1. Frankfurter, Felix, 1882–1965.   2. Black, Hugo LaFayette, 1886–
1971.   3. Judges—United States—Biography.   4. Civil rights—United States
—History.   I. Title.
KF8744.S563   1989
347.73'2634—dc20
[B]
[347.3073534]
[B]   89-35485
                                                                                      CIP

ISBN 0-671-47797-8

For my best friends,
Sara, Lauren, David and Marcia

Contents

THE
ANTAGONISTS

Introduction

THE NATION'S MOST COMPELLING political issues have often been translated into judicial questions placed on the docket of the U.S. Supreme Court. During the first fifty years of our constitutional history, the Court shaped the contours of our democracy, defining the responsibilities of the three branches of the federal government and their relationship to each other and to the states. In the last fifty years, the predominant business of the Supreme Court has been the protection of civil rights and liberties. During this period the Justices have attempted to draw the boundary between necessary governmental authority and the rights of individual citizens. No two members of the modern Supreme Court have been more important in developing the contemporary constitutional debate than Hugo Black and Felix Frankfurter.

Before their Court appointments in the late nineteen-thirties, both Black and Frankfurter had earned national reputations as political liberals, each enthusiastically supporting the social and economic reforms of President Franklin D. Roosevelt's New Deal. Frankfurter had further distinguished himself as one of the most vocal and effective defenders of individual rights of his generation. But shortly after Frankfurter joined Black on the Court in 1939, the two became embroiled in heated, often acrimonious debate over the meaning of the Bill of Rights and the role of the Court in protecting those rights. Their disagreements centered on crucial constitutional questions. Among them: Can the government de-

mand that a public school student participate in a patriotic ceremony? What is the correct constitutional standard of protection
for a criminal defendant? When and how should the Court enforce
the Constitution's equal protection clause on behalf of black
Americans? These issues continue to have currency, as the 1987
Senate confirmation hearings on Judge Robert Bork and the vitriolic presidential campaign of 1988 attest.

Justice Black led the Court's "activist" wing, insisting that the
Justices had a special obligation to protect minority rights. Justice
Frankfurter became the Court's leading exponent of the philosophy of judicial restraint, arguing that the country's best hope for
the protection of democratic values, including minority rights,
rested primarily with the elected branches of government, not the
Court. The central purpose of this book is to trace Black's and
Frankfurter's backgrounds, explain their very different responses
to fundamental constitutional questions and gauge the consequences of their work for the nation.

A second focus of this book is personal, not constitutional. I
have presented off-the-Court portraits of Black and Frankfurter in
an effort to understand them as individuals and as they interacted
with each other. For most of their twenty-three judicial years together, Frankfurter and Black fought tenaciously, their arguments
often tinged with anger and bitterness. Their strong wills and
opposing ambitions for the Court virtually assured deep disagreements that would set them apart personally as well as profession-
ally. But slowly, almost imperceptibly, the antagonists developed
a grudging mutual respect, heightened by their recognition that
they shared basic goals for the nation. And despite their many
public altercations, Black and Frankfurter became genuine friends,
each offering touching support for the other during times of personal need.

I have written this book for the general reader with the hope
that scholars will also find it both interesting and instructive. Since
Black and Frankfurter loom large in our constitutional history,
much has been written in articles and books on each of them.
Earlier scholarship has been extremely useful to me; I believe I
have added to the literature. I have based my study on primary
sources, particularly the papers of Black and Frankfurter. The book
contains quotations from previously unpublished correspondence

between Black and Frankfurter as well as that between the Justices and their colleagues, friends and families. I have also introduced other sources for the first time, including FBI files on Justice Frankfurter during the McCarthy era. Finally, I have interviewed family members, law clerks and members of the U.S. Supreme Court, including Chief Justice William H. Rehnquist and Associate Justices Harry A. Blackmun, William J. Brennan, Jr., and the late Potter Stewart, who provided insights into the personalities and work of the two extraordinary men who are the subject of this book.

Many people helped make this project a finished book. The late Luis Sanjurjo, my literary agent, and Esther Newberg, who succeeded Luis in representing me, encouraged me throughout the project. Alice Mayhew, my editor at Simon and Schuster, offered candid, always insightful, advice. Three colleagues in legal education graciously agreed to read the entire manuscript and provided excellent comments for its improvement: Professor Jethro Lieberman of New York Law School, Professor Harry Wellington of the Yale Law School and Professor G. Edward White of the University of Virginia Law School. My wife, Marcia, served expertly as a general reader who asked questions about the manuscript that lawyers tend to overlook. Over the several years of this project, I have benefited from the research help of the following New York Law School students: Cornelius Courtney, Randolph Iannacone, Blanche Lark and Carol Mann. I also want to thank members of the staff at New York Law School who helped with the manuscript: Maria Del Bagno, Debbie Denhart, Susannah Halston, Dawn Ingraham, Kathleen Mahan, Marie Newman, Mary lin Raisch and the faculty secretaries. Finally, I would like to express my gratitude for the assistance of the staffs in the manuscript divisions of the following libraries: Franklin D. Roosevelt Library, Hyde Park, New York; Harvard Law School Library, Cambridge, Massachusetts; Library of Congress, Washington, D.C.; Princeton University Library, Princeton, New Jersey; and the Yale University Library, New Haven, Connecticut.

Prologue

THE LARGE CAUCUS ROOM overflowed with Washington insiders, reporters, photographers, as well as plain citizens, straining to glimpse the star witness of the Senate's judiciary subcommittee. And at twelve minutes past ten o'clock on the morning of January 12, 1939, a short (five feet five), stocky, neatly dressed law professor from Harvard, the object of their attention, entered the room. He was Felix Frankfurter, who had been nominated a week earlier for the U.S. Supreme Court by President Franklin D. Roosevelt. On this dreary winter day, the third day of the hearings, the nominee appeared to be in a hurry to conclude the subcommittee's business and to take his seat on the highest court in the nation.

With the demeanor of a busy surgeon making his hospital rounds, Frankfurter briskly walked to the front of the room to shake hands with the subcommittee chairman, Senator M. M. Neely of West Virginia. Having dispensed with that formality, Frankfurter took his seat next to the distinguished Washington lawyer Dean Acheson, who was serving as his counsel. Photographers shouted to Frankfurter to strike one pose, then another. After a good-natured attempt at humor and accommodation ("I suppose that's constitutional," he told one insistent photographer), Frankfurter adjusted his pince-nez and settled down to the business of defending his honor and his nomination to the U.S. Supreme Court.

Frankfurter's slight pique at having to appear at the hearings was understandable, since he was the first nominee in the 150-year history of the U.S. Supreme Court to be subjected to a full inquiry by a Senate committee. After Roosevelt had named him to the Court, Frankfurter had at first politely but firmly declined the subcommittee's invitation (which he considered mildly audacious). The proposed public examination was in bad taste, he would later tell the Senators, and potentially damaging to the best interests of the Court which he expected to join. Professor Frankfurter had sent word to the subcommittee, therefore, that he preferred to remain in Cambridge, and he assigned his former law student, Dean Acheson, the task of representing his interests at the Senate hearings. At the time, his decision had seemed eminently reasonable and correct.

After two days of hearings, however, both Frankfurter and Acheson changed their minds. For neither man had anticipated the poisonous swill concocted for the committee by assorted oddballs, witch-hunters and anti-Semites who testified that Frankfurter's confirmation would threaten the Republic. The first witness, Collis O. Redd, the national director (and sole member) of the Constitutional Crusaders of America, had informed the committee that Frankfurter's ideas "correspond to the theories of Russian communism." A second witness, Mrs. Elizabeth Dilling, author of *The Red Network,* had charged that the nominee was part of a conspiratorial Communist network that included President and Mrs. Roosevelt, Supreme Court Justices Hughes, Stone and Brandeis, and two members of the Senate subcommittee itself. Between sobs and table-pounding, a Seneca Indian named Alice Lee Jemison had complained that Frankfurter and his fellow members of the American Civil Liberties Union had been responsible for legislation that undermined a "Christian government" and forced communism upon all American Indians. Other witnesses had opposed the nominee because he was a Jew or foreign-born or "a fixer" for an alien conspiracy.

When Frankfurter finally addressed the committee, he made it clear that he did not come before them as a supplicant, but as one who was certain of his rectitude and qualifications to serve on the U.S. Supreme Court. In his opening statement, the nominee put the Senators on notice that he, not they, would set the rules for the day's session. He would not, he announced, discuss anything he considered inappropriate. "I should think it improper for a nominee no less than for a member of the Court to express his personal views on controversial political issues affecting the Court," he told the Senators. His attitude and outlook on relevant matters had been fully expressed and were available to the members of the subcommittee in his publications, he said, and he had no intention of supplementing his past record with "present declarations."

Following that stern introduction, Frankfurter reviewed his professional background and acknowledged that he had served as legal adviser to the American Civil Liberties Union, the organization that had been attacked as subversive by several earlier witnesses. As a matter of "somewhat droll interest," he said, he had even attempted to help Mrs. Elizabeth Dilling, who had the previous day testified against him. With his approval, Frankfurter told the committee, the ACLU had issued a public protest after Mrs. Dilling had been denied the opportunity to speak on the radio because the broadcasting company disapproved of her planned unfriendly remarks about a Methodist bishop.

Not quite finished with the matter, Senator William Borah of Idaho asked, "What has been the relationship of the ACLU toward communism?"

"So far as I know," Frankfurter replied, "it has no relation to communism" except, he added, to see that Communists get their constitutional rights, along with Henry Ford, the Nazis and the Ku Klux Klan.

Had Frankfurter read the book *Communism,* written by the nominee's close friend, Professor Harold Laski? asked Senator Pat McCarran of Nevada.

"I have read it," Frankfurter replied.

"Do you subscribe to his doctrine as expressed in that volume?" asked McCarran.

Frankfurter objected to the question, suggesting that a satisfactory answer required a broad discussion of his own general views of government.

McCarran ignored the objection and demanded that Frankfurter respond to the question "whether you subscribe to the doctrine?"

In answer, Frankfurter shot back, had Senator McCarran read Laski's book?

"I have just casually glanced at it," was McCarran's somewhat befuddled reply.

"What would you say was its doctrine?"

"The doctrine is the advocacy of communism."

"You see," said Frankfurter with calm disapproval, "we could debate all day on whether that is in fact the doctrine of that book."

McCarran was temporarily embarrassed but not discouraged. He bore in, repeating his question, rephrasing it more provocatively in an effort to draw an intemperate response. "If it [Laski's book] advocates the doctrine of Marxism, would you agree with it?"

Frankfurter's blue eyes fixed coldly on McCarran. "Senator," said Frankfurter evenly, "you have never taken an oath to support the Constitution of the United States with fewer reservations than I have or would now, nor do I believe that you are more attached to the theories and practices of Americanism than I am. I rest my answer on that statement."

Defying Senate rules, the audience cheered and applauded Frankfurter for more than two minutes. The hearing, for all serious purposes, was over. Later that day, the subcommittee voted unanimously to recommend to the full judiciary committee the confirmation of the man whom the great Justice Louis D. Brandeis once called the most useful lawyer in the nation.

When President Roosevelt named Frankfurter to the Court, no responsible American could question the merit of the selection, but only why he had taken so long to make the nomination. Curiously, FDR had passed over the Harvard professor in 1937 when he first had the opportunity to appoint a Supreme Court justice. That year Roosevelt had named the rough-hewn populist Senator from Alabama, Hugo Black, whose zealous loyalty to the President's New Deal appeared to many to be the only palpable credential for his nomination. Almost two years after Black had taken his seat on the Court, important members of the Court itself, including the respected Associate Justice Harlan F. Stone, were chagrined by Black's brash style and idiosyncratic judicial positions.

Felix Frankfurter offered all of the tangible judicial prerequisites that Black so obviously lacked—legal scholarship, deep understanding of the Court, and breadth of vision built over years of study and hard experience as adviser to three Presidents. At long last, Roosevelt had nominated a man for the Court who honored that institution's history and high purpose. Here was no narrow-bore Alabama plaintiff's lawyer, no reformed Ku Kluxer, no stump politician dressed up in a black robe. No Hugo Black.

Frankfurter's Court appointment was hailed by liberal Democrats and anti–New Deal Republicans alike, and ranked, according to *The New York Times,* as one of FDR's most popular appointments during his entire presidency. Naturally, New Dealers responded enthusiastically to the nomination. Frankfurter had served as Roosevelt's confidential adviser, legislative draftsman and one-man employment agency for the administration. His public record on civil liberties had been the pride of liberals for more than two decades, highlighted by his defense of the lowly immigrant anarchists Nicola Sacco and Bartolomeo Vanzetti.

New Dealers and civil libertarians also found a multitude of nonpartisan reasons to salute the appointment. *The New Republic* noted the nominee's "abhorrence of the second rate in thought or action" and concluded that he was "the ideal choice" to succeed Justices Benjamin Cardozo and Oliver Wendell Holmes, Jr. "Frankfurter's whole life has been a preparation for the Supreme Court, and his appointment has an aesthetically satisfying inevitability," added *The Nation.* "No other appointee in our history has gone to the Court so fully prepared for its great tasks."

Support for the Frankfurter nomination from the other end of the political spectrum was no less impressive. In a poll of the conservative legal profession taken by George Gallup's American Institute of Public Opinion only a few months before the appointment, Frankfurter was preferred by more than five to one to fill the vacancy created by the death of Justice Cardozo. And two thirds of the same lawyers described themselves as "anti-Roosevelt."

Conservatives saw much in the nominee's often-expressed philosophy of judicial restraint that was reassuring. *Washington Star* columnist David Lawrence wrote approvingly of Frankfurter, who, he was convinced, rejected Hugo Black's radical politics that had merely been transferred from the U.S. Senate to the U.S. Supreme Court. Professor Frankfurter was too sophisticated a student of American history and too loyal to the country's traditional institutions for that. "From every point of view the President's nomination of Professor Frankfurter to the Supreme Court deserves high praise," the *New York Herald-Tribune* editorialized. "The Court needs its full membership to handle its heavy burden of work and it has been functioning this fall despite one vacancy—through Justice Cardozo's death—and the inadequacies of Justice Black as a jurist, reducing the Court, in effect, to a seven member basis."

As it turned out, the conservatives were more prescient in their forecast than the liberals, for Frankfurter's philosophy of judicial restraint proved to be his pervasive guide, and his record on civil liberties, so exemplary as a private citizen, would be less impressive as a Justice. Ironically, the former member of the Ku Klux Klan, Hugo Black, would become the libertarian hero and liberal leader of the Court—not Frankfurter.

No hint of the great future battles between Black and Frankfurter existed in January 1939. Then, the focus was exclusively on Frankfurter, who, appropriately, was taking the scholar's seat on the Court, filled by Cardozo and Holmes before him. Like his predecessors, Frankfurter had shared with the legendary Holmes (who had been his close friend and mentor) a view of the law as a living, vital force that must change with the times.

Members of the U.S. Senate were confident that Frankfurter, after taking the oath of office, would join the "liberal" wing* of the Court. But the newest Justice would do more than solidify the prevailing majority that had finally stopped judicial interference with New Deal economic and social reforms. Virtually every knowledgeable Court observer assumed at the time that Justice Frankfurter would *lead* a Court majority that would give the broadest scope to Congress's economic and social legislation while closely scrutinizing any governmental impingement on civil liberties.

---

* Although the terms "liberal" and "libertarian" are not, literally, interchangeable, they were commonly used at the time of the Frankfurter appointment to describe a Justice who gave the political branches a wide latitude to effect social and economic reforms while insisting that those political branches not interfere with individual liberties.

Chilling rains flooded cellars and sent swollen streams over low-lying roads in the District of Columbia on January 30, 1939. But the miserable weather was hardly the chief cause for despair. The morning papers reported that Adolf Hitler, addressing the Reichstag on the sixth anniversary of his rise to power, declared that Germany would stand by "its friend's side" if Mussolini's Italy was attacked. The real threat to world peace, Hitler claimed, was posed by "warmongers" and "agitators" in the United States like President Roosevelt's Secretary of the Interior, Harold Ickes.

The "warmonger" singled out by Hitler was, that wet Monday morning, ensconced in the marble courtroom of the U.S. Supreme Court to watch Felix Frankfurter, an Austrian-born Jew, take the oath of judicial office. The demand for seats from official Washington (four Cabinet members were in attendance), as well as from Frankfurter's friends and other admirers, was so great that Court marshals were forced to compromise requirements of safety and decorum by filling the aisles with additional chairs.

Precisely at the stroke of twelve, Chief Justice Charles Evans Hughes entered the chambers through the thick red draperies behind the bench, followed by the other members of the Court. A solemn Felix Frankfurter stepped forward and put his hand on the Bible offered by the Court clerk. In front of Frankfurter sat important representatives of his past—and future: Joseph Beale, one of the Harvard Law School professors who had first measured Frankfurter's brilliance; Marion Denman Frankfurter, the handsome daughter of a Congregational minister who had been his wife for twenty years; Dean Acheson, his counsel and frequent walking companion; Thomas Corcoran and Benjamin Cohen, two of Frankfurter's most illustrious recruits for the New Deal, who, with their former professor's advice and encouragement, had drafted some of FDR's most important economic legislation; Robert Jackson, U.S. Solicitor General and future Associate Justice, who would become Frankfurter's best friend on the Court and implacable foe of their common judicial enemy, Hugo Black; and Frank Murphy, U.S. Attorney General and future Associate Justice, who would reject the judicial philosophy of an embittered Frankfurter and follow the lead of Hugo Black in important civil liberties cases.

But the titanic constitutional struggles on the Court would come later. The moment belonged to Felix Frankfurter, who, in a clear, firm voice, took the judicial oath, walked to the high, cushioned chair to the extreme right of the Chief Justice, and sat down next to Hugo Black.

CHAPTER I

Felix

COFFEE WAS SERVED AT the prince's Paris villa in the Bois de Boulogne. Across the table from the prince and his constant companion, T. E. Lawrence, sat Felix Frankfurter. At the request of U.S. Supreme Court Justice Louis Brandeis, Frankfurter was to assure Arabia's Prince Feisal that as much as American Zionists wanted a Jewish homeland in Palestine, they were also committed to Arab rights in the region. Indeed, the thirty-seven-year-old Harvard law professor was prepared to go further and suggest to the prince that Jew and Arab should not only peacefully coexist in Palestine but should cooperate in economic projects that would bring prosperity to both peoples.

It was not an easy moment for Frankfurter, who on that spring morning in 1919 worried about his manners as much as the message he was to deliver. But once he had decided that he must, as a matter of protocol, accept the prince's offer of coffee in the late morning, and had discovered the coffee served to be of excellent quality, Frankfurter settled into the more familiar role of persuading an important public figure of the correctness of his opinion. He had trained for years for such occasions, first as the top student at Harvard Law School, later as assistant to Henry Stimson, the U.S. Secretary of War, and, remarkably for a man of so few years, as adviser to two U.S. Presidents. Frankfurter prided himself on his ability to impress men of power and wisdom with his fresh insights into complicated public problems. His weapons in arguments were threefold: a meticulous legal mind, a skeptic's respect for compromise in an imperfect world and an effervescent personality that built goodwill and confidence when even reason failed.

The prince listened intently to Frankfurter's views. American Jews shared the Arab world's antipathy toward colonialism, Frankfurter told Feisal, and shared a belief, built on religious tradition and history, in the dignity of man. American Jews could never, as a matter of principle, accept an agreement that benefited Jews at the expense of the Arab peoples. Arabs and Jews were natural allies, not only on the basis of tradition and principle, but now because of their common opportunity. Frankfurter showed Feisal the proposed Zionist borders for Palestine and spoke enthusiastically about plans for a joint hydroelectric project and irrigation system on lands then claimed by France for the Syrians. Jew and Arab could develop the land together, bringing prosperity—and peace.

Frankfurter rose to leave the villa, confident that the meeting had been productive. He and the prince agreed to put their remarks on paper, assured that there was much common ground for agreement. When Frankfurter returned to the Hotel Meurice, he immediately began composing his letter.

Frankfurter's activity in Paris that spring of 1919 was by no means confined to his discussions with Prince Feisal. There was the necessary "nursing" of Chaim Weizmann, the driving force behind the successful Zionist campaign for a Jewish homeland in Palestine. Frankfurter's task was to keep the temperamental Weizmann calm and rational in Paris while he and others moved the negotiations steadily forward. It was no easy assignment. "I've done my 'nursing' of men in my day and all kinds of temperaments—Stimson and Morgenthau and Pound and Wilson,"* Frankfurter wrote, "but Weizmann is the most difficult."

In Paris, as anywhere else he happened to be, Felix Frankfurter was perpetually in motion, reasoning, cajoling, charming his way through dozens of important challenges. One day it was lunch

---

* Henry Stimson, Secretary of War, 1911–1913, 1940–1945, Secretary of State, 1929–1933; Henry Morgenthau, Jr., Secretary of the Treasury, 1934–1945; Roscoe Pound, Dean of the Harvard Law School, 1916–1936; Woodrow Wilson, President of the United States, 1913–1921.

with Arthur Balfour, the author of the Balfour Declaration that had, on behalf of the British government, endorsed a Jewish homeland in Palestine. The next he would be deeply involved in line-by-line drafting of the charter of the International Labor Organization. Frankfurter, who represented the U.S. State Department in the negotiations, had the responsibility of making certain that the terms of the international agreement did not conflict with his government's internal constitutional obligations.

Regardless of the assignment, Frankfurter worked confidently, believing implicitly in his ability to find common ground among men of goodwill. For Frankfurter the enemy of productive negotiation was the man who stood on rigid self-righteous principle. And no one, in Frankfurter's opinion, exemplified that approach more than President Woodrow Wilson. Wilson's doctrinaire idealism, Frankfurter believed, doomed the post–World War I peace talks before they had even begun. The American President would fail, Frankfurter was certain, a victim of his own lofty rhetoric. No one could succeed in the real world of negotiation believing, as Wilson did, that he was "the personal instrument of God." Sunday school lectures had their place, but not at the conference table. "In no time it got to be a sordid pulling and hemming and hawing," Frankfurter observed, "and old hands at this kind of business, Clemenceau and Lloyd George, who knew that life is more complicated, that the tensions and tangles of Europe would be firmer and tougher than ever Wilson realized, just wore Wilson out and down."

Frankfurter himself was never exhausted by the negotiating process. He was convinced that his approach brought results—not total victory, but positive results in an untidy but essentially rational world. Prince Feisal's letter to Frankfurter shortly after their Paris meeting provided dramatic proof to him that his method and goal were exactly right for his times: "We Arabs, especially the educated among us, look with the deepest sympathy on the Zionist movement," Feisal wrote Frankfurter. "Our deputation here in Paris is fully acquainted with the proposals submitted by the Zionist Organization to the Peace Conference, and we regard them as moderate and proper. We will do our best, insofar as we are concerned, to help them through; we will wish the Jews a most hearty welcome home."

It was a singular triumph for Frankfurter. He had sat down with royalty, Arab royalty, to explore common ground for agreement. And the prince and he had done so civilly, rationally, gracefully. Although the future seemed foreboding, Frankfurter was optimistic—for himself and others like him who believed in deliberate, rational progress toward a better world.

Leopold Frankfurter had entered the rabbinical seminary in Vienna, as had six generations of Frankfurter men before him, to begin a life of scholarship and dedication to Judaism. But he cared more about the joys of opera and the theater than the lessons of the Talmud, and by his final seminary year it was apparent—to Leopold, at least—that he should not follow in the family's rabbinical tradition. He decided that he had neither the temperament nor conviction to complete his studies. Let his brother, Solomon, pursue the intellectual life. He would marry his sweetheart, Emma, raise a wonderful, joyful family and make a fortune in business. He did marry Emma, and together they raised a family of six children. But the dream of a fortune, like so many others, was not to be realized. He had too little head for figures and too much heart to compete in the cutthroat world of business. By the early 1890s, it was clear that his dreams would not be realized, in Vienna, at least. Having heard that opportunities were plentiful in America, Leopold set sail alone in 1893 for New York. Within a year he was urging his wife to pack for a new life in America. Despite a rising anti-Semitism in Vienna, Emma was reluctant to leave, but Leopold prevailed and she and their six children arrived at Ellis Island via steerage aboard the *Marsala* in 1894.

Felix, Leopold and Emma's third child, was twelve years old when the family settled in a cold-water flat in a German-Jewish neighborhood on New York's Lower East Side. Felix, who then could not speak a word of English, later told the story that he came home one day declaring, "This man Laundry must be a very rich man because he has so many stores."

Leopold began anew, selling linens door-to-door when the weather was warm and in the apartment during the cold months. But change of scenery did not affect his business fortunes. He was still the dreamer, a bit lazy, and more interested in the theater and opera than the dreary realities of the Lower East Side. When he did make a few extra dollars, which was not often, he bought fruit and delivered baskets to his poorer neighbors.

Emma Frankfurter took over the reins of power within her family. Even if Leopold had not been so weak, Emma would probably have dominated. Her appearance suggested her strong will: intense brown eyes, high cheekbones, full, unsmiling lips. She watched disapprovingly as her husband frittered away his days. She was determined that her children would not follow his example. She sent the two older boys, Fred and Otto, to work. And she told them all, not just Fred and Otto, but Felix, Paul, Estelle and Ella, that life was a serious, perilous enterprise. Jews had a particular responsibility, Emma believed, because they had to be better than the *goyim*. That meant longer work hours, higher standards and vigilant attention to duty.

Felix Frankfurter was acutely aware that his parents presented two vividly different models: "There are two distinct deep strains in me. I know the qualities I have from Father and those that are mine through Mother. My father loved *life*—he thought we were here for joy; joy was his emphasis. Mother's accent from childhood when the burdens of her parents' household fell not a little on *her,* marriage only making a transfer of the immediate interests of her cares, is duty."

Despite Emma Frankfurter's dominant influence on him, Frankfurter seemed to escape his mother's harshest mandates. Unlike his older brothers, Fred and Otto, he did not have to work to supplement Leopold's income. To be sure, Emma made certain that her son took life seriously. But there was more than one way to perform life's duties and in the Frankfurter family there was an acceptable male role model—Leopold's brother, Solomon, had succeeded as a scholar. He wrote extensively in the fields of philology, archeology and bibliography and held the prestigious position of director of the state library in Vienna.

Frankfurter was aware of his uncle's success, but of course he had to forge his own intellectual path in his own country. Fortunately, the Cooper Union was nearby. He traveled through time and space at the Cooper Union, devouring books on literature, politics and history, and he spent hours reading the periodicals from all over the world. He later compared his consuming interest in world affairs to John Stuart Mill's early mastery of Greek and Fritz Kreisler's of the violin: ". . . in me there was no such precocious gift, but early, certainly in the early teens, it became manifest that I was interested in the world of affairs. Why that shouldn't be as pronounced a predilection as playing the fiddle or reading Greek I don't know. Anyway, in my case it was."

The Cooper Union became Frankfurter's university. There were classes in history and geography and the natural sciences during the day. In the evening, beginning at eight o'clock, Frankfurter would treat himself to a two-hour lecture by an outstanding speaker, such as President Jacob Gould Schurman of Cornell, defending American imperialism in the Philippines. And after the formal lecture, the audience would spill out into the streets of the Lower East Side to continue the debate, Hyde Park style.

Between scheduled courses and lectures, Frankfurter would return again and again to the periodicals racks or go outside and, for a penny or two, purchase his own newspaper. The whole idea was to expand not only his knowledge but his world, and he was intent on doing so on a daily basis.

Frankfurter had his early political heroes, most notably the Democratic presidential candidate, William Jennings Bryan. When, in 1896, he heard that Bryan was scheduled to speak in Hoboken, he took a ferry across the Hudson and pushed through the crowd. He was not disappointed. Bryan mesmerized his audience, including young Felix, with his mellifluous voice, beautiful phrasing and romantic, hopeful message. Lecturing the crowd on the virtues of the common man, particularly the Midwest farmer, Bryan pointed an accusing finger at the evil bankers and Eastern big-city politicians who stood in the path of populist progress.

Frankfurter returned to the family apartment, excited and prepared to carry Bryan's fight to his own father, who supported William McKinley and the Republican party. Frankfurter never accepted his father's political views but later did admit that he had been carried away by Bryan's rhetoric. "Bryan was for me with reference to public affairs," he recalled, "what some actor or actress is to an adolescent girl." In other words, Bryan was a matinee idol to his infatuated supporter, the young Felix Frankfurter. Bryan was plagued, Frankfurter later concluded, by a rigid, doctrinaire view of the world that simply could not be squared with realistic human expectations. In years to come Frankfurter would condemn the philosophy and performance of other public men on similar grounds—among them President Woodrow Wilson and, a quarter of a century later, Hugo LaFayette Black.

As a teenager Frankfurter claimed heroes that he clung to for a lifetime. One was a middle-aged Irishwoman named Miss Hogan who taught Frankfurter at P.S. 25 on Fifth Street. At the time, Frankfurter's memories of Austria were still fresh, and the temptation to fall into his native language was overwhelming. But Miss Hogan's insistence on English in her classroom was enforced by verbal and physical sanction, including a few swift uppercuts to the boys who dared to respond to Felix in German. Miss Hogan's lessons on patriotism were rather more cerebral, and she found in Felix a devoted student. Indeed, when he was assigned his first public recitation in English upon his graduation from P.S. 25, Frankfurter selected William Pitt's speech on conciliation with America: "If I were an American, as I am an Englishman, I never would lay down my arms—never, never, never!" Patriotic fervor, first borrowed from others' speeches, soon entered Frankfurter's own vocabulary, and throughout his mature life he never shrank from praising *his* America and lecturing those around him on the opportunities that his adopted country offered.

The greatest gift that America gave Frankfurter was freedom, not just the formal constitutional liberties, but the everyday license to explore its streets and people and institutions. He relished it all, whether the chaotic Lower East Side scenes of pushcarts and peddlers or the elegance of the lecture hall in the Cooper Union where Lincoln had once delivered a famous speech. He embraced New York City, his city, and later thanked his parents for leaving him alone to discover it block by block for himself.

After P.S. 25, Frankfurter followed hundreds of bright, ambitious young immigrant men to the classrooms of the City College of New York. For the next five years Frankfurter attended the combination high school–college on Twenty-third Street and Lexington Avenue for four hours a day, five days a week. The courses in Latin and Greek and history were rigorous, but Frankfurter thrived on the challenge. Despite the heavy course load, he still found time to edit the college magazine, join the chess club and serve as vice president of his senior class. He was best remembered, however, for his skills as a debater representing one of the college's prestigious literary clubs, the Clionia Society.

"I shall never forget his stunning performance," one colleague recalled. "He looked so boyish. His neatness was striking. He spoke such sense. It was as though no opposition could have any significance. He was extremely courteous in manner but he pierced the arguments of his opponents with a deftness and finality that was devastating."

It was often difficult to distinguish the talk in the classroom and formal debate from that in the nearby coffeehouses where Frankfurter and his classmates continued their intense intellectual conversations. They placed no limits on subject matter or debating time. Over tea with rum and a piece of cake, through the night and early morning hours, they delighted and confounded each other arguing about Czarism and revolution and "everything under the sun." The experience was exhilarating but frequently frustrating as well. Frankfurter, even then, prided himself on his ability to cut to the core of an issue and recommend solutions closely linked to political realities. The trouble always came when he was engaged in debate with "speculative Russian intellectuals" who thought "they could reform the world over three glasses of tea." According to Frankfurter, "they couldn't do anything practical to bring [it] nearer their heart's desire because that required effort and subordination of one's own thoughts to the thoughts of other people." He tolerated their passion but detested their theoretical constructs and political naïveté.

In 1902, at the age of nineteen, Frankfurter graduated third in his City College class of 775. He had known for as long as he could remember that he wanted to be a lawyer, and he sat in on classes at New York Law School and New York University's School of Law. But he did not find the classes challenging and dropped out to work as a clerk for the reform-minded Tenement House Commission and to tutor slow high school students.

An agnostic throughout his life, Frankfurter had absolute faith in the opportunities presented by sheer chance. "I have always been of the view that what you want to do is have a general direction and then somehow or other chance takes care of you," he said.

"You want to put yourself in a position where a good chance can take care of you, but it's chance that takes care of you."

To make his point, Frankfurter recounted the story of how he ended up at the Harvard Law School. He had decided to enter Columbia Law School, and one day with ten dollars in his pocket he started toward Columbia's Morningside Heights campus. On his way Frankfurter met a buddy from his City College days who convinced him it was too beautiful a day to spend with application forms at Columbia. And so the two young men spent the day at Coney Island. Before Frankfurter could try again to enter Columbia, he fell ill with a severe flu. His doctor advised him to leave the congested city for the fresh air of the country. To Frankfurter anything outside New York City was country, and when the brother of an acquaintance suggested the Cambridge, Massachusetts, campus of the Harvard Law School, Frankfurter made up his mind. "I don't agonize over things," said Frankfurter. "I don't consult a thousand people. I don't dramatize life. You know, you just go."

Emma Frankfurter packed her son's trunk in preparation for his first year in the "country" at Harvard. Felix had never been to Cambridge or Boston before, and immediately upon arrival began to explore with the same delight and curiosity with which he had examined the wonders of New York City. There were free lunchtime concerts on campus, regular trips to the Boston Museum of Fine Arts and many hours spent at the Germanic Museum and library. On Friday afternoons he attended a debating class for law students given by Professor Charles Copeland ("Copey" to his student friends). "You go off like an alarm clock," Copeland gently admonished the fervent Frankfurter. "Don't talk so fast."

But Frankfurter did not slow down, whether talking or roaming from concert to lecture hall to library. He was consumed by the opportunities. He was also awed by his new classmates. They came from the Plains, and little towns in the Southwest, and elegant mansions in the nation's capital, the sons of railroad brakemen, Methodist ministers and Cabinet officers. A poor Midwestern classmate told Frankfurter about "gut rot" liquor, and another, from the Maine woods, confessed that he had thought all

Jews were "village peddlers" and was relieved to discover that Frankfurter, the first Jew he had actually met, was not.

All 211 of his classmates, he was convinced, were giants, both physically and intellectually. "The first day I went to my classroom," Frankfurter recalled, "I had one of the most intense frights of my life. I looked about me. Everybody was taller." And smarter, he thought. All seemed to answer their professors' intimidating questions with eloquence and a perfect command of the subject. "My god, this is a place for giants," Frankfurter said after hearing the recitation of one impressive classmate, "not for a little minnow like me."

At five feet five inches, Frankfurter could not do anything about this physical disadvantage. But he could still outperform the *goyim,* as Emma Frankfurter had warned that he must. And he did so spectacularly, standing at the top of his class at the end of the first year and maintaining that number one position for the entire three years he was at Harvard. One of his examination papers was so extraordinary that it was kept by a member of the faculty to be read aloud to later generations of Harvard law students.

Frankfurter took considerable satisfaction in his academic triumphs over his taller, seemingly more formidable colleagues. He remembered one tall handsome fellow "like a race horse in the Derby," and a second strapping student who was a great football hero. "These two fellows seemed to know everything," said Frankfurter, but then reported that both had flunked out at the end of the first year. The problem, Frankfurter archly observed, was that the football player considered the classroom to be like the football field. "You take the ball and run with it," he said, "but he didn't have the ball."

Frankfurter considered Harvard a perfect meritocracy where hard work and talent were rewarded, and all that was unworthy was discarded. Wealth did not matter. Neither did one's religion nor skin color nor, as Frankfurter put it, "your father or your face." The system was crucially weighted in favor of the best, that is, those like Frankfurter who could compete successfully in the classroom.

Frankfurter described with approval the process at work in selection and resignation from the *Harvard Law Review.* At the end of the first year the top students were selected for the *Review,* and if, at the end of the second, the high academic rank was not maintained, the member resigned. It was an unwritten rule, but among the honorable men on the *Harvard Law Review* it was rigidly observed. "In my day it happened that two sons of men of distinction and high influence in the country fell below the rank of excellence. They just resigned. That was all there was to it."

Frankfurter worshiped Harvard during his student days and for the rest of his life. Harvard students were the best, and Frankfurter was impatient with dissent from those who favored law schools in New Haven or elsewhere in the world. Legal education at Harvard was, he maintained, quite simply one of life's transcending human experiences.

If Harvard was Frankfurter's place of worship, the Law School faculty became his priesthood. "Giants they were," said Frankfurter, "and I revere their memory because they seem to me to represent the best products of civilization—dedication of lives of great powers to the pursuit of truth, and nothing else, complete indifference to all the shoddiness, pettiness and silliness that occupies the concern of most people who are deemed to be important or big."

The high priest was, naturally, Dean James Barr Ames. In class Ames could turn the most muddled question by a student into a pristine exposition of legal principle. With his elbow on his desk, and chin resting neatly in the palm of his hand, Dean Ames would reply to a hopelessly confused student inquiry, "If I understand what you mean, you are asking whether . . ." And the student then gratefully embraced the dean's restatement of the question.

Like other members of the faculty, Ames did not do his research in an individual office, but rather in the stacks of the law library. The dean invited interruptions by avid students like Felix Frankfurter, who remembered walking away "on clouds" from an intense, impromptu seminar with Ames.

When Frankfurter's third-year roommate, Morris Raphael Cohen, audaciously questioned Dean Ames's contribution to legal education, citing his relatively sparse publication record, Frankfurter rose indignantly to the defense. "What he left behind him is that which Pericles says in his funeral oration is the most important thing," said Frankfurter. "His deposit is in the minds of men. He excited and touched more first-rate minds in the profession of law, I suppose, than any man who ever had pupils."

While Frankfurter argued that Dean Ames had the most original mind and was the best teacher that he ever encountered, he also insisted that every other member of the Harvard Law School faculty was superb—superb in training, superb in presentation, superb in publication. The best.

Take Professor Joseph H. Beale. Frankfurter marveled at Beale, who by logic and facile verbal gyrations, could send his students through the most improbable intellectual hoops. His legal world had no blemishes, blotches or stray matter. Irreconcilable precedents were reconciled; ignorant, wrongheaded judges became, miraculously, a part of a seamless rational legal system. The professor could straighten out the greatest confusion, although Frankfurter knew that Beale's clarity belied the law's essential untidiness. "He was a theologian . . . rather than a lawyer—a legal theologian," Frankfurter recalled.

Jeremiah Smith, a former judge on the New Hampshire Supreme Court, was a plodder compared to the incredible Joseph Beale. He lectured rather than engaged in the more dynamic Socratic method, but he, too, took his high place in Frankfurter's hagiography. Like Samuel Williston, who wrote the seminal treatise on the law of contracts, Smith "instilled in one a passionate regard for truth-seeking."

The professor who most influenced Frankfurter's legal philosophy was the tall, handsome, bearded John Chipman Gray, an expert on the law of property. A man of the world, Gray was the only member of the law faculty who also practiced law, and he brought his practical insights and pragmatic philosophy of law to the classroom. Like Oliver Wendell Holmes, Jr., who fought with Gray in the Union Army, was his law partner and remained his close friend, Gray advocated a healthy skepticism about the rule of law. For Holmes and Gray, and later for Frankfurter, the law could only be understood within the broader context of society's political, economic and social fabric. To know the law's possibilities, one must study its limitations, which were closely linked to community expectations.

There was another member of the Harvard law faculty whose

influence on Frankfurter was profound, though Frankfurter never sat in his class. He was James Bradley Thayer, who had succeeded Holmes as Royall Professor at Harvard; he died the year before Frankfurter entered the law school. Still, Thayer's *The Origin and Scope of the American Doctrine of Constitutional Law* was as vivid and important to Frankfurter as any class of Beale's or Ames's or Gray's. Thayer's thesis became Frankfurter's judicial credo: that judges must exercise restraint in their decisions, mindful of the strength and wisdom of the popularly elected legislators who passed the laws the jurists interpret. Assume, Thayer suggested, that legislators are rational men acting with competence and in total good faith. It followed, *a fortiori,* that judges should overturn legislative mandates rarely, and only on the most compelling constitutional grounds.

Behind the Thayer premise was the fear that courts, and most of all the U.S. Supreme Court, would lose both their prestige and their power if they dared to challenge a popular mandate frequently. It was far better, both in terms of sound judicial interpretation and preservation of the Court's power, to ration constitutional judgments cautiously. To do otherwise would risk the accusation that courts were no different from the political branches of government and would invite rough political counterattack by Congress and the President. Like Thayer, Justice Holmes counseled against excessive judicial ambition, and that philosophy of judicial restraint became the foundation of Frankfurter's own jurisprudence.

By the time he graduated from law school in 1906, Frankfurter's perspective was vastly different from that with which he had entered Harvard three years earlier. To be sure, his insatiable intellectual curiosity continued at full force. But now Frankfurter had added an important dimension to his universe. His ruminations about law and public policy were no longer confined to Cooper Union lectures and nocturnal debates in Lower East Side coffeehouses. He was comfortable conversing with the most respected members of the legal profession and counted among his friends Dean James Barr Ames and classmates from some of the most influential families in the country.

Throughout his pre-Court career, Frankfurter balanced his role as an "outside" Jewish intellectual with his obvious pride in at-

tracting the company of certain members of the WASP establishment. He could, therefore, become an outspoken advocate of
liberal causes (and be labeled a "radical" for his efforts) at the same
time that he maintained close friendships with Justice Oliver Wendell Holmes, Jr., and Henry Stimson, who served as both Secretary
of War and Secretary of State. When he became a member of the
Harvard Law School faculty, Frankfurter appeared to reconcile the
roles of outsider and elitist without noticeable discomfort or compromise.

Frankfurter confessed that he had "a quasi-religious" feeling
about the Harvard Law School, nurtured to full strength during his
three years there as a law student and sustained for the rest of his
life. Harvard offered Frankfurter the world, at least the world that
he wished for his fellow man. Rigorously bound by a strict professional code that demanded the best performances by the most
gifted students, Harvard allowed sons of ministers and Lower East
Side linen salesmen to mingle with high government officials and
work toward common goals. Those goals, for Frankfurter, included
not only a mastery of technical legal skills but a commitment to
the highest ideals of a profession dedicated to the rule of law.
Holmes's hopes became his liturgy: "If you believe in great
things," said Holmes, according to one of Frankfurter's favorite
quotations, "you may make other people believe in them."

There was, however, the mundane problem of earning a living.
Even with his superb grades from Harvard, Frankfurter did not find
many doors open at the major New York law firms. Most still
excluded Jews, and it was only with the strongest recommendation from Dean Ames that Frankfurter was made an offer by the
firm of Hornblower, Byrne, Miller and Potter. He was the first Jew
the firm had hired and even after he had begun working there,
Frankfurter was quietly advised by one partner to change his
name. But Felix remembered his mother's words—"Hold yourself
dear"—and refused to deny his Jewishness at Hornblower or anywhere else. He wanted to be accepted by WASP society and institutions on his terms. Frankfurter's attitude was complicated and
not completely sorted out, even in his own mind. He always insisted that his religion was an accident of birth, and that he, like
everyone else, should be judged on merit. But he forced the issue
at Hornblower, where the firm's anti-Semitic reputation was a

significant challenge for him. Once he had broken down the barrier at Hornblower, however, Frankfurter was bored and looked elsewhere for stimulation.

Within months of his arrival at Hornblower, Frankfurter was told by Dean Ames about an opening in U.S. Attorney Henry Stimson's office. He could be the public's lawyer, not the lawyer for some stuffy corporate client at Hornblower. Nothing could hold more appeal for the public-spirited young Frankfurter.

Frankfurter joined Stimson, and the chemistry between the two was, improbably, perfect. Henry Stimson came from wealthy patrician New York stock: austere, socially correct and rigidly dedicated to the practice of law at the highest professional and ethical level. His public behavior was as fastidious as his private life. As U.S. Attorney, he prosecuted overreaching corporations with the same scrupulousness as he tried common criminals. There were no deals and no illegal searches under Henry Stimson.

Young Felix Frankfurter offered Stimson total dedication and a supple, brilliant mind that Stimson relied on for years for both legal and political advice. He stood out intellectually, even among a coterie of extraordinarily talented young assistant U.S. attorneys that included Thomas Thacher, a future solicitor general of the United States, and Emory Buckner, one of the finest New York attorneys of his generation. Frankfurter was also fun, whether talking animatedly about the latest world political crisis or puffing, far behind the competition, in a foot race at Stimson's home near Huntington, Long Island.

For his part, Stimson taught Frankfurter the art of meticulous trial preparation. That meant preparing "the other fellow's case at least as well as your own." Analyzing legal problems from "multiple perspectives" was a particular forte of Frankfurter's, apparent in his work for Stimson and in later years. Stimson also stressed the importance of voluminous supporting factual materials that buttressed the oral argument in court, again a lesson that Frankfurter's mind, with its penchant for detail, absorbed naturally. Finally, there was Stimson's omnipresent sense of fairness and decency, traits that fitted neatly within Frankfurter's ideal image of the practicing attorney.

When Teddy Roosevelt, who had appointed Stimson, did not seek another presidential term in 1908, Stimson returned to private

practice in New York, taking Frankfurter with him. In 1910 Roosevelt urged Stimson to enter elective politics, and Stimson obliged
by successfully seeking the Republican nomination for the New
York governorship. And Frankfurter, twenty-eight years old, became Stimson's chief political strategist and speechwriter. Unfortunately, Stimson's solid reformist ideas did not project well on
the political hustings. The candidate failed to heed TR's instruction
that "a campaign speech is a poster, not an etching." Stimson lost
resoundingly in the general election, and he and Frankfurter returned to the private practice of law. But the call to Washington
was only months away for Stimson, and so, too, for his protégé,
Felix Frankfurter.

Washington in those days still impressed visitors as an over-
grown Southern town, languid in pace, parochial in style. President
Taft did little to shake its lethargy. His three-hundred-pound bulk
moved slowly and his ideas were never far behind. The greatest
challenge to keen observers of the Washington scene was to sum-
marize Taft's ineptitude with clever aphorisms. "Oh, if only Taft
knew the joys of leadership," exclaimed Teddy Roosevelt, his chief
rival within the Republican party.

Taft had attempted to make political peace using a time-honored
method: the appointment of a staunch TR supporter to the Cabinet. Henry Stimson, a Roosevelt loyalist, was therefore named
Secretary of War. And Felix Frankfurter, a Stimson loyalist, was
appointed law officer for the Bureau of Insular Affairs in the War
Department.

Frankfurter shared TR's sentiments about President Taft but did
not let his dim view of the Taft administration spoil his first professional experience in the nation's capital. He was gliding at the
highest political altitude of his young life. As counsel for the Bureau of Insular Affairs, Frankfurter dealt with the broad legal issues
arising within the United States possessions, from Puerto Rico to
the Philippines. Questions of U.S. treaty obligations, as well as
constitutional issues arising from the governance of nine million
people living in the insular possessions, came to Frankfurter's desk
for review, analysis and argument, sometimes in the U.S. Supreme
Court.

His unofficial but no less important function as the War Secretary's confidant delivered its own rewards. Frankfurter was called in regularly by Secretary Stimson to sit in on meetings of the War Department's top brass. Though he never mastered the meanings of the insignia on the uniforms, he escaped embarrassment by simply addressing everyone at the meetings as "General." Fortunately, he was not required to speak often and he saved his comments for his personal debriefing with the Secretary.

Frankfurter closely watched "Mr. Stimson," as he always called the Secretary in private as well as public. He learned from Stimson how to "nurse" reluctant colleagues toward his point of view. It was a talent that Frankfurter later claimed for himself and one that would be the hallmark of his own *modus operandi.*

Frankfurter traded effectively on his reputation as a "Stimson man," talking confidently of his meetings at the White House with high-ranking officials and other well-connected operatives on the Washington scene. Soon enough he began to acquire friends in high places under his own intellectual steam. One crisp fall morning in 1911, for example, Frankfurter rode to work with U.S. Attorney General Cornelius Wickersham, and the two engaged in a lively conversation that covered Spanish jurisprudence, the virtues of early-morning exercise, the sugar trusts and Herbert Croly's *Promise of American Life,* the book that had become the foundation of TR's New Nationalism. Even then, Felix knew that his intellect drew men of greater position and worldly experience to him. But that same quality of mind, Frankfurter's strength, was also his concern. He admitted to his diary that he and Attorney General Wickersham had similarly facile, perhaps too facile, minds: "Wickersham has a vivid, fresh, agile, prehensile mind, but I suspect pretty much as superficial as my own, with considerable ability to mobilize effectively and quickly all his intellectual assets."

The lively conversations on public policy and private pleasures continued unabated at the house on Nineteenth Street where Frankfurter lived. The residence belonged to Robert Valentine, the Commissioner of Indian Affairs. But the house was Valentine's in name only; it became known, in fact, as the "House of Truth," proudly offered as an intellectual haven for official Washington's brightest minds. Besides Valentine and Frankfurter, the hosts included Winfred Denison, an Assistant Attorney General, and Lord

Eustace Percy, seventh son of the seventh duke of Northumberland, then on the staff of the British Embassy.

The guest list at the House of Truth was its most impressive feature. Felix did his part, bringing to the house, among others, the already legendary Justice Holmes. Upon arrival in Washington, Frankfurter had presented a letter of introduction to Justice Holmes from his Harvard mentor, Professor John Chipman Gray, and a lifelong friendship began. Most of the time Frankfurter went to Holmes's residence to sit before the fire or in his study, listening—unusual for Frankfurter—to the great man's flow of ideas on history and the future of the republic. Holmes, like so many others in official Washington, soon became a regular guest at Frankfurter's House of Truth, joining a list that included Cabinet members, Ambassadors and Justices of the U.S. Supreme Court. Louis Brandeis stopped by often. Felix compared Brandeis to Lincoln in his depth, force and correct political sympathies, but wished that he had Lincoln's "patience, his magnanimity, his humor."

Frankfurter solidified his close relations with Brandeis and Holmes as he did with so many others throughout his life—with the force of his ebullient personality and his keen intellect. But he also employed flattery, using the English language in creative ways to praise those he very much wanted to please. To Justice Holmes he wrote:

> It is, I think, a wise habit of our Puritanism to withhold appreciation from the living, for thus only the most puri-fied sincerity will break through the dam of reticence. And so I do not even apologize for saying that from the first time in contact with you, as a freshman in the Law School, through your Common Law, you had for me—the only sure canon of truth—"the gift of imparting ferment." That this bounty would be enriched by the passion and persuasiveness of the living fire is a good fortune that makes my indebtedness everlastingly alive.

The deification could be excused here for this was, after all, Justice Holmes. But later the flattery took on wholesale value as Frank-furter effusively praised lawyers, professors, politicians and law clerks with equal fervor and conviction.

One guest at the House of Truth, in particular, captured a dispro-
portionate amount of his attention, though she was neither Cabinet officer nor Supreme Court Justice. Her name was Marion
Denman; she was the tall, attractive daughter of a Congregational
minister in Longmeadow, Massachusetts, whose family's roots in
the United States predated the American Revolution. Physically
and genealogically, Marion and Felix were a mismatch. But they
shared values, if not backgrounds, and Marion, a Phi Beta Kappa
Smith College graduate, possessed a bright, inquiring mind and an
energetic agnosticism that suited Frankfurter perfectly. Forgetting
his mother's sermons on vigilance in a hostile gentile world, he
pursued Miss Denman avidly. His exuberant style was reminiscent
of his father, Leopold. When Emma Frankfurter learned of her
son's infatuation, she, predictably, did not approve. Indeed, Emma's disapproval of the six-year courtship and later marriage was
a source of prolonged anxiety for her son.

Frankfurter's Washington was not, of course, merely an endless
round of parties and high-level meetings with government officials. To be sure, he was enjoying himself enormously. He was
also formulating his own philosophy of law and society, gener-
ously influenced by Holmes and Brandeis, but slowly and unmistakably containing his distinctive imprint. "If facts are changing,"
Frankfurter told those at the twenty-fifth reunion of the *Harvard
Law Review* in 1912, "law cannot be static. So-called immutable
principles must accommodate themselves to facts of life, for facts
are stubborn and will not yield." Legislation must, he insisted, be
molded to changing social and economic realities and, therefore,
be experimental. As long as social and economic-reform legislation
was reasonable, Frankfurter asserted, it should withstand constitutional challenge.

The speech borrowed from the views of Brandeis, who strongly
believed that legislative reform must follow social and economic
changes. New studies exposing the detrimental effects on workers
of unhealthy industrial conditions and long hours demanded legislative response. Frankfurter applauded new industrial regulations
as proper exercises of the legislative function. The legislation
should not, he asserted, be interfered with by a conservative judiciary unhappy with the result. Courts had to curb their ambition

in these circumstances, cautioned Frankfurter, articulating a philosophy of judicial restraint that reflected his readings as a law student of James Bradley Thayer and Oliver Wendell Holmes, Jr.

The clearer his political vision for reform, the more frustrated Frankfurter became in the Taft administration. Henry Stimson's talent for clean, forceful thinking was wasted, and so, thought Frankfurter, was his. Frankfurter longed for the passion, dynamism and, most of all, the sense of national purpose that only Teddy Roosevelt promised.

"The air I breathe here—outside of home—is fetid," he complained. "I feel myself cramped, of dubious fitness in the current of things. I chafe that I am not where I long to be. I have the sniff of the fight and find myself a cog in the bureaucracy. I want to be out of here, even or perhaps because the third party fight is a folly —to me it's real, the odds are challenging, the requirement power of ideas and ideals as political ammunition too stirring a fancy of mine to sit remotely by."

In 1912 Roosevelt broke from the Republican party, promising government regulation for the common good, and Felix Frankfurter wanted to join the ranks of the Bull Moosers. But Frankfurter's boss, Stimson, counseled his young protégé against it. Frankfurter's long-range best interests, Stimson strongly suggested, were tightly linked to his continued service with Stimson in the Taft administration. In particular, Stimson wanted Felix to work with him on government regulations of a series of water-power projects that were within the War Department's jurisdiction.

Dutifully, Frankfurter stayed on, quietly supporting Roosevelt's third-party candidacy but devoting full time officially to Stimson's War Department. After Woodrow Wilson's election, however, Frankfurter knew that he would soon leave his government post, and only waited for the appropriate opportunity. By 1914 he was actively considering two options: to become a practicing lawyer in New York or to join the Harvard Law School faculty. Powerful advocates lined up on both sides.

Stimson and Holmes favored law practice, largely out of concern that Frankfurter was not suited to the academic life. "You have the greatest faculty of acquaintance—for keeping in touch with the center of things," wrote Stimson, "for knowing sympathetically men who are doing and thinking, of almost all men—certainly all young men that I know. I query whether that most valuable faculty would not be to a great extent lost at the law school."

But the thought of serving private commercial clients and putting money "in other people's pockets" did not appeal to Frankfurter in 1914 any more than it had when he had first started practice in the Hornblower firm. He also did not think the lawyering process would sustain his idealism. "I can't quite become a crusader for the rule in Shelley's case or shipwreck a friendship," he wrote his old Law School friend, Emory Buckner, "through disagreement on a picayune point on pleading."

The Harvard Law School, on the other hand, had always held a reverential fascination for Frankfurter. And now that Professor Roscoe Pound was in Cambridge promoting the view that there was a natural partnership between law and the social sciences, Frankfurter had reason to believe that his work there could have a high public purpose. Pound and Brandeis believed that Felix's talents were best served at the Law School.

"I have decided to go to Cambridge if they want me," Frankfurter wrote a skeptical Justice Holmes. "I would not go up there for a conventional professorship. Academics are neither my aptitude nor the line of my choice—so far as one chooses. The thing is rather different and what challenges me is to bring public life, the elements of reality, in touch with the university, and, conversely, to help harness the law school to the needs of the fight outside."

In 1914 Frankfurter returned to Harvard, aspiring to be the citizen-academic, with the earlier Louis Brandeis, the citizen-lawyer, as his role model. He would continue to analyze and comment on the great issues of the day, not from the War Department or the House of Truth, but from one of the world's great universities. Harvard, he hoped, would provide him with the resources and the perspective to make a substantial contribution to the public dialogue. Professor Frankfurter would thereafter engage in sustained thinking on important public policy issues and would make the ride from Cambridge to Washington a shuttle service, freighting his ideas and protégés to the seat of government for the next two and a half decades.

Although he agonized over it, Frankfurter viewed his decision to go to Harvard as only a five-year commitment. The challenge of the classroom would be formidable, he knew. But once he had mastered the academic materials and had caught the rhythm of dialogue with his students, Frankfurter assumed that he could cut his academic life to half time and freely roam toward other important causes.

In the summer of 1914, however, he concentrated on academic business, spending long hours in the stacks of the Harvard library catching up on cases in criminal law and public utilities, the subjects he would be teaching. He gloried in the leisure of reading the law carefully and without interruption, so unlike his "intellectual hand-to-mouth" experience in Washington, where he had always rushed to meet deadlines. At the War Department he had never been satisfied that his research was thorough enough, even when preparing for an appearance before the U.S. Supreme Court. At Harvard it would be different.

"I like it lots," Frankfurter reported during his first semester at Harvard. He was a natural teacher, extending his probing conversations, so familiar at Washington receptions and in government offices, to the students at the Harvard Law School. To be sure, his students were not subjected to the tight theoretical exercises of a Professor Joseph Beale or the perfectly controlled dialogues of a Dean James Barr Ames. Unlike Beale or Ames, Frankfurter had an incorrigibly discursive style that would not be bound by traditional classroom rules. He linked cases to relevant political, historical and sociological fact, out of conviction that only in the broader context could the law be truly understood. And he allowed his own and his students' minds to wander creatively, searching for insights and mental adventure. At his best Frankfurter could lift the brightest students (and he did favor the brightest) to new intellectual plateaus. And even when he failed to accomplish that feat, Professor Frankfurter was marvelously entertaining. Francis Plimpton, the future lawyer-diplomat, described the experience: "You learn no law in Public U/That is its fascination/But Felix gives a point of view/And pleasant conversation."

From the beginning of his academic career, Frankfurter found it impossible to confine himself to his law books and his students. During his first semester he was already shuttling to New York and Washington regularly. The idea that Frankfurter could ever be far from the center of things, as Stimson and Holmes had feared, turned out to be a ludicrous miscalculation. Through voluminous correspondence, conversations and regular meetings, Felix kept up with two hundred best friends and three dozen causes. Some of his friends, such as the brilliant English scholar Harold Laski, worried. "I don't find him able to sit down solidly to a single thing," Laski wrote Justice Holmes. "He wastes the time that ought to be given to the permanent work that is in him in writing fine letters to antiquated New York lawyers with doubts about the Constitution. . . . To New York three times a week is a drain I wonder whether even he can stand."

Laski might as well have fretted about the inability of the blue whale to swing from trees. Frankfurter was incapable of focusing exclusively on a single task. His peripatetic intellectual nature had served him wonderfully well in Washington and would do so again in Cambridge. A quarter of a century later, however, when he sat on the U.S. Supreme Court, Frankfurter would find that one single-minded colleague, Justice Hugo Black, unaffected by Frankfurter's learning and experience, would pose a formidable obstacle to his achieving his goals for the Court.

Although Frankfurter lacked total dedication to scholarship at Harvard, he could articulate his philosophy of law with clarity and considerable force. In 1915 he lectured an American Bar Association audience on the use of the law as an instrument for reform. The law should not, Frankfurter warned, be an end in itself but rather a means for society's improvement. ABA lawyers, therefore, should not sit comfortably back and bank their fees but should be in the forefront of the battle. He made a special plea to young lawyers. "We make of them clever pleaders, but not lawyers, if they fail to catch the glorious vision of the law, not as a harsh Procrustean bed into which all persons and all societies must inexorably be fitted, but as a vital agency for human betterment."

For his part, Frankfurter became deeply immersed in the constitutional challenge to major social and economic-reform legislation of the day. His work followed that of his mentor, Louis Brandeis, who in 1908 had successfully defended the constitutionality of an Oregon statute providing a maximum-hours limitation for women workers. The Brandeis brief had consisted of two pages of abstract constitutional argument and one hundred pages of economic and social fact showing in precise detail the detrimental effects of long hours on female workers. After Brandeis's appointment to the U.S. Supreme Court in 1916 Frankfurter took up the cause, representing without fee Florence Kelley's National Consumers' League in three cases involving challenges to state maximum-hours and minimum-wage legislation.

The cases had first been argued by Brandeis in 1914 but the Court had postponed decision pending reargument in 1917. In two of the cases, involving minimum-wage legislation for women workers, however, the Oregon Attorney General had moved for a decision on the basis of the written briefs. Frankfurter was appalled, convinced that his oral argument before the Justices could be the difference between success and failure.

Not one ever to stand by complacently, Frankfurter wired the Chief Justice of the United States:

"MY DEAR MR. CHIEF JUSTICE I SHALL CALL AT YOUR HOUSE AT ABOUT NINE O'CLOCK SATURDAY MORNING NEXT IN THE HOPE THAT YOU'LL BE FREE TO SEE ME ON A MATTER OF CONSIDERABLE PUBLIC IMPORTANCE. RESPECTFULLY YOURS FELIX FRANKFURTER."

Frankfurter had calculated that Chief Justice Edward White was a man of at least modest curiosity and that a telegram from Harvard Professor Frankfurter about a matter of "considerable public importance" would arouse his interest. Anticipating the meeting, Frankfurter boarded the Federal from Boston and arrived at White's house on the next Saturday morning. He was immediately escorted to the Chief Justice, a large, genial Louisianian whose political skills significantly exceeded his legal scholarship. White devoted the first few minutes of the meeting to general conversation including an inquiry about the number of Harvard Law students from the South and a lamentation on the tragic consequences of the Civil War on the Confederacy. Then he asked Frankfurter to state his business.

Frankfurter believed implicitly in his instincts and his instincts that Saturday morning told him to lay out his mission in the most intimate terms. He told White that what he had to say was in the nature of a confessional.

"Well, that was a masterstroke," Frankfurter later recalled. "I felt at once as though the whole church was enfolding me. He [the

Chief Justice] came nearer, more intimately, and he said, 'Tell me. Just speak freely.' "

Frankfurter then told the Chief Justice of his concern that a decision on the written briefs alone could shield the Court from crucial aspects of the case that would come out in the give-and-take of oral argument. White pondered the professor's point and then asked if oral argument would take care of his concern. Yes, Frankfurter replied. The following Monday a Court order set a date for oral argument.

When he appeared before the Court, Frankfurter knew that he faced a group of conservative Justices who opposed any state regulations that interfered with the "liberty of contract" between employer and employee. They believed that the employer of, say, one thousand textile workers should be free to negotiate working conditions with individual employees based on the theory that employer and employee possessed equal bargaining power. Associate Justice James McReynolds, young, bright, deeply conservative and viciously anti-Semitic, was by far Frankfurter's most hostile interrogator. Repeatedly hectoring Frankfurter, Mc-Reynolds interrupted his argument that the ten-hour-maximum regulation was constitutional.

"Ten hours! Ten hours! Ten! Why not four?" McReynolds snarled.

Frankfurter paused dramatically, then calmly addressed McReynolds. "Your honor," said Frankfurter, "if by chance I may make such a hypothesis: if your physician should find that you're eating too much meat, it isn't necessary for him to urge you to become a vegetarian."

He savored the moment, delighting for years in the memory of Justice Holmes loudly exclaiming, "Good for you!" Other observers were equally impressed by the unflappable young Harvard professor. "He [Frankfurter] lectured the court quietly," *The Nation* reported, "but with a due sense of its indebtedness to him for setting it right where it had been wrong and giving it positive opinions where uncertainty had been clouding its mental vision."

The Justices voted 5–2 to uphold the constitutionality of Oregon's maximum-hours law and split 4–4 on the minimum-wage regulation, thereby leaving in place the lower court decision declaring the law constitutional. Frankfurter did not have much time to reflect on this turn of judicial events since he was, typically, already on his way to another appointment. That same year, 1917, Frankfurter's appointment calendar not only listed the U.S. Supreme Court but the War Department as well.

Secretary of War Newton D. Baker, an old Frankfurter colleague at the National Consumers' League, had asked him to serve as his counsel and mediator of domestic industrial disputes. On an extended leave from Harvard, Frankfurter was dispatched to the West, where strikes and potential strikes threatened the war effort. He lived out of a suitcase for weeks at a time, trying to bring management and labor together in the copper mines of Arizona, the oil fields of California and the spruce forests of the Northwest.

In every dispute Frankfurter attempted to import his analytical classroom approach to the bargaining table. He insisted on reason, not absolutes, and was most successful when he found like-minded negotiators. The senior attorney in one dispute, a graduate of the Harvard Law School, received particularly high marks from Frankfurter. "We were products of the same kind of teaching at the Harvard Law School, the same rational way of trying to analyze a problem and see what the factors are in order to reach an accommodation," Frankfurter remembered. "The upshot was that he saw that this wasn't a fight for immortal principles. This was a situation calling for the give-and-take of sensible people."

Later, on the Court, Frankfurter despaired when confronted by Justice Black, who was not Harvard-trained and did not seem to appreciate his subtle distinctions and sensible compromises. "Every time we have that which should be merely an intellectual difference," Frankfurter once complained after a judicial conference, "it gets into a championship by Black of justice and right and decency and everything, and those who take the other view are impliedly always made out to be the oppressors of the people and the supporters of some exploiting interest."

For the younger Frankfurter, however, there were also times when a call for justice and right and decency was not only tolerated but demanded. Two such occasions occurred in 1917. The first involved Tom Mooney, a labor leader who had been convicted and sentenced to death for alleged complicity in a bomb explosion that killed ten people in a San Francisco Preparedness Day parade. Frankfurter had been appointed counsel to the presidential commission investigating the Mooney case, and he filed a report to President Wilson charging that Mooney's conviction had been obtained by perjured testimony. In recommending to the President that Mooney be granted a new trial, Frankfurter argued: "War is fought with moral as well as material resources. We are in this war to vindicate the moral claims of unstained processes of law, however slow at times such processes may be. These claims must be tempered by the fire of our own devotion to them at home."

Soon after he had completed his report on Mooney, Frankfurter was again asked by the President to investigate an alleged injustice, this time involving a thousand striking miners in Bisbee, Arizona. The miners had been rounded up by a local vigilante group, loaded on cattle cars and dumped in the New Mexico desert without food or water. Frankfurter concluded that the treatment of the miners was "brutality and injustice in the raw."

The Mooney and Bisbee reports inspired American conservatives to label Frankfurter a dangerous radical, a reputation that would stalk him for the next two decades. Even Teddy Roosevelt turned on his former adviser, suggesting that Frankfurter's attitude was suspiciously similar to "Trotsky and the other Bolshevik leaders in Russia." Frankfurter immediately challenged the former President to reconsider his rash judgment on the basis of facts, not "blind passion."

Frankfurter's service to the Wilson administration was not confined to the domestic scene. He was asked to accompany former Ambassador Henry Morgenthau, Jr., on an international mission publicized by the State Department as "an effort to ameliorate the conditions of the Jewish communities in Palestine." In fact, it was a bold attempt to disengage Turkey from the Central Powers. The mission failed. The timing was wrong and so was the personal matchup between Frankfurter and Morgenthau. "My knowledge was critical and analytical," Frankfurter said confidently, "and his was just general, hot-air impressions."

By late spring of 1919, Felix Frankfurter, thirty-seven years old, could speak authoritatively about matters of state and international peace. He commanded the respect of Prince Feisal and President Wilson, Justice Holmes and Arthur Balfour. He was dedicated to human progress at as rapid a rate as scientific truth

and public education would allow. A thinking progressive, he refused to pledge his permanent allegiance to any ideology or political party, preferring to test others' ideas against his own and
ultimately trusting his reasoned judgment.

The Paris peace talks had disintegrated into hopeless feuding
among the great powers, and Frankfurter held Woodrow Wilson
primarily responsible. The President, he believed, was too rigidly
moralistic and lacked the necessary negotiating tools or the understanding to make a lasting peace. But Frankfurter was not discouraged. Possibilities for progress at home and abroad seemed
unusually promising. Having been away from Cambridge for almost two years, Frankfurter looked forward to his return to Harvard and a new set of challenges. And he anticipated with pure
excitement his reunion with the love of his life, Marion Denman,
whom he planned to make his bride.

Marion Denman was plagued by tension throughout her life.
Even as a promising young graduate of Smith, she seemed uncer-
tain of her role and direction. She first became secretary of the
fashionable Spence School in New York City, but nursing the elite
did not suit her. In search of socially useful work, she trained at
the New York School for Social Work, joined the suffragette cause
and enlisted in the Red Cross's War Camp Activities Bureau. All
were interesting activities, but none suggested a calling.

Marion was courted zealously by Felix Frankfurter in those
years. She certainly suited him intellectually, though she was cautious and reflective, while he leaped fearlessly into every conversation. Her interests were more literary than his, but that just
added perspective to his conviction. What Frankfurter tried, but
failed, to give Marion in return was his sense of joyful adventure.
He knew problems and pain but appeared to bounce out of them
with his confidence intact. Not so with Marion, who never could
shake deep feelings of insecurity.

Despite the obstacles, Felix and Marion's love affair was touch-
ingly poetic and frequently rapturous. Each offered the other intense emotions that they dared not share with anyone else. Felix
became Marion's "little boy" who was consumed by his love for

her. "You are dearer than dear—peace of peace and joy to Life," he wrote her. "O, how I do love Beloved Marion."

Marion returned home one day to find flowers and four notes from Felix. She cried as she never had before and confessed that "I shall never learn how to love you as you love me." She wanted to learn so much from him, particularly how to take pleasure in life. She knew that she could not pass quickly "from a habit of pain and sorrow to a habit of joy." But she was confident that she had picked the right mentor. "I shall learn the habit of joy from being loved much, in a thousand ways," she wrote. "Dear Felix, you've been the only person in my life for so long."

Marion's letter was written in 1919, six years after she had met Felix at the House of Truth. From the beginning of the relationship there was strain amid bursts of passion. The main problem, as they both knew, was the cross-fertilization of pure Yankee stock with that of a Lower East Side Jewish immigrant. Frankfurter held fast to his belief that his Jewishness did not matter. But when he and Marion talked about their future together, he reluctantly admitted that race and religion were relevant, at least in his mother's mind. And because Emma Frankfurter cared so much, so did her devoted son. Shortly after his father's death in 1916, Frankfurter had declared the affair over. "Mother loved the only sight she had of you," he explained. "But alas: You in yourself were also a symbol—the symbol of difference in 'race' and 'faith' and all the other separating institutions born of the past. . . . I could not destroy what was left of zest and strength in her—most was expected of me and there you are. . . ."

The breakup was unbearable for him and shortly afterward he rushed back to her. A marriage proposal followed but Frankfurter continued to worry about his mother's feelings. After dinner with Brandeis, he reported to Marion the Justice's reservations about the impending marriage: "You hit him [Brandeis] hard, the very first time he saw you—he has a quick and wise eye—very hard. And yet when you think how bothered he would be by you-me you can get some measure of what the racial symbol means to my Mother. Gosh!!! I suppose I ought not to bother you—but I ought not to shine the candor of trying to make you see and feel just what it is I've asked of you, just what you and I are up against. . . ."

Marion and Felix were married in the chambers of Judge Learned Hand in the summer of 1920. Judge Benjamin Cardozo of the New York Court of Appeals presided and, at the couple's request, kept his remarks to a tactful minimum. Emma Frankfurter did not attend.

Felix's love for Marion never faltered, through a childless marriage and Marion's periodic bouts of depression. He courted her until his death, fluttering happily about her, proudly insisting that his friends recognize her extraordinary character and talent. But Marion never overcame her feelings of inadequacy. Indeed, having the indefatigable Frankfurter as a mate only made matters worse. At times she would fend him off with a gentle putdown. Her loquacious husband had only two faults, she said: First, he always got off the subject and, second, he always got back onto it. She asked half-desperately: "Do you know what it's like to be married to a man who is never tired?"

Frankfurter began the marriage with a concession to his newly acquired domesticity. He worked at their home on Brattle Street whenever he could, forgoing his great pleasure in long conversations with students in his Harvard office. But he could not be contained at home or anywhere else. And Marion, like Josephine Black, who also suffered severe emotional depression during her marriage to a brilliant attorney with boundless energy, endured pain privately while her husband moved from one impressive public success to the next.

"Evidently we are the most reactionary country in the world right now," Frankfurter had written his friend Walter Lippmann from Paris in the spring of 1919. When he returned to Harvard in the fall, Frankfurter witnessed the grim reality of his observation. A. Mitchell Palmer, the U.S. Attorney General, offered leadership appropriate for that hysterical time, authorizing so-called "Palmer raids" on suspected subversives. Thousands of persons, mostly aliens, were rooted out of Communist offices, labor union headquarters, bars and cafés in thirty cities across the country, arrested without warrants and thrown into local jails under shameful conditions. In one instance, in Detroit, eight hundred men huddled in total darkness; they were forced to share a single toilet and were refused food for twenty-four hours. Perfunctory administrative hearings followed and then, frequently, deportation.

Historians labeled the frenzied hunt "the Red Scare," a period when official tyranny was excused and public dialogue frozen. Like its latter-day counterpart, McCarthyism, the post–World War I government action intimidated ordinary citizens while punishing those who were unorthodox in thought. Left-wing political organizations and nascent labor unions were targets and so, inevitably, were those who questioned the government's moral and legal authority. Felix Frankfurter questioned that authority openly and with increasing militancy and was, therefore, a marked man.

Actually, Frankfurter's notoriety among conservatives predated the Red Scare, and could be traced directly to his Mooney Report. Teddy Roosevelt had never forgiven Frankfurter for his criticism of the labor leader's conviction; certainly those of a conspicuously narrower political stripe would not. After the war, Frankfurter made their task easy. He seemed to pop up in the center of every controversy. On Armistice Day, 1919, he presided at a huge rally in Boston's historic Faneuil Hall, organized specifically to promote support for U.S. diplomatic recognition of the Soviet Union. Frankfurter told the overflow crowd that he knew he would be labeled a Bolshevik for his participation; he did not have to wait long to realize his prophecy.

A few days later, Frankfurter received a telephone call from Thomas Nelson Perkins, legal counsel to the Harvard Corporation and a senior partner in Boston's prestigious law firm of Ropes, Gray and Gorham. "What's this Communist meeting you presided over?" asked an angry Perkins. Before Frankfurter could respond, Perkins read a letter from an irate Harvard alumnus, "a man of influence and large property" who objected to the university's "red professors" and had been "after Laski and you . . ." Perkins continued his recitation of complaints over lunch with Frankfurter, reporting that other prominent Harvard alumni had expressed disapproval of Frankfurter's politics and had issued subtle threats that their financial support for Harvard might not continue. "Why do you rock the boat?" Perkins asked plaintively.

Frankfurter threw the question back at Perkins. Why not ask the real "boatrockers," the reactionaries who were sponsoring the

reign of terror in the country? They were the problem, not Frankfurter, whose moderate position—and diplomatic recognition of
Soviet Russia was a moderate position—should be encouraged.
He would not be intimidated by alumni threats, he told Perkins,
and neither should high-level Harvard officials. "You know as well
as I do," he said, "that at present there is raging a form of lynch
law in the North, much more ominous, because less crude, than
the well-known brand of the South. I should feel like a poltroon if
I suppressed my convictions . . . because . . . some people would
shy off from contributing money." Convinced of the correctness
of his position, Frankfurter did not hesitate to lecture Perkins.
"Sanity and goodwill do not just happen in this world," he said.
"They must be fought for and won."

His courage was not always appreciated, even by his friends.
Holmes told Frankfurter that he, too, believed in academic freedom, but noted that freedom, used unwisely, could hurt the academic institution. Learned Hand did not think Frankfurter had
chosen a propitious time to make such a public show of his controversial views. Despite the warnings, Frankfurter forged ahead, ex-
hibiting a nerve and conviction that should have embarrassed his
apprehensive counselors.

He joined ten others in publishing *Report Upon the Illegal Practices
of the United States Department of Justice.* The report was so devastating that, after reading it, Charles Evans Hughes, former Republican
presidential candidate and perhaps the most respected member of
the bar, likened the Justice Department's abuses to "the worst
practices of tyranny." With his Harvard Law colleague Professor
Zechariah Chafee, Frankfurter came to the defense of twenty alien
victims of Palmer raids who were scheduled for deportation, but
had been denied procedural safeguards that the government itself
had promulgated. After reading what he considered an irrefutable
criticism by Chafee of a U.S. Supreme Court decision, Frankfurter
signed a clemency petition on behalf of three men convicted under
the Espionage Act for publishing alleged subversive leaflets. That
the three men were the unsuccessful defendants in one of the
most famous free speech decisions ever handed down by the U.S.
Supreme Court did not make Frankfurter's action less controversial.

At the same time Sidney Hillman, the harassed leader of the

Amalgamated Clothing Workers, called Frankfurter for help. His striking union was under attack by government attorneys in Rochester, New York, who sought an injunction permanently forbidding the strike, substantial damages and a ruling that Amalgamated had engaged in an illegal conspiracy. If the prosecution succeeded, Hillman believed his union would be finished, and so, at least for the moment, would progressive trade unionism in the United States. Frankfurter led the union's defense team but faced a trial judge who was unmoved, to say the least, by the Harvard professor's appeal to economic and sociological data that underscored the legitimate needs of the city's industrial workers. The permanent injunction and damages against the union were granted. The pragmatic Frankfurter advised his client not to appeal in such a hostile atmosphere. A compromise was worked out that eliminated damages against the union and enabled Hillman's organization to survive.

In large part because of the firm resistance of Frankfurter and others to the Red Scare, the worst government abuses were successfully challenged, and the nation gradually returned to the "normalcy" of President Warren Harding. But for progressives like Frankfurter "normalcy" was far from satisfying. The business of America was business even before Calvin Coolidge coined the phrase, and the cry for broad economic and social reforms was barely audible, a faint echo from a distant past.

Frankfurter found the choice of presidential candidates offered by the two major parties in 1924 disheartening. Coolidge, the Republican standard-bearer, made indifference to reform a political virtue. Attorney John W. Davis, nominated by the Democrats, had represented his corporate clients flawlessly, but lacked a social conscience, Frankfurter concluded.

The nation desperately needed the ideas and dedication of a reform candidate and in his *New Republic* article "Why I Shall Vote for La Follette," Frankfurter gave his reasons. First, he attacked both major party candidates for ignoring the most compelling public issue of the day: the gross economic disparities between America's most and least affluent citizens. Second, he deplored the government's economic imperialism directed toward the poor countries of Latin America. Finally, he condemned the Democratic party's reliance on the "solid South" which he characterized as "the greatest immoral factor of American politics." Senator Robert La Follette of Wisconsin promised a program of economic and social progress in which government responded to the legitimate claims of America's industrial and agricultural workers. Frankfurter had a ready answer for those who chided him for supporting a doomed third-party candidacy: "If the clarification of American politics through the formation of a new party is required to make our politics more honest and more real, then all the talk of 'throwing one's vote away' is the cowardly philosophy of the bandwagon."

The same year that Coolidge was elected President, Frankfurter was named Byrne Professor of Administrative Law at Harvard. The endowed chair was tacit recognition that Frankfurter had accomplished what he had set as his goal when he had joined the faculty in 1914. He had become the nation's foremost citizen-academic, a professor with a limitless public-interest portfolio. Even before he had taught his first class, he had known that his most important lectures would be addressed to audiences far from the Harvard campus. He would apply the law to significant public problems and his forums would range widely—from his Bisbee and Mooney reports to his advocacy of state minimum-wage and maximum-hours legislation before the U.S. Supreme Court to his plea for political reform in the pages of *The New Republic*.

In 1920, while Frankfurter was abroad, Nicola Sacco and Bartolomeo Vanzetti were arrested, convicted and sentenced to death for the robbery and murder of a paymaster and his guard outside the factory of the Slater Morrill Shoe Company in South Braintree, Massachusetts. Later, despite the persistent urging of friends, Frankfurter refused even to discuss the convictions of Sacco and Vanzetti. As he had told Marion repeatedly, he abided by a self-imposed rule that he would abstain from any discussion of a case in which he had not read the trial record. He was not tempted by banner newspaper headlines or animated discussions at social gatherings. In 1925, however, Frankfurter relented, partly at the urging of Mrs. Glendower Evans, one of Justice Brandeis's oldest friends, and partly because William G. Thompson, a Harvard Law graduate and an attorney Frankfurter greatly respected, agreed to represent Sacco and Vanzetti.

At the time of their arrest, Sacco and Vanzetti carried weapons that the prosecution later linked with the bullets found in the bodies of the murdered men. Prosecution witnesses placed the defendants at the scene of the crime; defense witnesses said they were elsewhere when the murders occurred.

What elevated the trial of Sacco and Vanzetti above that of an ordinary robbery-murder were the participants in the proceedings. The virulence of the Red Scare was at its height, and the defendants, both Italian immigrants with well-documented records of draft resistance and anarchist politics, served as ripe targets for those in and out of government who wanted to cleanse the country of subversive influence. Judge Webster Thayer, a Dartmouth man and Odd Fellow, made no secret of his contempt for the defendants. He allowed the prosecutor to put Sacco and Vanzetti's politics on trial and made no objection to the prosecutor's ethnic slurs.

Prosecutor Frederick Katzmann's decision to try Sacco and Vanzetti's politics as much as their alleged crimes suited the defendants' trial counsel, Fred Moore. Moore, who claimed a long list of left-wing clients, believed implicitly in the need to take the class struggle to the courtroom. Judge Thayer referred to Moore, who wore sandals in his courtroom, as "that long-haired anarchist from the West." And Moore did little to play down his radical reputation, often ignoring intricate procedural points in favor of his larger ideological cause.

The trial lasted for almost seven weeks, but when Judge Thayer charged the jury, he made it clear that a quick guilty verdict was in order. Matching the prosecutor in his broad political appeal, the judge contrasted Sacco and Vanzetti with U.S. soldiers in World War I who accepted the call to duty "in the spirit of supreme American loyalty." Five hours after Thayer's final instruction, the jury returned guilty verdicts against both defendants.

"Did you see what I did with those anarchistic bastards the other day?" a proud Judge Thayer asked a friend shortly after the trial. "I guess that will hold them for a while." The guilty verdict certainly did send Sacco and Vanzetti to prison and, ultimately, to their death. But the verdict also galvanized the liberal and left political communities in the United States and abroad as no other event during the decade. Solid citizens of the center and moderate left, including Felix Frankfurter, joined anarchists, Communists and other left-wing fringe groups to protest the judgment in the Dedham, Massachusetts, courtroom.

Frankfurter was not moved by the shrill political rhetoric that followed Sacco's and Vanzetti's convictions. He was, rather, drawn into the case by a legal argument raised in 1925 on appeal by Thompson, the defendants' new attorney. As grounds for a new trial, Thompson presented an affidavit of a ballistics expert who had been a key prosecution witness at the trial. The expert, Captain William H. Proctor, former head of the Massachusetts State Police, had given testimony at the trial that suggested the bullet found in the body of one of the victims had come from Sacco's gun. In his affidavit, however, Proctor declared that the prosecutor had coached him in his testimony in a way that gave the jury the mistaken impression that Proctor believed the bullet found in the victim's body had come from Sacco's gun. In fact, Proctor was not certain of this. What Proctor had said was that the bullet that killed one of the men was of a type that *could* have been fired from Sacco's revolver.

In his affidavit Captain Proctor blamed the prosecutor for the misleading testimony presented at the trial. According to Proctor, he told the prosecutor of his doubts about the origin of the fatal bullet. But the prosecutor had insisted that Proctor take the witness stand and testify in a way that both prosecutor and witness knew was misleading. When Prosecutor Katzmann did not issue a flat denial of Proctor's accusation, Frankfurter became convinced that Katzmann had acted unethically and strongly suspected that other perversions of justice would be found in the trial record. He read all six thousand pages of it, and his suspicions turned to rage. In an article in the *Atlantic Monthly* that followed, Frankfurter denounced the entire proceeding.

The Frankfurter attack was published in book form later that same year, 1927, and instantly became a minor classic in trial analysis. In 110 tightly reasoned pages Frankfurter laid bare the weaknesses in the prosecutor's case, the biases of the prosecutor and trial judge and the critical failure of the state appellate court to correct the errors. And Frankfurter put his case to the public systematically and seemingly without emotional appeal. But by the book's end no reader could ignore the author's righteous indignation. On the prosecutor's and trial judge's bias Frankfurter wrote: "By systematic exploitation of the defendants' alien blood, their imperfect knowledge of English, their unpopular social views, and their opposition to the war, the District Attorney invoked against them a riot of political passion and patriotic sentiment; and the trial judge connived at—one had almost written, cooperated in—the process." On Judge Thayer's judicial opinion rejecting arguments for a new trial: "His 25,000-word document cannot accurately be described otherwise than as a farrago of misquotations, misrepresentations, suppressions and mutilations." On justice: "Perfection may not be demanded of law, but the capacity to correct errors of inevitable frailty is the mark of a civilized legal mechanism."

Frankfurter's criticism of the Sacco-Vanzetti trial presented in narrow compass his legal philosophy as well as his strongest professional skills. He began with facts taken from the trial record, facts about the murders, facts about witnesses' testimony, facts about the judge's instruction to the jury. These facts were carefully arranged to persuade the reader that a particular result was demanded. Facts, for Frankfurter, served the vital purpose of educating the public and, ultimately, inciting the citizenry to take action in the public interest. And the action called for in the Sacco-Vanzetti case was nothing less than the preservation of the integrity of the legal process.

Frankfurter challenged, welcomed really, opposition from any quarter. And that opposition massed quickly with a spokesman from the very center of Harvard's establishment. He was Harvard President A. Lawrence Lowell. It was not the first time that he and Professor Frankfurter had clashed. Earlier in the decade Lowell had attempted to establish a Jewish quota at Harvard and Frankfurter had challenged it. The antipathy that Frankfurter felt toward Lowell highlighted his deep ambivalence about the WASP establishment. He openly courted selected members, such as Holmes and Stimson, yet lashed out at others, like Lowell, on issues that clearly marked him as an outsider.

The trouble with Lowell, Frankfurter later said, quoting a classmate of the Harvard president, was that he was "incapable of seeing that two wops could be right and the Yankee judiciary could be wrong." Then another formidable adversary joined the fray; he was John H. Wigmore, Dean of the Northwestern Law School and author of the generally accepted treatise on the rules of evidence. Wigmore wrote a letter to the *Boston Transcript* that accused Frankfurter of shoddy reasoning and wrong results. Within hours of the publication of the Wigmore letter Frankfurter was in front of a typewriter preparing the reply that the *Boston Herald* had promised to hold its presses to print. By many accounts, including Frankfurter's, his published response "pulverized" Wigmore. In *Felix Frankfurter Reminisces,* the concluding page of the chapter on Sacco and Vanzetti quotes Lowell: "Wigmore is a fool! Wigmore is a fool! He should have known that Frankfurter would be shrewd enough to be accurate."

Frankfurter surely got the better of the argument, not only with Wigmore but with Lowell as well. But Lowell had the last word. The Harvard president headed a three-member committee appointed by the Massachusetts governor to consider clemency for Sacco and Vanzetti. Not surprisingly, the committee found that the defendants had been properly convicted and sentenced to death.

"Sacco gone, Vanzetti going," a radio announcer reported shortly after midnight on August 23, 1927. Felix and Marion Frankfurter heard the bulletin as they aimlessly walked the streets of Boston. Marion collapsed. Felix helped his wife that night but could not help himself for days after the executions. He was "like a madman," reported a friend. "He was really beside himself."

After the trauma of the executions had subsided, Frankfurter reiterated his belief that a grave injustice had been done. But the trial that radicalized hundreds of thousands around the world did nothing, ironically, to shake the basic allegiance to the legal system of a prime mover in the controversy, Felix Frankfurter. In fact, the injustice that Frankfurter believed to have been perpetrated only strengthened his resolve. Justice must follow injustice. The integrity of the legal system must be protected. Reform, not revolution, was called for and Frankfurter continued to offer his services.

Frankfurter had spent most of his adulthood looking in vain for a national leader who could effect broad social and economic reform. In Franklin Delano Roosevelt he found a political leader whose capacity for leadership was worthy of his total devotion. The friendship between the two men began in earnest during FDR's first term as governor of New York and lasted until Roosevelt's death, a full six years after he had appointed Frankfurter to the U.S. Supreme Court.

Roosevelt and Frankfurter's friendship dated back to their early Washington days when Frankfurter worked in Henry Stimson's War Department and Roosevelt served as Assistant Secretary of the Navy. The two regularly attended meetings together, exchanged memos and spoke frequently by telephone. Years later, Frankfurter recalled that Roosevelt had impressed him as the outstanding administrator in the Navy office. Although Frankfurter and Roosevelt continued to see and write each other sporadically over the years, their friendship was casual, no more intense than Frankfurter's friendships with hundreds of others. When Roosevelt was elected New York's governor in 1928, however, Frankfurter's interest in Roosevelt quickened.

"Dear Franklin," Frankfurter wrote shortly after the gubernatorial election, "Your victory is a great source of consolation and hope. To have the direction of New York affairs in your hands in immediate succession to [Al] Smith assures such momentum to those standards of government which Smith and you typify as to secure for them almost the force of a tradition. For you have, as Smith has, the conception of government which seems to me indispensable to the vitality of a democratic government, namely, the realization that the processes of government are essentially educational."

Frankfurter's favorite New York governor in 1928 was still Al Smith, and, in private, he expressed doubts about Roosevelt's intellectual capacity and conviction. But gradually Frankfurter became convinced that Roosevelt possessed the essential qualities for political leadership. He was bright, tough, resourceful, reform-minded and pragmatic. Roosevelt also knew that government leadership required, as Frankfurter had written, the talent to educate the public. When FDR introduced public utility and water power reforms, for example, he did so openly, creating a dialogue with the voters that elevated both public awareness and government standards.

After Roosevelt was reelected governor in 1930 by a landslide, he was considered a likely Democratic presidential candidate in 1932. By this time Roosevelt and Frankfurter had become extremely good friends. Being close to a progressive political leader with a promising future was obviously attractive to Frankfurter. But Roosevelt found the friendship to his substantial advantage as well. Professor Frankfurter offered effusive encouragement and sophisticated advice on political tactics and legislation. "Felix has more ideas per minute than any man of my acquaintance," Roosevelt said. "He has a brilliant mind but it clicks so fast it makes my head fairly spin. I find him tremendously interesting and stimulating."

One morning in 1932 after Frankfurter and the President-elect had talked the night away at FDR's Hyde Park estate, Marion Frankfurter scolded her husband for conducting the nocturnal seminar as he would have done for eager Harvard law students. In the world of ideas, Felix replied, there is no hierarchy. Professor Frankfurter was offering advice, and the new President, pencil in hand, was paying close attention.

The Frankfurter style never changed. There was the inexorable rush of suggestions—about appointments, legislation, broad policy—all elaborately packaged in tufts of flattery. When Roosevelt was governor, Frankfurter had suggested members for state commissions, strategies for investigations, and had offered congratulations for announced policies ("You have vindicated courage in government . . . ").

Roosevelt's presidential election brought a new wave of Frankfurter advisories. First, the President-elect was compared to Woodrow Wilson in his ability to "mobilize the will and wisdom of the nation" and to TR in his "extensive and intimate knowledge of his countrymen." Then Frankfurter told Roosevelt that a President's Cabinet was like a symphony and the individual members depended upon their leader (Toscanini came to Frankfurter's mind) to draw out their best qualities. Secretary of State Cordell Hull seemed just right in temperament and outlook, Attorney General Tom Walsh was "the embodiment of Justice" and Labor Secretary

Frances Perkins "is not only the best possible woman for your cabinet but the best man for her job."

Frankfurter also offered his prescription to overcome the deep malaise of the Depression, and it was bound closely to the new President's pragmatic leadership. He hoped that FDR would find "some felicitous way of indicating that our greatest need is to resume employment and the way to resume employment is to resume employment." He took his practical approach one step further by asserting that "the budget will be balanced when business recovers rather than this foolish theory of magic that business will recover by balancing the budget."

Though Roosevelt kept his own shrewd counsel on all policy and personnel matters, he did enjoy Frankfurter's company and "seminars." It was natural, therefore, that Roosevelt would conclude that Frankfurter himself should become a part of the New Deal administration that he supported so insistently. The President offered Frankfurter the position of solicitor general, the government's chief advocate before the U.S. Supreme Court. FDR tried to entice Frankfurter with the argument that he would be much more likely to be named to the U.S. Supreme Court from the solicitor general's office than from the Harvard Law School. But Frankfurter, after consultation with Holmes and Brandeis, turned Roosevelt down, largely, he said, because he thought he could be of greater service to the President outside of the administration. He preferred to pump ideas and other men into the New Deal— rather than to be totally consumed by the technical business of government litigation. "You are an independent pig," FDR wrote Frankfurter after he learned of his decision, "and that is one reason I cannot blame you!"

Frankfurter began immediately to prove to the President that his decision had been the right one. With the critical assistance of two of his Harvard protégés, Frankfurter helped draft the Securities Act, which provided much-needed protection for the public against misinformation and unscrupulous operators in the securities market. But Frankfurter's label as "the most influential single individual in the United States" by the National Recovery Administration's director, General Hugh Johnson, had less to do with his drafting skills than with his recruitment record. He always seemed to have just the right young lawyer to place in FDR's new agencies. They were called Felix's "happy hot dogs" and appeared to have gotten their jobs after the professor had put in a good word for them.

Frankfurter denied undue influence and pointed out that he did nothing more for his friend the President than he had done for scores of other friends in prominent Boston and New York law firms. "It was the most natural thing in the world," said Frankfurter. "If you want to get good groceries in Washington, you go to Magruder's, or in New York to Park and Tilford, or in Boston to S.S. Pierce. If you wanted to get a lot of first-class lawyers, you went to the Harvard Law School."

By 1935 the New Deal had begun to hoist America out of its worst depression, but the major tools that had done the job—the social and economic legislation—had come under increasing scrutiny. The complaining business community, which, ironically, had greatly benefited from the remarkable recovery, intensified its attack on "that man in the White House." One weapon at hand was the constitutional challenge to the New Deal legislation, since the conservative majority on the Supreme Court was hostile to the welfare state philosophy of the Roosevelt administration. Indeed, the Court had already begun to dismantle the early legislative underpinnings of the New Deal by striking down the National Industrial Recovery Act, the Bituminous Coal Act and the Agricultural Adjustment Act.

Franklin Roosevelt did not fail to notice the paradox of being one of the most popular U.S. presidents in history yet consistently frustrated by a handful of Justices who rejected his social and economic programs on constitutional grounds. In 1936 Roosevelt prepared for reelection, which seemed assured, and a successful challenge to the conservative Court majority, which did not.

The problem with a challenge to the Court was not FDR's conclusion—that the Court majority had wrongly thrust itself in the path of popular legislation. That view had long had the wide support of constitutional scholars. Professor Frankfurter of Harvard, perhaps the leading scholar on the issue, could point to a list of publications dating back almost twenty years to document the proposition that U.S. Supreme Court Justices should not, as a matter of principle, substitute their social and economic philosophies for those of the popularly elected legislatures. And that, Frankfurter had written, was precisely what the anti–New Deal Court majority was doing.

The problem for Frankfurter (and ultimately, for Roosevelt) centered on the constitutional process for change. Frankfurter counseled patience, hoping that the Justices' mortality or good sense would correct the wrongheadedness of the Court majority. If that failed, however, Frankfurter recommended a constitutional amendment.

But Roosevelt considered the amendment route too slow and cumbersome, preferring quick legislative action. The President proposed a bill that he described as a reform measure to relieve the overburdened Justices of the U.S. Supreme Court of their onerous workload. It was, in fact, an attack on the conservative Court majority that had declared much of FDR's New Deal economic legislation unconstitutional. Expressing sympathy for the Justices' problems, the President offered to relieve every Justice over seventy years old of his job or appoint another Justice to halve his assignments. Had the President's proposal been accepted, he could have appointed six new Justices.

Two weeks before the announcement of the President's proposal, Roosevelt wrote Frankfurter that he would soon "shock" him. But Roosevelt carefully avoided discussion of his judicial-reform idea with Frankfurter before presenting it to the public. The President knew that Frankfurter would have doubts about the proposal. The Court-packing plan came too close to tampering with the constitutional process itself to have received Frankfurter's unqualified endorsement. After he heard FDR's announcement, Frankfurter put the best possible interpretation on the President's action:

> Dramatically and artistically you did "shock" me. But beyond that—well, the momentum of a long series of decisions not defensible in the realm of reason nor justified by settled principles of Constitutional interpretation had convinced me, as they had convinced you, that means had to be found to save the Constitution from the Court, and the Court from itself. . . . There was no perfect way out. . . . But I have, as you know, deep faith in your instinct to make the wise choice. . . .

As if he needed to prove his unwavering loyalty to Roosevelt, Frankfurter took an oath of public silence on the controversial issue and privately sent the President materials and suggestions on how best to succeed in his effort. The Court-packing plan failed, but Roosevelt soon would convert the Court by his own appointments. And eighteen months after the demise of the Court-packing plan, the President placed a phone call to his dedicated supporter, Felix Frankfurter, to inform him that he would nominate him for a seat on the U.S. Supreme Court. Frankfurter stood in his Cambridge apartment in his underdrawers when the President's call came through. "All I can say is that I wish my mother were alive," said the usually voluble Frankfurter.

The appointment was Roosevelt's third to the Supreme Court but was, by far, the most popular among civil libertarians. Hugo Black's Klan membership as a young man and scholarly capacity were still questioned. Stanley Reed, the second Roosevelt appointee, had been an effective solicitor general but seemed, at best, a moderate on civil liberties issues. Frankfurter was entirely different, set apart from his predecessors by an exemplary record. Further, his preeminence in the constitutional law field would assure libertarians, so they reasoned, of someone who could stand up to the formidable Chief Justice Hughes in judicial conference.

When news of the Frankfurter appointment spread through New Deal Washington, Tommy Corcoran burst into Harold Ickes's office at the Department of the Interior with two magnums of champagne. A group soon gathered that included three future Court appointees—Robert Jackson, William O. Douglas and Frank Murphy. "We were all very happy," Ickes later wrote. "All of us regard this as the most significant and worthwhile thing the President has done. He has solidified his Supreme Court victory, and regardless of who may be President during the next few years, there will be on the bench of the Supreme Court a group of liberals under aggressive, forthright and intelligent leadership."

Frankfurter would not have quarreled with Ickes's conclusion, since he seemed to have been training for the leadership role of the liberal wing of the Court during his entire professional life. But only four years later it would be clear to all that the prediction of Ickes and his friends was wrong. There would be a cohesive liberal group on the Court, but they would not be led by Frankfurter, who would pose increasingly hostile opposition. The leader, inconceivable at the time of Frankfurter's Court appointment, would be the former populist Senator from Alabama, Hugo Black.

CHAPTER II

Hugo

THE YEOMAN FARMERS HAD straggled into Ashland on foot and
horseback and in rickety wooden wagons to hear Reuben Kolb
preach a radical brand of political reform. The common farmers of
this poor, rural northeast Alabama county, Kolb warned, could
never receive a fair day's pay for a fair day's work as long as the
banks, railroads and wealthy corporations dominated their economic lives. If elected governor in 1892, Kolb promised that he
would redress the economic order by promoting the welfare of
farmers in the overwhelmingly rural state. Kolb lost three gubernatorial elections in that decade, at least one through the fraudu-
lent manipulation of the vote by the powerful interests he had
regularly denounced. But for years after Kolb's speech in Ashland
that spring evening, those who heard it—and those who only
heard about it—remembered his message.

Hugo Black was only six years old when Reuben Kolb appeared
in his hometown of Ashland, and did not claim to have heard him
speak. But Black missed very few of the populist orators who
followed Kolb to Ashland's square. And when he returned to his
boyhood home to declare his candidacy for the U.S. Senate in
1926, Black would rail against the populist demons of an earlier
generation: the banks, railroads and corporations that continued to

prosper at the expense of the farmers of Clay County who barely eked out a subsistence income.

The crowd milled with restless excitement in Ashland's square. Hugo Black, now a successful trial lawyer in Birmingham, had chosen to enter big time politics where he had begun his political education. Above the crowd, posters with the fresh, intense profile of the forty-year-old Black were tacked to every utility pole in town, and hundreds of the candidate's pamphlets were distributed by friends and Black family members. Eight-year-old James Black and his sister, Lucyle, carried their uncle's slogan—Hugo Black for U.S. Senator—on simple homemade signs.

There was one significant addition to the political landscape of Ashland in 1926 that was entirely absent in Reuben Kolb's time. Mingling with the farmers and friends and family of Black were men who, the previous night, had worn long white sheets at a rally in the square. They were members of the Ku Klux Klan whose goals were identical to those of the farmers and Black family members and friends: to hear and support Ashland's favorite son.

When Hugo Black rose to speak to the exuberant crowd on March 20, 1926, he first paid tribute to his father "who cherished hopes for my success," and his mother, "whose worn and wrinkled hand pointed my way to the truth and light and faith." Then he got down to political business. The times, said Black, called for a candidate who had not lost the common touch, who could understand and sympathize with the common men and women of Clay County. He reminded his audience that he had been born to generations of farmers and educated in the public academy at Ashland. He declared himself the candidate of the common people.

Black did not hide his scorn for his two chief rivals. Both were dedicated members of the state Democratic party's conservative establishment, Black said. Both had known power, one as a former governor, the other as the heir apparent to a family political dynasty whose members had served conservative political interests in the U.S. Congress for more than thirty years. Both came from wealthy families with considerable holdings in Birmingham's booming coal and steel industries. Both, in sum, represented the vested interests that had dominated Alabama politics for generations and had, Black charged, oppressed the dirt farmers of Clay

County. "Shall we return to the old shackles," asked Black, "cut from our people by sacrifice and blood, and say that the great common people of America can only be represented by the rich or by the sons of distinguished fathers?" Not if the voters of Alabama supported Hugo Black. He was not an attorney for the railroads or the utility companies or the corporations. He did not inherit wealth or a conservative political creed. Hugo Black was the son of a farmer, and he shared the interests of the common folk of Alabama. He favored low tariffs, cheap fertilizers, strict prohibition enforcement and no immigration. "The melting pot idea is dangerous to our national inheritance," Black declared. "I oppose further immigration, and believe our nation would be greatly benefited by closing the gates until we can educate and Americanize those already here."

The picture of the dedicated, decent friend of the common man was, as it turned out, the perfect prescription for victory. Aligning himself with the powerless, Black carved out a magnificent piece of political real estate, leaving his powerful and wealthy opponents to scrap for the rest. In the months that followed, Black carried out his senatorial campaign with the shrewdness, single-mindedness, energy and high intelligence that distinguished his career both before and after he won his seat in the U.S. Senate in 1926.

Black's ancestors left their native Ireland in 1800, fugitives of the failed rebellion, to settle in South Carolina. His mother, Martha Toland Black, was educated at an academy, a sign of privilege for a young Southern girl, and her brother became a prosperous lawyer after moving to California. The Tolands made no secret of their disapproval of the marriage of Martha to plain, uneducated William LaFayette Black of Clay County, Alabama. The marriage was, according to the Tolands, slightly beneath Martha's social station. Martha told her children that she had married her husband on the "rebound" after her true love, William's brother, Columbus, had been cut down by Yankee gunfire at Gettysburg while fighting gallantly by Lee's side.

When speaking to her children of her husband, Martha did not speak admiringly or even lovingly. In fact, Hugo was vividly aware at an early age that his adored mother did not love his father and that their marriage gave Martha no happiness. Fayette, as Hugo's father was called, made his living as a country storekeeper and farmer, as had his father before him. By Clay County standards, William earned a very good living indeed. The Blacks' general store and farm virtually composed the little post-office station of Harlan, where Hugo LaFayette Black was born. William ran the general store, supervised the planting of cotton and corn and oversaw the work of the two tenant farmers on his land. Among some family members it was known that Fayette had built and furnished his modest five-room farmhouse with his profits as a "moneylender" to the tenant farmers and sharecroppers in the county.

Martha Toland Black milked the cows, prayed regularly and endured her husband's bad temper and frequent drinking sprees. She raised her eight children strictly but with care and love and ambition. Martha believed that education was important and that it should begin at home. And so into Fayette Black's rough, clapboard house, Martha imported volumes of Victor Hugo and Sir Walter Scott. Indeed, her eighth, last and favorite child, Hugo, was named after the author whose book Martha happened to be reading at his birth. And the Scott novels, dominated by the ideals of honor and chivalry and noblesse oblige, became a part of Hugo Black's early fantasy life.

At Martha's insistence, the LaFayette Blacks moved to the Clay County seat of Ashland when Hugo was three. With a population of 350, Ashland boasted an academy, a combination high school and junior college, where Martha was certain that her children could receive a better formal education than could possibly be provided by Hugo's older brother, Lee, on the family farm at Harlan. Fayette opened a general store opposite the Ashland courthouse square, and he prospered on a larger scale than he ever had in Harlan, selling general merchandise to farmers on credit and exacting high interest rates in return. He voted with the downstate conservative Democrats, unaffected by the populism that swept the county in the last decade of the nineteenth century. Martha's life centered on her children, who would, she determined, succeed in ways and on a scale that neither she nor her husband could dream of for themselves

Hugo did well enough at the Ashland Academy, but his more valuable education was received in the courthouse square listening to aspiring local and state politicians. From Black's earliest memory, politics held a special fascination for him. At the age of nine Hugo was already deeply absorbed in the politics of Clay County and devoured election news the way today's boys master baseball statistics.

Young Hugo was equally intrigued with the activity inside the Clay County courthouse where the county's best lawyers, like three-hundred-pound Martin Lackey, seated on a specially built cane-bottomed chair, harangued local juries. Hugo listened intently to the arguments, matching wits with the cream of the Clay County bar. Whenever an attorney argued a case, Black played the same challenging game, testing his silently conceived arguments against those actually put forward to the judge and jury. Hugo won more victories in his mind than the best attorney in the county.

Although Hugo cared early and deeply about politics and law, his older brother Orlando posed a formidable alternative role model. By the time Hugo was fourteen, Orlando had already completed studies at the Birmingham Medical College and graduated from the medical department of the University of the South at Sewanee, Tennessee. Shortly after graduation, Orlando established a successful practice in Wilsonville, Alabama, joined the Democratic party, the Knights of Pythias, the local Baptist church, and was listed in *Notable Men of Alabama*.

Hugo dutifully abided by the wishes of his mother and also enrolled in the Birmingham Medical College. But his mother's best wishes and his brother Orlando's guidance could not overcome Hugo's intense aversion to the study of medicine. Finally Martha Black relented and allowed Hugo to attend the University of Alabama Law School at Tuscaloosa. In the two years that Black and his twenty-two classmates studied law, the school's two faculty members lectured on legislation and legal rules. Black later admitted that his formal legal education could not compare to the revolutionary case-method approach that had been introduced at Harvard. But it would do. Black graduated with honors and stood ready to realize his boyhood dream: to emulate his heroes in the Clay County courtroom.

After a brief, disappointing attempt to establish a profitable practice in Ashland, Black headed for boisterous, booming Birmingham. Settled shortly after the Civil War, the city grew dramatically, supported primarily by a steel industry drawing on the nearby rich coal and iron ore deposits and the ready supply of cheap labor. With Birmingham's reputation as the industrial capital of the South came the more dubious title of "Murder Capital of the World." The city was, in fact, the South's version of the wide-open, rough-edged frontier towns of the West.

But Birmingham also offered opportunities for energetic and ambitious young professionals like Hugo Black. To be sure, Black's career began slowly. After he arrived in Birmingham in 1907, Black shared a room in a boardinghouse with three other men. He rented office space from an established Birmingham attorney, spent much of his time investigating claims for a mail-order insurance company and waited impatiently for paying clients to walk in the door. He also joined every civic club that would have him and taught Sunday school at the First Baptist Church—wise investments of time for a newly arrived attorney from Clay County with no connections and no clients.

Soon enough, Black received his first big break when he appeared in the courtroom of Judge A. O. Lane, a former mayor of Birmingham, to plead the case of a black convict who claimed to have been forced to serve as a laborer leased to a local steel company for twenty-two days beyond his prison sentence. Black's client, Willie Morton, had been the victim of the convict-leasing system which was openly condoned by the city's judicial establishment and avidly supported by the city's steel industry in search of the cheapest labor available. The chances of a black convict's successfully challenging the system did not seem promising. But Willie Morton was Hugo Black's first legitimate client, and the young lawyer attacked the case with the zealous intensity that would be a hallmark of his entire professional career. Spending weeks researching the law, Black came to court fully prepared to deal with the barrage of anticipated procedural maneuvers of his opposing counsel, William Grubb. Each time that Grubb, a leading member of the city bar, attempted to lure Black into an irrelevant pleading that could spell defeat for his client, Black would demur softly but firmly. After an entire day of Grubb's procedural thrusts and Black's controlled parries, Judge Lane peered down at his friend Grubb and said, "Well, they didn't work, did they, Billy?"

Black won a $150 judgment and more. Judge Lane was so impressed with the young attorney's performance that he shortly arranged for twenty-five-year-old Hugo Black to be appointed to the part-time position of municipal court judge. News of the appointment spread quickly through Black's hometown of Ashland. A Birmingham newspaperman who happened to be in Ashland at that time reported the town consensus opinion that Black's rise "to the responsible position which he now holds is a striking example of the recognition which his pluck and energy has secured." Despite Judge Black's meager $1,500 annual salary, all Ashland was certain that the appointment represented only the first modest rung on young Hugo's ambitious career ladder.

The municipal court in Birmingham served as the way station for the city's underclass—prostitutes, petty thieves, gamblers, drunks and drifters—and the city provided accommodations to match. The court was a single ugly, dirty room with a cage at the rear to hold the hapless prisoners. The *Birmingham Age-Herald* assigned a reporter to the court, not because of the importance of the proceedings, but for the opportunity it offered for lively—and condescending—commentary. The *Age-Herald*'s Charles Mandy described with cheerful smugness the constant, depressing line of blacks that trudged through Black's courtroom. But slowly the reporter's daily column began to offer grudging respect for the man in charge.

Judge Black's courtroom opened promptly at 8:30 A.M. every business day. Always courteous, Black listened impassively to tales of wife-beatings, brawls, binges, swindles and slashings. He meted out $25 and $50 fines to minor flim-flam artists and thieves, dealt sternly with drunks (a $500 fine and a 90-day sentence for violation of the city's prohibition law) and kept a steady eye on the number of cases he disposed of daily. Black studied people, not rules, and relied more on common sense than anything he had learned in law books at Tuscaloosa. He carefully weighed the testimony of those appearing before him, even if they were ignorant and black. Occasionally he took their word over that of a white policeman without speech or fanfare but a simple, "I am inclined to believe you and you may go."

The work in the police court offered Black the judicial title and assured him good publicity in the *Birmingham Age-Herald.* But the calendar was tedious and the pay inadequate. After a year and a half in the job Black resigned to pursue his private practice, now thriving, on a full-time basis. Before long, however, even the steady stream of clients and increasingly larger fees did not fully satisfy Black's ambition and energy. He decided to run for the office of Jefferson County solicitor, the county's chief criminal prosecutor.

In 1914, a reform-minded Jefferson County solicitor could have his choice of challenging targets: the county's burgeoning crime rate or the scandal-ridden fee system. Homicides were not indigenous to northern Alabama, but the corruption bred by the fee system there had no rival, even in other parts of the state where it existed. Instead of paying sheriffs and county clerks regular salaries, Alabama legislators had passed a law providing for a system of state payments based on the number of prisoners in jail awaiting trial. Since officials in the system were paid on a daily basis, dishonest sheriffs often ordered mass arrests of lowly blacks accused of nothing more ominous than shooting craps. Once the accused was in jail, neither sheriff nor clerk had much incentive to move the process forward. Hundreds of blacks arrested on minor gambling charges could languish in jail for months without protest from a single law-enforcement officer.

For the fifteen years that he had been county solicitor, Harrington Heflin had exhibited no discernible concern about the crime rate or the fee system. Heflin, overshadowed by his flamboyant brother, Congressman J. Thomas Heflin, found his normal duties difficult enough without attempting risky reforms. Besides, the bar and the established businesses of Birmingham had few complaints.

Black began touring the county in his Model T Ford six months before Heflin or his two other opponents gave serious thought to the race. In each town, Black headed for the general store or village square, introducing himself and asking his new acquaintances what they expected from their county solicitor. Always courteous and concerned, Black thanked them, promised to work hard if elected and left a stack of his pamphlets for their friends.

By the time his opponents finally began to campaign, Black had already overcome his relative anonymity, having systematically canvassed the entire county and distributed his simple but effective cards and pamphlets at every stop. In sum, he was running at full stride before his opponents had left the starting blocks.

Black's opponents attempted to make up lost ground by placing large ads in Birmingham's daily newspapers, promising their dedicated service to the voters of Jefferson County. Black, poised for battle like the superb trial lawyer that he was, immediately responded. Cultivating his underdog role, Black claimed that he represented the ordinary citizens of the county, not "a few capitalists or a ring of politicians." At the same time he placed small teaser ads in the same Birmingham newspapers with his photograph and the announcement, "This man is your *next* solicitor."

When the large city dailies threw their support to Heflin and Black's other opponents, Black declared he was beholden to no establishment publication or other vested interests. He reminded the voters that he was the candidate of the common men and women of Jefferson County. Finally, as the campaign wound down, it was clear to Heflin that the race had narrowed to a contest between the incumbent and twenty-eight-year-old Hugo Black. On election day, Black polled more than two thousand votes than Heflin and left the other challengers far behind.

Once in office, Solicitor Black took dead aim at the corrupt fee system, releasing five hundred petty offenders incarcerated on mere suspicion and kept there because of the greed of their jailers. On his first day in office Black declared they were not law violators but unfortunate victims of the fee system. Shortly afterward, Black began to clear the clogged docket; he and his two assistants tried eleven capital cases during their first week of official duties.

What he had heard canvassing the county during the campaign suggested to Black that Jefferson County voters were concerned not only about crowded dockets and capital crimes but also about illegal liquor trafficking. For Black, professional responsibility and private moral code merged with the result that he prosecuted whiskey interests with a special vengeance. His most celebrated case involved a major whiskey ring that reportedly had smuggled more than $600,000 worth of illegal alcohol into the small town of Girard, Alabama, just across the Chattahoochee River from Columbus, Georgia. Acting on a tip, but without a search warrant, state officials had raided several buildings in Girard and found thousands of gallons of booze hidden behind false doors and walls and hanging by ropes in barrels submerged in the Chattahoochee. In all, twenty-two separate cases arose out of the Girard raids. When six defendants indicted as ringleaders failed to appear at trial, Black, who had been appointed special prosecutor by the state attorney general, ordered the immediate destruction of every barrel and bottle confiscated. Claiming that the defendants had forfeited their legal rights by failure to appear in court, Black personally supervised the emptying of the whiskey into the Girard gutters. The next day, the *Birmingham News* featured Black on the front pages as "the man of the hour," photographed in shirtsleeves and straw hat, proudly pouring out the moonshine.

Black's aversion to liquor was due in large part to his bitter family history. He remembered his mother's unhappiness after his father's binges, and he mourned the death of his favorite brother, Pelham, a victim of a riding accident while inebriated. His aversion was so strong, in fact, that it caused this future civil libertarian to take questionable legal actions such as the destruction of the seized goods in the Girard case. A second incident occurred after the Alabama legislature passed an anti-liquor-advertising law over protests that the law violated the First Amendment freedom of the press. Solicitor Black immediately announced that he would strictly enforce the new law, threatening to shut down newspapers and newsdealers that defied it. Black eventually defended the constitutionality of the law in the state supreme court, successfully arguing that the legislation was a proper exercise of the state police power.

The whiff of official wrongdoing always seemed to capture Solicitor Black's attention, and the news out of the steel town of Bessemer in 1915 suggested the grossest transgressions. An extraordinarily high volume of confessions had been reported, and Black suspected foul play by the police department. A special grand jury convened by Black confirmed the county prosecutor's worst suspicions. Confessions had been beaten out of prisoners by police in a manner that would, the grand jury reported, have

shamed "the most uncivilized and barbarous community." Black
prisoners were led out of their cells late at night, tied to doorknobs
and hacked with a buckle-ended leather strap until they collapsed
in their own blood. Many of the helpless prisoners had been jailed
on only the vague suspicion of lawbreaking. Their persecutors
were two senior members of the Bessemer police force who had,
it was revealed, been carrying out their barbarous practices for
years.

The grand jury's final report could have been torn from an opinion by U.S. Supreme Court Justice Hugo Black a quarter of a century later: "A man does not forfeit his right to be treated as a
human being by reason of the fact that he is charged with or an
officer suspects that he is guilty of a crime. Instead of being ready
and waiting to strike a prisoner in his custody, an officer should
protect him. . . . Such practices are dishonorable, tyrannical and
despotic, and such rights must not be surrendered to any officer or
set of officers, so long as human life is held sacred, and human
liberty and human safety of paramount importance."

A Bessemer citizens' group supported the grand jury's findings
but disgruntled city officials faulted the young prosecutor, not their
police force. "There are ways to ask a white man questions,"
grumbled Alderman Moss Crotwell, "and I never talk to a negro
working for me in the manner that Black spoke to me." Ironically,
eight years after Black had come to the defense of the black victims
of the Bessemer police department's "third degree," he would join
the most rabid and destructive racist organization of twentieth-
century America: the Ku Klux Klan.

By June 30, 1917, the prison population in the county jail had
been cut by 277 since the day Black took office, the monthly food
bill by $2,000 and the court docket by 2,660 cases. It was progress
by any objective standard. But those most interested in the activities of the solicitor—the sheriffs, clerks and others who had benefited from the desultory administration of Black's predecessor—
were not impressed.

Led by Black's defeated opponent, Harrington Heflin, anti-Black
forces took advantage of a technicality in the state law to embarrass Black and, ultimately, to force him from office. Under existing
Alabama law, Jefferson County was entitled to two prosecutors,
the county solicitor and the circuit solicitor, with overlapping legal

authority. In 1917 Heflin and friends encouraged the circuit solicitor to challenge Black's authority in court. Shortly afterward, observers in the state court witnessed the bizarre spectacle of the county solicitor telling the court that the government was ready with its case and the circuit solicitor promptly standing up to tell the same judge that the government was not prepared for trial. The challenge soon deteriorated into an argument over whether Black or the circuit solicitor could hire Black's assistants. Resolution of the dispute ultimately came in the state's highest court, where, remarkably, Black was told that he did not have the authority to hire his own staff. Understandably disgusted, Black quit, publicly stating that he could no longer carry out his duties effectively.

The *Birmingham Ledger*'s editorial that followed Black's resignation was sympathetic: "Hugo Black has left a good record as chief prosecuting officer and legal counsel of Jefferson County. He has given speedy trials and kept down the population of the county jail. He has vigorously enforced the laws. Mr. Black's chief claim on the gratitude of the people is his record of attempting to pry loose from the county some of the treasury spoilage systems which have been fastened on it by generations of legislative lawgrowing and the interest of the office holders. . . . In the end his own position became unsatisfactory to him and he gave up that post rather than have subordinate men not of his selection. This was the manly thing to do."

Black's reputation as a top trial lawyer was, by this time, firmly established and a lucrative private practice presented an attractive alternative to public office. But by 1917 World War I had erupted, and Black, though thirty-one and protected from the draft, answered the call to service. To his profound disappointment, Captain Hugo Black never came closer to the front than Fort Sill, Oklahoma. By the time he had completed his training in Oklahoma and California, the Armistice was at hand. A year after volunteering for service, Captain Black returned to Birmingham to enter private law practice.

The fact that Black had not seen action at the front did not dampen his patriotism or his willingness to talk to civilian audi-

ences about the Great War. He had spoken at length to American
officers as well as to those of our European allies, Black told a
Birmingham audience, and he could assure them that the dough-
boy was a superb soldier. At home "the spirit and patriotism of
the men were wonderful," Black reported, "even though there was
much disappointment that many did not get the opportunity to
take their shot at the Hun."

The young man who had left Birmingham a beleaguered public
prosecutor had returned to the city a respected private citizen
whose views on war and law, school bonds and the Bible were
widely solicited in a remarkably short time. In supporting a $5
million school bond, Black was quoted in the *Age-Herald* as believing "in the little frame schoolhouse built and maintained from the
common fund of the common people." He rejoined his fellow
Masons, Moose and Odd Fellows and once again awoke at sunrise
every Sunday to prepare his favorite lessons for the class at the
First Baptist Church (for example, "The Dramatic Life of Moses,
Dramatic in Birth, Dramatic in Life, Dramatic in Death").

Rejecting corporate clients and retainers, attorney Black quickly
attracted a large clientele among the blue-collar workers who were
injured in the mines, textile factories and other industries in and
around Birmingham. Representing the common workman was a
matter of principle with Black; it was also very good business. By
1925 Black was earning more than $40,000 a year. He did so largely
by working on a contingency-fee basis, taking a percentage of the
jury verdict if he won, nothing if he lost. He did not lose often,
frequently winning unprecedentedly high jury awards: $3,000 for
a hernia victim, $10,000 for a fireman with an injured leg and
$25,000 for an employee with an eye injury. The court reduced the
$25,000 jury verdict to $6,000, concluding that "passion and not
reason dictated the amount of the verdict," but at the same time
commending Black for presenting his client's cause "in the most
forcible manner."

"Old Ego," as his courtroom opponents derisively called Black,
was so good that he appeared to handicap himself before trial. "I'll
take the jury in the box," Black would tell the judge, seemingly
indifferent to jurors who might be prejudiced against his client. But
even his feigned cockiness contributed to his shrewdly calculated
strategy: by accepting jurors without question, Black immediately

established a trusting relationship with the people who would decide his client's fate. His gesture also suggested that his case was so strong that his arguments were virtually superfluous.

Black's bravado was backed by meticulous preparation for trial, not only on the technical points of law but also on the weaknesses of his opponent's witnesses. "Hugo could get more out of witnesses than anybody I ever saw," said one admiring attorney. "Never lied. Just took stabs and hit the heart. Could see what you or your witness was scared of and, without telling you he had it, make you believe he did have it when he might not. He could do one hell of a lot with a blank piece of paper."

Furiously competitive, Black relished a trial against a powerful adversary, even if his client's case was weak. With a reputation and record to match Black's, attorney Borden Burr seemed the prohibitive favorite to win one trial against Black. The problem for Black was that Burr possessed clear evidence that Black's client was stone-drunk at the time he lost a leg in a mining-car accident. During the trial Burr was the picture of confidence, loudly chortling as Black struggled to present his client's case. Finally, Black walked over to his client, handed him his crutches, and gingerly helped him struggle to the front of the jury box. Pulling up the worker's empty pants leg, Black spoke softly to the jurors, tears welling in his eyes. "That's not funny to me. Not funny at all. But did you hear Mr. Burr? He laughed and cackled all over this courtroom." Then Black took his client's arm and said, "Go on, son, you can sit down now. Let me help you." By the time Black had returned to the counsel table, jurors were openly crying. A short time later the jury returned a record-setting award for Black's client.

For the most part, however, Black did not need such histrionics to win his cases. His trial preparation was thorough; his phenomenal memory retained both fact and legal technicality with flawless consistency. Moreover, Black genuinely believed in his clients and welcomed every opportunity to punish corporations that remained insensitive to the legitimate needs of their lowly employees. Protection of the common man was a favorite Black theme in the Birmingham courtrooms, later on the floor of the U.S. Senate and, finally, in the conference room of the U.S. Supreme Court.

Despite his growing professional reputation in Birmingham, Black remained an outsider to the city's establishment. And for all

of his proletarian fire, Black seemed to want establishment acceptance. Since childhood, Black had made critical choices—to excel
in school, to become an attorney—that conformed to his mother's
firm ambitions for him to enter a profession. Black himself strad-
dled the line between individuality and conformity. He was the
outspoken defender of the common man at the same time that
he befriended members of the legal establishment and sought the
company of hail-fellows in a half dozen civic organizations.

When it was time for marriage, Hugo Black selected a very
uncommon mate—Josephine Foster. Josephine's father, Dr. Sterling Foster, had studied for the ministry at the University of the
South and later at Princeton and the University of Edinburgh. Her
mother, Anne Patterson, grew up in one of Mobile's most prominent political families, as the daughter of Josiah A. Patterson, a
lawyer, judge and member of Congress. The Fosters' wedding had
been reported prominently on the society page of the Mobile daily
newspaper, which noted that President Grover Cleveland had sent
a telegram of congratulations, as did every member of the President's Cabinet.

An attractive brunette with penetrating blue eyes, Josephine
Foster flaunted a vivacious nature and independence of mind that
confounded her parents and attracted clusters of young men wherever she went. She grew up on Birmingham's fashionable South
Side and attended Sweetbriar Academy in Virginia, a preparatory
school for generations of genteel Southern women. During World
War I, Josephine joined the Navy as a yeomanette and was stationed in New York City. Upon her return to Birmingham, Josephine, twenty-one years old, met Hugo Black, thirty-four.

Black was immediately love-struck. "She just seemed to have a
sweet nobility about her," Black later recalled. "She just seemed to
reflect a spiritual quality." He approached the courtship as he did
all matters he deemed important during his lifetime: with total
dedication and confidence that he would prevail. As with so many
of his challenges initially, this one was daunting. Josephine had
been carefully groomed to take her place in comfortable Southern
society. Her parents came from conspicuously conservative political stock and did not favor a marriage for their daughter to a
commoner from Clay County, and certainly not one thirteen years
her senior.

Hugo pursued Josephine relentlessly. "I had never seen any man before with so much confidence," Josephine later recalled. "He assumed that I was fated to marry him and that everybody else was out of the picture. He was like an irresistible force; he just kept coming at me." Josephine's family and friends thought Hugo was crude and common. But Josephine kept her own counsel and was soon mesmerized by Black's mind and charm and complete devotion to her. "Although many men had been in love with me before," she said, "nobody ever looked at me with such total adoration."

They were married on February 23, 1921, a day that Hugo Black would always remember with supreme satisfaction. "If I have accomplished anything real in this world," he later told his son, Hugo, Jr., "it was talking your mother into marrying me." Until Josephine's untimely death at the age of fifty, Hugo Black's love and devotion to his wife was sustained with fairy-tale intensity. She was the perfect mate: beautiful, gracious, loyal and noble, a Sir Walter Scott fantasy come true. Josephine was much more, of course—a life companion who offered her husband emotional security and a quiet, creative intellect that naturally complemented his aggressive brilliance.

With his marriage to Josephine Foster, Hugo Black edged closer to Birmingham's establishment. He bought a two-story house on the city's South Side and added a country club membership to his list of affiliations. Meanwhile his young bride became active in the Junior League, doing good works in the company of women from other socially prominent families.

For the next four years Black's law practice prospered as never before, primarily as a result of his fabulously successful personal-injury work. Occasionally Black took a controversial case outside of his personal-injury practice. The most celebrated involved the murder of a Catholic priest by a Methodist minister named Edwin Stephenson, whom Black defended. The essential facts were not disputed: Stephenson shot the priest on the front porch of his rectory and then walked to the police chief's office to confess. Black claimed self-defense for his client in an argument heavy with racial and religious overtones. The jury was told that Stephenson had been enraged by the news that the priest had performed the marriage ceremony of Stephenson's daughter and Pedro Gussman, a Puerto Rican and a devout Catholic. Shortly before Gussman took the witness stand, Black ordered the courtroom blinds to be lowered so that Gussman's swarthy complexion appeared even darker. And though Black presented his client's case with characteristic attention to technical detail, his final appeal to the jury contained pointed references to Gussman's religion and racial heritage. The jury acquitted Stephenson, and Black later credited his courtroom victory to the poor performance of an inept prosecutor. Others, however, remembered the case not for the prosecutor's ineptitude, but for Black's blatant appeal to the jury's prejudices.

At the same time that Black was accused of prejudicial appeal in the Stephenson case, he also represented numerous black laborers injured in industrial accidents. Whether in the Stephenson murder trial or his more typical personal-injury cases, Hugo Black's single objective was to win a verdict for his client, without regard to religion or race. Indeed, Black once pleaded the case of a black convict injured in a mining accident all the way to the U.S. Supreme Court, offering to argue it without compensation if the Court would assume incidental costs. Black was convinced that the convict had been a victim of injustice at the hands of a negligent mining company and insisted that his client was entitled to a hearing before the U.S. Supreme Court. Without dissent, the Justices accepted Black's argument.

Secure in his profession and at home, Black began to think once again about public service. In 1923 he seized an opportunity to prosecute bootleggers that would put him on the front pages of every newspaper in the state. The assignment followed the confiscation of ten thousand quarts of illegal liquor by federal agents in the port of Mobile. Unable to find a sufficiently zealous and competent Republican prosecutor, U.S. Attorney General Harlan Fiske Stone and his assistant, Mabel Walker Willebrandt, chose Democrat Hugo Black. In one of the bitterest legal conflicts in the state's history, special prosecutor Black faced twenty-one attorneys who represented the defendants. For two months at trial Black argued that the defendants, who purported to be engaged in "bona fide" grocery and restaurant businesses, were, in fact, "engaged in bona fide bootlegging." At trial's end, eleven defendants were convicted of bootlegging as charged.

In the same year that he prosecuted the Mobile bootleggers, Black joined the Robert E. Lee chapter of the Ku Klux Klan, which counted among its members many of Birmingham's lawyers as well as hundreds of miners and other laborers who comprised Black's clientele and juries. Black later explained his Klan membership in terms of professional and political expediency.* Largely overlooked in his and others' analyses of Black's motives was the fact that the Klan appealed to an idealistic side of its members' nature as well as to their base, violent instincts. Black never supported the Klan's violence. He was, however, susceptible to the organization's more positive appeals: to a strict moral code that denounced bootleggers, protected the so-called purity of Anglo-Saxon America and exalted the role of the common laborer too often victimized by manipulative corporate powers.

Hugo Black had dreamed of high political office as a boy in Ashland, and now, as his career and ambitions seemed boundless, that early dream suddenly appeared possible. U.S. Senator Oscar Underwood, Alabama's senior statesman, announced in 1925 that he would not seek reelection. Black carefully considered his political opportunity, but so did two men who, if they entered the race, would do so as prohibitive favorites over the relatively unknown Birmingham attorney. The first frequently mentioned candidate for Underwood's seat was Thomas Kilby, who had served as governor and could draw on extensive financial resources from his prosperous steel business as well as from longtime corporate political supporters. The second potential candidate presented even more formidable credentials than Kilby. He was John Bankhead, Jr., whose family members had represented Alabama in Congress for more than thirty years and who was backed by the family coal-mining fortune.

Eleven years earlier, Black had confronted similar political odds when he challenged Harrington Heflin, the incumbent Jefferson

---

* Black resigned from the Klan in 1925, a month before he declared his candidacy for the U.S. Senate. The resignation was fully approved by the Klan, which preferred that candidates it endorsed not be active members.

County solicitor. In that race Black had devised a brilliant strategy that included early and constant contact with voters in every area of Jefferson County, a clever, low-budget publicity campaign and the insistent claim that he was the common man's candidate. The strategy had worked in 1914; Black prepared to duplicate it on a larger scale in 1925.

Six months before either Thomas Kilby or John Bankhead, Jr., announced his candidacy for the Senate seat, Black opened his campaign. Investing in two Overland Whippet automobiles—one for southern Alabama and one for northern Alabama—Black worked laborious campaign days, shaking hands with voters in fifty-seven of the state's sixty-seven counties. In each tiny town Black would start at the general store. "I would introduce myself and talk to the people in the store," Black recalled, "and try to find out their needs, their wants." Depositing a stack of "Hugo Black for U.S. Senate" automobile cards and windshield stickers on the counter, Black then would head for the town square in search of a checker game. "I believe I can whip either one of you fellas," he would boast good-naturedly. Quickly Black's credentials as a top checker player—and serious political candidate—were established. In each town and rural crossroad Black would carefully identify men and women who were highly respected in their communities and ask for their support. A friendly farmer would usually offer Black a bed for the night; at sunrise the next morning, farmer and candidate would begin a new day's chores.

"I am personally of the opinion that there have been so many millionaires and corporation lawyers in the United States Senate," Black wrote a distant relative in December 1925, "that the people rarely ever have a representative. It is my ambition to give them one. I have been in 50 counties in Alabama and the situation looks good to me." Noting the forces against him, Black added, "I shall probably have the unanimous opposition of the Catholic Church. Several years ago, when a Methodist preacher in Birmingham shot a Catholic priest, I successfully defended the Methodist preacher. There is no chance of them forgiving me for that. Owing to my prosecutions of the liquor ring at Mobile, Alabama, and at Girard, Alabama, there is no chance of my getting support of the wet. My hopes, therefore, rest on the DRY—PROTESTANT—PROGRESSIVE VOTERS of the state of Alabama."

Kilby and Bankhead entered the race in the early months of 1926 with pompous, ponderous pledges of service to the great people of Alabama. Meanwhile, Hugo Black continued his one-man road show, speaking at a well-publicized meeting of voters in Abbeville, at the Florala county fair (between the sacred harp singing and the fiddlers' contest) and, on Wednesday and Sunday nights, to local church groups.

While his two chief opponents ignored his candidacy, Black pounded out his core campaign theme—that the ordinary voters of Alabama deserved a Senator who would stand up to the conservative, vested interests of the state, represented by Bankhead and Kilby. "I ask the fathers who love their children, citizens of Alabama who prize the freedom of American opportunity to strike at this idea that only the rich, the powerful, the sons of the great can serve the state," Black told an audience in Cleburne. "It is true now and I believe it will be true hereafter, that the humblest son of the humblest citizen, born in the humblest surroundings can lift his eyes toward the star of hope. So may it ever be!"

Belatedly, both Bankhead and Kilby realized that Black's vigorous campaigning and constant, though indirect, assaults on their candidacies had propelled him into the position of front-runner. They counterattacked, sneering at Black's self-promoted image as the poor man's candidate. Attorney Black's Birmingham law practice, they claimed, produced an annual six-figure income. With bite and humor, Black quickly retorted that "there is not one of the candidates who couldn't buy all I have and get their stenographer to give me a check without missing it."

Less than a month before the election an admirer wrote Black that "you have those Bankheads scared within an inch of their life." Black replied, "I agree with you that the Bankheads are astounded. I believe we have them beat, however, and I am going every minute." Black had accurately calculated that Bankhead posed the main threat to his election, and he devoted the last weeks of the campaign to pointed attacks on his chief opponent. He told a rally in blue-collar Bessemer that the Bankheads expected "a line of royal succession" and exhorted the crowd to reject the notion that "the road to the U.S. Senate shall be paved with gold."

Since both Bankhead and Black advocated cheap fertilizers, good roads, prohibition enforcement and restricted immigration, the election ultimately became a contest of campaign styles, slogans and strategy, and John Bankhead, Jr., was no match for Hugo Black. Throughout his campaign Black had repeated with rising zeal his call for a crackdown on bootleggers and "the closing of all doors to immigration." Those appeals, together with Black's militant defense of the workingman against the wealthy, captured the organized support of the powerful Alabama Ku Klux Klan. In order to stave off last-minute Klan defections, Black openly criticized New York Governor Al Smith, a Democratic presidential aspirant, an outspoken foe of prohibition and a Catholic.

On the night of August 10, 1926, Hugo Black stood outside the *Birmingham News Age-Herald* building intently watching a screen flash the election returns. The final tally showed Black with 71,916 votes and his nearest challenger, John Bankhead, Jr., with 49,841. He carried 42 of the state's 67 counties; Bankhead won only 19. But at the critical moment of victory Black walked away from the crowd. "There are times that are so important in a man's life that he wants to be alone," he later explained. "I was asking the people of my state, people I knew and loved, to give me the chance to play a part for them in one of the highest offices in the nation."

Three weeks after his Democratic primary victory (tantamount to election in Democratic Alabama at that time), Black stood triumphantly before three thousand hooded Alabama Klansmen in their large Klavern on Twentieth Street in downtown Birmingham. Grand Dragon James Esdale proudly introduced Black and Bibb Graves, who had won the Democratic gubernatorial primary, as "the men who have been chosen by the Klansmen of Alabama to come out into the forefront." Both Black and Graves were presented with Klan passports. Rising to accept the passport and thank the Klan for its political support, Black pledged allegiance to the organization's high principles. With florid rhetoric he expressed admiration for the Klan's dedication to "American manhood and womanhood, revering virtue of the mother race, loving the pride of Anglo-Saxon spirit—and I love it—true to the heaven-born principles of liberty which were written in the Constitution of this country, and in the great historical documents, straight from the heart of Anglo-Saxon patriots." He bid farewell "with my love and

my faith from the bottom of a heart that is yours." Black's orator-
ical flourish was greeted by tumultuous applause. His political dues
dramatically paid, Black never again publicly acknowledged his
debt to or sympathy with the Klan.

U.S. Senator Hugo Black and his wife, Josephine, moved to a
modest District of Columbia house with their two small boys in
1927. At twenty-seven Josephine was the youngest hostess and
one of the most attractive among the Senators' wives. She accepted her sudden lofty social status—meeting ambassadors from
the great European capitals and attending elaborate dinners for
Washington's official elite—with bemused pleasure. But her greatest joys were her home and family, and Josephine spent most of
her time caring for Hugo, Jr., and Sterling, planting her garden and
offering her husband, the junior Senator from Alabama, a loving
and sometimes puckish perspective on his serious business of law-
making for the nation.

Black approached his Senate duties cautiously, aware that he
had much to learn. His election had passed virtually unnoticed by
the national press. In reporting the new faces in the Senate *The
New York Times* left Black for last. Preceding him were Robert
Wagner of New York, a prominent Democratic leader in the state
senate, and Carl Hayden of Arizona, Alben Barkley of Kentucky
and Millard Tydings of Maryland, all moving to the Senate from
their seats in the House of Representatives.

Black had openly promised his constituents that he would maintain a low profile at first, accepting his committee assignments
dutifully, learning the Senate's rules and procedures and, most of
all, listening to his more experienced colleagues. At home, in the
quiet of his study, Black prepared for the day when he would lead,
annotating the works of Jefferson, underlining key passages of
Aristotle's *Politics* and absorbing the economic theories of Veblen
and Adam Smith.

During his first term Black took few legislative initiatives and
rarely spoke on the floor of the Senate. He took assiduous care of
his constituents, setting aside several hours a day to respond to
their concerns in letters and meetings. His most impassioned
speech to his colleagues was inspired by a slur on the Confederacy:

"Let the Senator from Maryland [William Bruce] hurl his darts and charges thick and fast. Let him drop his loaded shrapnel into their midst, and still, when the din of the explosion is ended, the people of the South will be there, back in their homes on the hillsides and in the valleys, responding to the same old Anglo-Saxon principle of loyalty to law and decency and government which seems to entitle them to be the particular object of the animadversions of the Senator from Maryland."

There was always a deeply serious side to Black's work and, even as he played to his Southern constituency, he remained resolutely committed to his view that the ordinary taxpayers were regularly manipulated and abused by wealthy special interests. As a member of the Senate's Interstate Commerce Committee, he voted against the nomination of a railroad lawyer to the ICC. He also opposed the nomination of Charles Evans Hughes to be Chief Justice of the United States because of his representation of wealthy corporate clients in his New York practice.

Black's suspicion of lobbyists for powerful utility companies prompted his call for a Senate investigation. So did his criticism of the U.S. Shipping Board's too-close link to the shipping interests the board presumed to regulate. In both instances Black's demands for investigations were postponed but not forgotten, and in his second Senate term Black would make good on both pledges.

The colleague whose work most influenced Alabama's junior Senator was George Norris, the great progressive from Nebraska. Norris's deep distrust of powerful corporate interests matched Black's own, and the Nebraskan's ability to articulate his views and translate them into meaningful legislation enormously impressed him.

Black and Norris shared an interest in Muscle Shoals, the large dam constructed during World War I on the Tennessee River in northern Alabama, and both were determined to prevent private utility companies from controlling its future. Norris proposed a government-operated Muscle Shoals; Black wanted private ownership that would insure the manufacture of cheap fertilizers as well as electric power for Alabama farmers. In his first major speech to the Senate, Black put his potent rhetorical skills to work in support of his position: "When the farmer comes in after a hard day's work following a mule on some red-clay hillside and finally puts his tired limbs to rest on an old-fashioned feather bed, he can lie there and pass into dreamland, with the sweet hope and fancy that his children's children may someday get fertilizer as cheaply as they are getting it in Germany today."

Norris expanded his legislative proposal to include a provision for the manufacturer of fertilizer and Black announced that he would vote for the Norris bill. Both Norris's and Black's efforts proved futile, since President Coolidge silently vetoed the measure, but the two Senators would continue to work together to fight their common corporate enemies.

During his first senatorial term Black quietly shed two groups of supporters that had been instrumental in his 1926 election. Significantly, the strength of both groups, the Ku Klux Klan and the prohibition forces, had diminished precipitously. After his dramatic post-election address to the Alabama Klan in Birmingham, Black made no attempt to court Klan support. And though he remained a teetotaler, Black gradually succumbed to the tide of national opinion opposed to prohibition and publicly supported a referendum on the issue. That stand naturally infuriated Alabama's Anti-Saloon League, whose members threatened to throw their support in the 1932 Democratic primary to Black's longtime rival, former governor Thomas Kilby. By this time Black was no longer the outsider but the effective representative of the people of Alabama. He handily won renomination in the Democratic primary, carrying fifty-two of the state's sixty-seven counties.

Looking back on his career in the U.S. Senate, Black confessed disappointment in his first-term performance, which he considered of only modest, parochial worth. The second term was profoundly different. Now an experienced legislator comfortably ensconced in office, Black marched confidently forward, sure of his abilities and dedicated to the service of the nation. The timing was fortuitous, since Black could now work under the inspirational leadership of the first Democratic President in twelve years, Franklin D. Roosevelt.

Though their American roots were buried in widely divergent social strata, both Black and the patrician Roosevelt viewed the Great Depression with unmitigated horror. Roosevelt responded with One Hundred Days of creative government, introducing new ideas, legislation and hope. Black applauded FDR's New Deal and voted for virtually every measure that the administration sponsored. But he bristled at the idea that he was a rubber stamp for the President—even this President whom he so admired.

In fact, Black offered his own cure for the nation's economic paralysis. After reading the works of the English writer G. D. H. Cole, as well as those of Stuart Chase, Black was persuaded that a mandated thirty-hour-maximum workweek would rescue the unemployed. He reasoned that the restricted workweek would spread the need for jobs without significantly sacrificing the income of the individual laborer. Black announced his bill for a thirty-hour week in the Senate and patiently shepherded it through the upper chamber, but to no avail, since the measure was never fully supported by the Roosevelt administration. Ultimately, the administration succeeded with its own bill, the Fair Labor Standards Act, which provided for minimum wages and maximum hours. Throughout Black's failed efforts, FDR made it a point to assure him that his ideas had been instrumental in advancing the administration's own thinking and that the final legislation was a product in large part of the Alabama Senator's efforts.

Black was of greatest service to the President, however, in undertaking Senate investigations that exposed the abuses of three corporate groups: the private shipping operators, the major commercial airlines and the gargantuan utility holding companies. In each Senate investigation Black displayed his finely honed trial lawyer's talent. Working for days, often without sleep, Black confronted his witnesses with sharply focused questions and a forceful impatience when they meandered from his predetermined line of inquiry.

The first investigation involved a peculiarly ill-conceived government program to rehabilitate a sagging merchant marine fleet held over from World War I. The plan had included generous subsidies for private U.S. shipping corporations, ostensibly for purposes of carrying the U.S. mail. Black's committee mandate was to investigate and cancel such contracts if they did not serve the public interest.

The first witness before Senator Black's subcommittee was Henry Herberman, the president of the Export Steamship Company. Under intensive interrogation by Black, Herberman spun an incredible tale of abusive privilege at the government's expense. Herberman had never operated ocean ships before the government offered its lucrative contracts. He nonetheless devoted very little time to mastering the business but a great deal to living well on the government dole. His expense account for one month alone was $11,360, with meal vouchers (during the Depression) of $75 a day. When he visited Washington, Herberman made it a point to stay at the same hotel as the chairman of the government shipping board and found generous ways to show his affection (by picking up the chairman's $500 tailoring bill, for example). For his efforts Herberman had received $45,230,151 in subsidies during the Coolidge and Hoover administrations. From August 1928 to June 1929 Herberman's ships carried precisely three pounds of mail, a cost to the American taxpayer of $234,980 per pound. By the end of Black's interrogation, Herberman's personal physician was by the witness's side, taking his pulse at regular intervals.

In all, Black questioned fifty shipping executives, uncovering rampant waste in the highly subsidized government program. The shipping investigation was quickly followed by a second Black subcommittee assignment, this one to scrutinize the government's airmail contracts with the commercial aviation industry.

The passage of the McNary-Walters Act in 1930 had severely limited open bidding by operators for airmail contracts by giving the U.S. Postmaster General broad authority to extend existing routes as he saw fit. Postmaster General Walter Brown had wielded his new power in a way calculated to favor the large carriers such as American and United, at the expense of the small independent companies.

Black's investigation showed that lobbyists for American and United had helped draft the quasi-monopolistic provisions of the McNary-Walters Act that were of great financial benefit to the major carriers. Under the new legislation, for example, American was able to extend its routes 4,415 miles, all without competitive bidding.

After months of hearings, Black reported to a nationwide radio audience that a web of collusion existed in which twenty-four of twenty-seven airmail contracts were divided among three giant holding companies. In one year these companies and Northwest

Airways received 97 percent of all government airmail subsidies. Black also showed at his hearing that the commercial-aviation industry was fat with inflated salaries and stock options for its own executives as a result of the government contracts.

Frederick Rentschler, vice-president of the board of United Aircraft, testified that he held corporate shares worth $1.5 million and was compensated with salaries and bonuses in one year alone of $429,999. "If you had not got the $40 million for carrying the mail," asked Senator Black, "is it your judgment that salaries and bonuses amounting to $400,000 a year to one man could have been paid?" "Possibly not," Rentschler answered.

With the airline contract investigation, Black emerged from his relative obscurity in the Senate to capture headlines across the country. His encyclopedic command of the materials on the government-airline relationship was impressive, as was his dominance over the parade of witnesses that appeared before him. Another side of Black also surfaced: the single-minded investigator who was not above the use of fakery or strong-arm methods, as the situation demanded, to achieve his objective.

"The chairman [Black]," wrote one observer, "sits back easily in his chair, puffs slowly on his cigar, rolls his large, open eyes quite innocently, and with a wise smile, undertakes to refresh the memory of a squirming witness." Black was labeled a "hunch player" who fired questions confidently even when he did not know where his inquiries would lead. "Once in a while," noted one reporter, "he hooks a fish." Black's flamboyant, sometimes guileful, stratagem was contrasted with that of earlier Senate investigators like the patient, plodding Tom Walsh who had exposed Teapot Dome. In a tactic he had used so successfully in Birmingham courtrooms, Black sometimes coached testimony out of reluctant witnesses, convincing them that he already had all the facts and only awaited confirmation. At one session Black conspicuously referred to a piece of paper in his hands, giving the impression it had all of the facts Black needed. The witness then told his story. Later, reporters found that the piece of paper referred to a totally unrelated matter.

When William MacCracken, former Assistant Secretary of Commerce and then a lobbyist for the airlines, refused to divulge documents concerning his clients, claiming lawyer's privilege, Black stalked to the Senate floor with a motion ordering its sergeant at arms to arrest MacCracken, two airline executives and a clerical employee for attempting to destroy evidence needed by his committee. Shortly after the Senate passed Black's motion, MacCracken was arrested, released in the custody of his lawyer, then fled, claiming Black's committee had no legal authority for its action. Black immediately prepared another resolution, again passed by his Senate colleagues, ordering MacCracken's rearrest. In the meantime Black hauled the three remaining defendants before his committee and confronted them with missing letters retrieved by postal clerks who, at Black's direction, had searched three hundred bags of trash in MacCracken's office building. Two of the defendants were later freed, but MacCracken and a fourth were sentenced to ten-day jail terms for contempt of the Senate.

At a luncheon meeting in the White House during the investigation, President Roosevelt urged Black to push his investigation to the limit. As a result of Black's work, the President transferred the airmail contracts from the commercial carriers to the Army Air Corps. That decision proved disastrous—several unprepared and ill-equipped Air Corps pilots died tragically in blizzards in the winter of 1934—and Roosevelt ultimately returned the mail contracts to the private carriers. That embarrassing turn of events did not, however, diminish Black's stature as an investigator in the public's—or the President's—eye.

The shipping and airmail contract hearings had offered Black splendid opportunities to display his investigative skills on the national stage. But those performances were merely out-of-town tryouts compared to the major production of 1935. In that year the Roosevelt administration sponsored a bill with the so-called "death sentence" provision, which effectively eliminated octopus-like public-utility holding companies that spanned the continent. The holding companies, some controlling utilities in dozens of states, countered with a $20 million campaign to defeat the measure. Partly as a political tactic, partly to educate the public, the administration asked Senator Black to conduct an investigation of the holding companies' lobbying efforts.

It was the ideal assignment for Black, who detested both the powerful holding companies and their omnipresent Washington lobbyists. Black began the investigation by pursuing a tip furnished by Congressman S. J. Driscoll, whose district included Warren, Pennsylvania. Driscoll told Black that he had received over 800 telegrams opposing the bill, attributed to residents of Warren. The congressman became suspicious as he noted that the names of most of the senders began with "B." Black subpoenaed the manager of the Western Union office in Warren, who testified that a representative of one of the nation's largest holding companies had dictated 1,300 telegrams, picking names from the Warren city directory. That testimony was followed by others that revealed a nationwide pattern of written protest against the administration's bill, orchestrated in its entirety by the holding companies themselves, without the approval or knowledge of the thousands of voters the correspondence appeared to represent. Under Black's questioning, an officer of one holding company admitted that staff members of his company from 26 states had met to plan a telegram-and-letter campaign costing $700,000, much of it for bogus wires and letters opposing the legislation. Of 14,782 messages opposing the bill from four states—New York, Pennsylvania, Florida and Texas—all but three were paid for by the utility companies.

Black's subpoena of thousands of Western Union telegrams brought a fusillade of criticism from members of the bar and press that claimed an unconstitutional seizure of private property. The response from Black was an impassioned speech on the Senate floor defending his action and denouncing the utilities lobby. If any court ruled against his committee's subpoena power, Black warned, he would immediately introduce legislation to deprive the transgressing court of its jurisdiction.

Black dealt with other obstacles to his investigation with similar resolve. Howard Hopson, president of Associated Gas and Electric Company, had ignored or evaded Black's committee for weeks, though he did appear before the friendlier House committee investigating the same subject. Finally Black persuaded the Senate to cite Hopson for contempt and directed service of the subpoena on the utilities executive as he left the House committee hearing room.

Once he had captured Hopson, Black wasted no time in subjecting his reluctant witness to a sizzling interrogation. "We intend for you to state the facts," Black sternly instructed Hopson, "and you are going to do so." When Hopson tried to point out that the administration's lobbying efforts were as intense as the holding companies', Black curtly interrupted. "That's enough," said Black. "We don't care for your opinion on the administration's acts." Hopson pleaded for mercy after Black confronted him with a foot-high stack of telegrams opposing the bill. "You have me on the hip," said Hopson, "because you have copies of these things and I have not."

At the close of the day's testimony sympathetic journalists reported Hopson "gasping and indignant" and his attorney demanding a stop to Black's "third degree." In fact, Black also made some members of the Washington press corps covering the hearings uncomfortable. They noted with distaste Black's talent for grabbing headlines, and some questioned his integrity. "My impression of the man is that he is essentially cheap," wrote one correspondent covering the hearings. "He is smart as the devil. He has one of the shrewdest minds in the Senate. But I wouldn't trust him farther than I could throw a cow by the tail. His orbit is that of a small town lawyer, more aptly, a small town prosecutor."

But neither Hopson nor reporters hostile to Black's aggressive style could deny the blunt facts that his interrogation produced. Hopson admitted that he had managed his company's campaign against the legislation, an effort costing approximately $900,000. He increased or decreased his company's advertising in newspapers in direct proportion to their sympathy with the utility's legislative position. On several occasions Hopson boldly dictated editorials to cooperative newspapers, including the Hearst chain, which were printed almost verbatim.

Distrustful of the print media, Black appealed for public support in a nationally broadcast radio address. Beginning with the statement that "there is no constitutional right to lobby," Black built his case with blocks of facts documenting the abuses of the utility lobby. Later he wrote an article for *Harper's Magazine* further defending his investigative methods and goals. "Special privilege," he wrote, "thrives in secrecy and darkness and is destroyed by the rays of pitiless publicity."

The Public Utilities Holding Company Act was passed by Congress and, despite the elimination of some of the administration's strongest restrictions, led to the dismantling of the holding-company empires within three years. No single person, of course, could take credit for the passage of the bill, but Senator Hugo Black stood very high on President Roosevelt's list of heroic legislators. As he began to plan his reelection campaign, FDR turned to Black to welcome him into his inner circle of political advisers.

Alf Landon of Kansas, the Republican presidential standard-bearer, did not pose much of a threat to FDR's reelection, as it turned out. But neither the President nor his advisers, including Senator Black, took the election for granted. Campaigning through the Midwest for Roosevelt, Black reported back that he encountered enthusiastic crowds wherever he went. Black was so ebullient that he risked offering the President a little unsolicited advice. "Millions of people are anxious to vote peace," Black wrote. "If you could and would leave with the people in your last speech, preferably near the close, your firm determination to keep our people at peace, I believe that it would be a most effective climax to a magnificent campaign." The President responded cordially, but noncommittally, to Black's suggestion and then promptly handed the Republicans the worst election defeat in modern American presidential history.

In marked contrast to Felix Frankfurter's correspondence, that between Black and Roosevelt is remarkably sparse over the five-year period that Black served in the Senate and Roosevelt was in the White House. Black sent the obligatory letter of congratulations to Roosevelt after his nomination in 1932: "You are the unquestioned choice of the people." For the next four years, however, Black only sent a handful of telegrams and notes to the President, urging support for his thirty-hour-a-week legislation or protection of farm prices or requesting committee authority to examine income tax reports during his airmail contract investigation. Unlike Frankfurter's voluminous correspondence with the President, Black's never gave the slightest hint of sycophancy or maneuvering for presidential favor.

And yet, Black was always available when the President needed him, and the President needed him badly after he announced his Court-packing plan in February 1937. "It was the French King, Louis XIV, who said, 'L'état, ç'est moi'—'I am the state,'" snorted the New York Herald-Tribune. "The paper shell of American constitutionalism would continue if President Roosevelt secured the passage of the law he now demands. But it would only be a shell." Chief Justice Charles Evans Hughes and Associate Justice Louis Brandeis, the two most respected members of the Court, openly opposed the President's plan. Even the President's devoted friend Felix Frankfurter wavered.

But not Hugo Black. Without hesitation, the Senator from Alabama threw his unequivocal support to the President and willingly took FDR's case to the people. In a carefully calibrated radio address, Black reminded his listeners that the U.S. Constitution provided for a system of checks and balances, and one of the checks on an irresponsible judiciary, Black pointed out, was the right of Congress to increase or decrease the number of members on the U.S. Supreme Court. "Neither the people who wrote nor the people who approved the Constitution ever contemplated that the Supreme Court should become all powerful and omnipotent," Black said. And that, Black suggested, had become the unfortunate reality since five conservative members of the U.S. Supreme Court had dominated the nation's constitutional jurisprudence. "The time has arrived when those who favor fitting laws to modern needs in order to correct and cure social and industrial injustice must face their problems squarely and fairly. Everybody knows that Supreme Court decisions by a bare majority have for years been thrown as impassable barriers in the way of the solemn and well-matured legislative plans supported by the people."

It was a vintage Black speech, based on a bold constitutional interpretation unabashedly critical of his political enemies and concluding with an appeal to the American people to reject elitist control of their institutions. Though an effective address, it did not carry the day for FDR's Court-packing plan. But Roosevelt did not have to wait long for relief from the conservative Court majority. Within months, one of the five conservative Justices, Willis Van Devanter, retired.

After almost five years in office the President was able to make his first Court nomination; it was Senator Hugo Black. But the President's pride in the selection of his loyal New Deal legislator soon turned to chagrin as revelations of Black's early membership in the Ku Klux Klan were publicized by reporter Ray Sprigle of the *Pittsburgh Post-Gazette*. While public pressure mounted for the withdrawal of the nomination, Roosevelt kept a studied silence, subtly shifting the burden of proof to the nominee himself.

At 9 P.M. on the first Friday in October 1937, Hugo Black sat erect in an antique chair in the living room of his friend Claude Hamilton, prepared to make the most important speech of his life. Before a battery of six microphones and fifteen radio announcers and technicians, Black admitted to thirty million radio listeners across the nation that he had been a member of the Robert E. Lee Chapter of the Ku Klux Klan in Birmingham, Alabama. In a tense eleven-minute talk, Black said that he had joined the Klan in 1923 but had resigned from the organization before he had taken his seat in the U.S. Senate in 1926. The radio address (second in ratings only to the abdication speech of Edward VIII) came six weeks after President Roosevelt had named Black as his first nominee to the U.S. Supreme Court and less than two weeks after Black's KKK membership had been revealed in the series of articles in the *Pittsburgh Post-Gazette*.

The confession of Klan membership consumed barely a minute of the Black speech; the former trial lawyer devoted far more time to an attack on religious bigotry in the United States. The strategy rankled Black's opponents in the press. "The effort of Senator Black to suggest that he is the real protagonist of tolerance and that his enemies are intolerant is perhaps the greatest item of effrontery in a uniquely brazen utterance," wrote the *New York Herald-Tribune*.

But Black's radio address received a far different review from a more important source. "It was a grand job," FDR declared privately. "It did the trick. You just wait and see." Within days, Roosevelt's political judgment was confirmed. The first Gallup poll after the Black radio address showed that a majority of Americans thought that Hugo Black had vindicated himself and deserved to take his seat on the U.S. Supreme Court.

That view had been held steadfastly by Professor Felix Frankfurter of the Harvard Law School since the day Roosevelt had nominated Black. Despite Black's meager legal training, Frankfurter was confident that the Court nominee possessed a fine mind "and the humility which leads to growth and understanding." When the revelation of Black's membership in the KKK hit the front page of every newspaper in America, Frankfurter had expressed only sympathy. He had acknowledged the realities of Alabama politics in the early twenties when Klan membership was a necessity for an aspiring office holder. "Poor Black," Frankfurter wrote a friend shortly after the *Pittsburgh Post-Gazette* series had begun. "I suspect he long ago outgrew clanism and couldn't tell the truth by merely telling the facts."

Soon after Black took his seat on the Court, Frankfurter was given a most unusual assignment: to tutor Black on the intricacies of constitutional law. "Do you know Black well?" Justice Harlan F. Stone asked Professor Frankfurter. "You might be able to render him great assistance. He needs guidance from someone who is more familiar with the workings of the judicial process than he is."

Frankfurter attacked his new professional task vigorously. "I used to say to my students," Frankfurter wrote Black, "that legislatures make law wholesale, judges retail." In other words, Frankfurter was telling Black, he must tone down his opinions. He was no longer a political reformer but a judge, and would have to show more restraint in his new role than he had as a populist legislator.

When he was in Washington, which was often, Frankfurter would take Black aside at dinner parties and genially but insistently make his point. And when Black left the room, Frankfurter would press his case with the passionate love of Black's life, his wife, Josephine. "She is altogether a grand person," Frankfurter later observed, "with a keen realization of the psychological aspects of the situation and with unusual talents for mitigating difficulties and softening hard feelings."

What concerned Frankfurter, aside from the gap in Black's knowledge of constitutional law, was the perceived danger that Black would feel intimidated and isolated by his more learned brethren. "Various experiences of his life have been calculated to make him a bit of an Ishmaelite—to expect every hand to be raised against him, and therefore at times to be unwarrantly suspicious when nothing but friendliness is intended," Frankfurter wrote. Frankfurter subtly passed that message to Justices Stone and Brandeis, but to a third Black colleague, newly appointed Justice Stanley Reed, Frankfurter reverted to a more direct appeal. "I took the bull by the horn," Frankfurter later reported, "and told Stanley Reed that he must not allow Black to interpose the barrier of formality between them, and that, as a matter of fact, Black will gradually soften to influences of friendliness and affection." After a round of teas and dinners with Josephine and Hugo Black, Frankfurter was certain that his tutorials were working. "I have high hopes for the future," Frankfurter told the President.

Frankfurter treated Hugo Black as he did so many of his students at the Harvard Law School who were bright, eager and, with careful attention from the professor, capable of vast learning. But Professor Frankfurter had failed to do his homework. Had he studied Black's prosecutorial record at the Mobile bootleggers' trial, or his 1926 senatorial campaign, or his Senate investigation of the utilities lobby, he would have known that Mr. Justice Black would hardly be putty in his professorial hands. Frankfurter's kindly, slightly patronizing estimate of Black's abilities would be one of the greatest miscalculations of his professional life and would have profound consequences for his and the nation's future.

CHAPTER III

Saving Souls

EVERY WEEKDAY MORNING, JUST after dawn, the lone, hulking figure of Associate Justice Harlan Fiske Stone could be seen walking from his palatial northwest Washington residence up Massachusetts Avenue and then returning home for breakfast and a day of work. Sometimes he was joined by Marquis Childs, the ambitious, respected journalist for the *St. Louis Post-Dispatch*.

As the two took their early-morning exercise, Justice Stone talked to his companion about his concerns for the Court. Stone, a strong-minded, plainspoken man, told Childs that he feared the Court was in danger of repeating one of the most tragic mistakes in its history. Only two years earlier, in 1935, the Court majority had very nearly provoked a constitutional crisis by tossing out one piece of New Deal legislation after another in the name of constitutional orthodoxy. Stone, usually joined by Justices Cardozo and Brandeis, had condemned the Court majority for substituting their political views for the legislature's and claiming they were merely interpreting the Constitution.

The Court majority had shifted by 1937 so that New Deal legislation was safe from further interference by politically conservative Justices. But the basic problem of judicial legislation, as Stone saw it, had arisen again. This time the threat did not come from the right, but from the political left on the Court, represented by President Franklin Roosevelt's first appointee, Justice Hugo Black.

Stone conceded that Black was bright enough and certainly

hardworking. But he lacked judicial experience or even the broad-based legal practice that would have prepared him for the Court's work. His raw intellect and aggressive methods had served him well in the U.S. Senate. And that was part of the problem—Justice Black seemingly had not changed roles. He was still the populist legislator bent on making economic and social policy with slashing attacks on his colleagues and the vested corporate interests he accused them of protecting. Black's early Court opinions, full of bold ideas and devastating criticism of the status quo and his brethren who maintained it, were an embarrassment to Stone and other, more experienced judicial colleagues.

Black had not yet completed a full year on the Court before he had written more dissents during the term than any other member. That fact alone suggested to Stone that the former Senator did not fully appreciate the history and tradition of the Court or the required subtlety of movement by the Justices. Audaciously, Black had even dissented from an unsigned opinion supported by all eight of his colleagues. By tradition, that simply was not done.

Black's transgression occurred in a case in which the Indianapolis Water Company complained that its rates to consumers had been set too low by a state regulatory commission. The water company had asked the federal courts to set aside the commission's decision, arguing that the rates established were so low as to be confiscatory. The Supreme Court majority accepted the utility company's argument, in effect, and sent the case back to the federal district court for a new rate-making analysis with the clear directive to take into consideration the water company's rising costs. Presumably, with the increased costs considered in the valuation, the public utility would be able to demand a greater return through consumer billing.

Justice Black's written disagreement with his brethren covered nineteen pages. In that space the Court's newest Justice questioned the competence of federal courts to review state utility rates, then committed further judicial heresy by asserting that a corporation should not be protected by the due process clause of the Fourteenth Amendment. Black saved the most powerful attack in his opinion, however, for a denunciation of the established valuation system, tacitly approved by the Court majority. "Wherever the question of utility valuation arises today," Black wrote, "it is ex-

ceedingly difficult to discern the truth through the maze of for-
mulas and the jungle of metaphysical concepts sometimes
conceived, and often fostered, by the ingenuity of those who seek
inflated valuations to support excessive rates."

Black's scorn and distrust of the Indianapolis Water Company,
a monopoly, were abundant. His sympathy for "the people of
Indianapolis in their efforts to obtain fair and reasonable water
rates" was full and undisguised. But in taking sides with "the little
guy" against the corporate utility, as Black had so often done during his entire professional life, the Justice laid out one of the most
sophisticated critiques of the prevailing rate-making structure in
the Court's history.

Even Justice Stone privately admitted that Black's attack on the
utility valuation structure was exceptional. Indeed, Stone suggested that the opinion may have been ghostwritten by someone
more adept at such analysis than Black. The name of Harvard-
trained New Dealer Thomas Corcoran, who had broad experience
and knowledge in the public-utilities field, was mentioned.

Admiring the substance of the dissent, Stone nonetheless was
totally dismayed by its existence. Didn't Black realize that he was
discussing issues that were not even raised on appeal? And didn't
he understand that a Justice, and an inexperienced one at that, did
not attempt to overturn a long-standing, generally accepted Court
premise in a single dissent? The law changed slowly, cumulatively,
building on the collective wisdom of a Court whose accomplishments were measured in decades, not days.

Stone found the Black dissent in the Indianapolis Water Company case disconcerting, but the worst was yet to come. For in a
second dissent that term Black submitted a small treatise to follow
his earlier notion that the Fourteenth Amendment did not protect
corporations. His position was disarmingly straightforward: The
Fourteenth Amendment was drafted after the Civil War to protect
the recently freed slaves. It was only later, in a period when the
U.S. Supreme Court looked with extravagant favor on corporations, that the Justices discovered a new meaning for "persons" in
the Fourteenth Amendment that included Standard Oil and other
corporate giants. That was wrong, Black concluded, and that judicial error of sixty-four years' standing should be corrected. Immediately. The amendment, wrote Black, "followed the freedom of a

race from slavery," and when it was submitted to the people they "were told that its purpose was to protect weak and helpless human beings and were not told that it was intended to remove corporations in any fashion from the control of state governments."

Marquis Childs listened intently to Justice Stone's criticisms of Black's opinions during their early-morning walks together, and on January 22, 1938, Childs's *St. Louis Post-Dispatch* readers also learned about the Justice's views. "The *Post-Dispatch* has been privileged to gain an inside view of the Court," Childs wrote, "and of the concern for its future of the members who feel keenly the importance of its integrity and continuity." Childs adopted Justice Stone's position of judicial restraint, then discussed the difficulty posed by a neophyte jurist like Black. "A new man on the bench," Childs wrote, "who has had no judicial experience and only a comparatively limited legal experience is not a help to his colleagues in the first two or three years."

"Just what is needed to educate the public," Stone told Childs after reading the article. But why not deliver the message to a national audience? Stone asked. And that is exactly what Marquis Childs did four months later.

In an article in the May 1938 issue of *Harper's Magazine* entitled "The Supreme Court Today," Childs laid out Stone's complaints in considerable detail and revealed, for the first time, that the complaints were directed explicitly at Justice Black. The theme was again judicial restraint, the need, as Childs put it, for the Court to pass on large constitutional issues "with great caution and extreme reluctance." Black did not seem to understand the judicial exercise, handicapped as he was by a lack of legal knowledge and experience "that have led him into blunders which have shocked his colleagues on the highest Court." The journalist then made the same patronizing point metaphorically: "It is as though a comparatively inexperienced player had stepped into a fast game, say tennis or pelota, and, ignoring the rules, made vigorous passes at every ball with a piece of board."

With the publication of the article, the tight little world at the U.S. Supreme Court was shattered. A Justice had been attacked openly and in very personal terms. And the attacker, a journalist without formal legal training, was so well informed that the conclusion was inescapable that the journalist's informant was a member of the Court. When reporters discovered that Childs had been taking early-morning walks with Justice Stone, the Justice's phone began to ring.

"I am calling from a pay station," a desperate Gertrude Jenkins, Justice Stone's secretary, shouted into the receiver to Marquis Childs. "Reporters are hounding me. What shall I say?"

"Deny everything," Childs snapped.

"I always told the Judge he talked too much," Miss Jenkins sighed before hanging up.

Gertrude Jenkins did deny everything on Justice Stone's behalf, but nobody was fooled. The press linked Stone with the Childs article, and soon Black supporters and detractors were scrambling for opportunities to have their own say on the matter.

The only person who seemed totally unperturbed by the furor was Justice Hugo Black. A friend of Stone's, Irving Brant, assured Black that Stone "did not remotely support the statements made by Mr. Childs." Brant wrote Black that "the Childs article, I presume, is a composite of information given him from various sources and his own deductions, but I can assure you that if it is based in any part on statements made by Justice Stone, he has completely twisted their implications."

"I can assure you," Black replied coolly, "that I am not disturbed in the slightest by the matter to which you referred."

Harlan Fiske Stone's discomfort over the incident passed and his hopes for the future of the Court were significantly lifted by the news that Professor Felix Frankfurter of Harvard was actively being considered as the President's next Supreme Court nominee. Stone had earlier asked Frankfurter to engage Hugo Black in a friendly tutorial on the proper role of the judiciary. And now it seemed that Stone would have Frankfurter nearby to help civilize the renegade Black. In fact, Stone had operated effectively behind the scenes to accomplish that result. At Roosevelt's invitation Stone had visited the White House to discuss a replacement for Justice Benjamin Cardozo, who had died during the summer of 1938. Stone spoke of Frankfurter's eminent qualifications to serve on the Court and the need to select Justices with the intellectual gifts and training to make the Court truly distinguished. The President could do no better than Felix Frankfurter, whose potent mind and liberal bent would serve as an effective foil to the formidable and more conservative Chief Justice, Charles Evans Hughes.

Frankfurter dressed casually in an alpaca coat and slacks for his first judicial conference, but upon entering the well-appointed conference room, he was chagrined to find that all his new colleagues wore suits. At the lunchtime break Frankfurter rushed home, changed into a suit and returned for the afternoon session. He was greeted by Chief Justice Hughes, who had also made a lunchtime change of dress, and now wore *his* alpaca coat.

That small gesture suggests one of the minor reasons that Charles Evans Hughes became a great Chief Justice of the United States. Tall, full-bearded and austere in appearance, Hughes was always the gentleman, and he showed an acute sensitivity toward his judicial colleagues, as Felix Frankfurter discovered that very first day at the Court. But Hughes's leadership qualities ran much deeper. His reverence for the Court as an institution was inspirational, and his conduct of the day-to-day affairs of the Court was no less impressive. He absorbed facts and identified legal issues with phenomenal efficiency and thoroughness. His presentation of the cases to the other Justices in conference, therefore, became a verbal instrument of considerable power.

As Chief Justice, Hughes assigned the writing of the opinion for the Court when he was in the majority, and that authority gave him subtle but not insignificant influence. Selecting the colleague who was most likely to bring to an opinion Hughes's own views as well as the skill to preserve a majority vote required a political savvy that the Chief Justice possessed in full measure. That talent was readily apparent in the spring of 1940 when the Chief Justice assigned the majority opinion in *Minersville School District v. Gobitis* to Felix Frankfurter. The opinion, written barely more than a year after his appointment, would indelibly mark Frankfurter's judicial career.

The school board in the small Pennsylvania community of Minersville had required that all public school children salute the American flag before classes began each weekday morning. Although the overwhelming majority of Minersville students routinely accepted the rule, Lillian and William Gobitis, ages twelve and ten, did not. The Gobitis children had been raised by their father, Walter, as Jehovah's Witnesses and had been taught to refuse to worship false idols. In Chapter 20 of Exodus, it was written: "Thou shall not make unto thee any graven image, or any likeness of any thing that is in the heaven above, or that is in the earth beneath, or that is in the water under the earth:/Thou shalt not bow down thyself to them, nor serve them." According to the Gobitis reading of Exodus, Chapter 20, saluting the American flag was therefore forbidden by God, and the punishment for ignoring the biblical command was annihilation.

Lillian and William Gobitis did not join their classmates in the early-morning patriotic exercise and were subsequently expelled from the public school. Their father, as a result, brought a lawsuit against the Minersville School Board, charging that the board had prevented his children from freely exercising their religious beliefs in violation of the First Amendment of the Constitution.

"Our beloved flag, the emblem of religious liberty," wrote U.S. District Judge Albert Maris in his opinion supporting the Gobitis position, "apparently has been used as an instrument to impose a religious test as a condition of receiving the benefits of public education. And this has been done without any compelling necessity of public safety or welfare." The Maris opinion was upheld unanimously by the U.S. Court of Appeals for the Third Circuit. By the time the U.S. Supreme Court granted certiorari in the *Gobitis* case, the Gobitis family could count among the advocates for their cause leading members of the national bar and academic community. Grenville Clark, chairman of the American Bar Association Committee on the Bill of Rights, worked on the Supreme Court brief as did Professor Zechariah Chafee of the Harvard Law School, one of Felix Frankfurter's civil libertarian comrades-in-arms during the twenties.

The case had first been heard in Judge Maris's courtroom in 1937. When the Supreme Court listened to arguments in April 1940, the western world had been radically transformed by the violent ambitions of Adolf Hitler. The Nazi blitzkrieg had devastated large chunks of Europe, and observers on both sides of the Atlantic were dreading the imminent Battle of Britain. In those portentous times the plea by the attorney for the Minersville School Board defending the flag salute as a legitimate form of patriotism assumed a special poignancy.

The *Gobitis* case presented two conflicting elemental Frankfurter values for calm judicial resolution. The first had been argued by the attorney for Lillian and William Gobitis: In the United States it was an article of faith as well as law that every citizen was entitled to freedom of belief and expression without fear of government intrusion. No American living in 1940 could make a greater claim to upholding that seminal proposition than Felix Frankfurter, for he had dedicated much of his professional life to the defense of civil liberties. If civil libertarians had gained promotions military style, Frankfurter would have been a five-star general at an early age with battle ribbons for his Bisbee and Mooney reports, the Distinguished Service Cross for his role in founding the American Civil Liberties Union and the Medal of Honor for his defense of Sacco and Vanzetti.

But against his strong libertarian beliefs Frankfurter struggled with his equally firm conviction that the judicial branch of government should exercise restraint in reviewing the acts of the popularly elected branches. He had held that view since he had studied law at Harvard under the influence of James Bradley Thayer. And even when as a young man he had published eloquent tracts on civil liberties, he did so with the understanding that the people—through enlightened leadership in the legislative and executive branches—must defend those liberties and not leave that defense to the courts. The Gobitis children's argument could only succeed if the Supreme Court rejected a public school requirement, enforced by a publicly responsible school board, that all public school children, including Lillian and William Gobitis, salute the American flag. Affirmation of the requirement of the school board need not be seen as an abandonment of Frankfurter's libertarian ideals. It could be argued, rather, that those ideals were best preserved by the electorate, not the Court. A flag-salute requirement was a silly rule, but Frankfurter, the civil libertarian who might have opposed it as a member of a small-town school board, might not as a member of the U.S. Supreme Court declare it unconstitutional.

There was a third Frankfurter value at work, which proved to be decisive. Frankfurter was a patriot first and last, and no amount of sophisticated judicial philosophizing could cover up the deep debt that he felt to his adopted country. As he freely admitted, the convert was more zealous in preaching the faith than the native-born, and this Jewish immigrant who did not speak English when he arrived at Ellis Island in 1894 was an unabashed zealot. "I can express with very limited adequacy," he once said, "the passionate devotion to this land that possesses millions of our people, born like myself under other skies, for the privilege this country has bestowed in allowing them to partake of its fellowship."

Frankfurter was the only Justice who regularly whistled "Stars and Stripes Forever" as he walked through the corridors of the Supreme Court building. Shortly before his death he instructed his chosen biographer to tell readers "how much I loved my country." The United States had allowed this Austrian Jew, this outsider, to enter the highest echelon of governmental power, and he never forgot it. Other outsiders, like Jehovah's Witnesses, he seemed to reason, should learn the lessons of Americanism as well.

At the judicial conference following oral argument in the *Gobitis* case Chief Justice Hughes spoke first. "I come up to this case like a skittish horse to a brass band," he said. "I am disturbed that we have this case before us. There is nothing that I have more pro-found belief in than religious freedom, so I must bring myself to view this case on the question of state power." Having posed the issue skillfully, the Chief Justice concluded that "the state can in-sist on inculcation of loyalty. It would be extraordinary if in this country the state could not provide for respect for the flag of our land."

Both Justices Black and Murphy had doubts about the wisdom of the school board regulation. But Black and Murphy, as well as other Roosevelt appointees William O. Douglas and Stanley Reed, eagerly awaited the view of Felix Frankfurter, who, by training and experience, had earned their respect on civil liberties issues above all others, including the Chief Justice. Frankfurter did not need to belabor his devotion to civil liberties; it was a matter of public record. Here, he said, the Court was confronted with two clashing constitutional rights: the individual's right to free exercise of religion and the state's right to teach patriotism. For Frankfurter, the only foreign-born member of the Court, a public school's prerogative to nurture national loyalty was constitutionally unassailable.

Did any member of the Court seriously think the framers of the First Amendment would have forbidden a flag salute? Frankfurter had no doubt they would not, nor should the Court in 1940. His statement dominated the conference, and seven members of the Court, including every Roosevelt appointee—Black, Douglas, Murphy and Reed—voted with him.

On the eve of World War II, the Court's *Gobitis* opinion undoubtedly would be read with particular care by scholars and lay citizens alike. The Chief Justice's assignment, therefore, became critically important. A safe choice would have been Stanley Reed —intelligent, cautious, centrist. Or the Chief himself. Hughes, in fact, was Frankfurter's choice. The Chief Justice kept his own counsel, however, and without hesitation gave the assignment to Frankfurter. He made the choice, he said, "because of Frankfurter's moving statement at conference on the role of the public school in instilling love of country in our pluralistic society." Although he never said so, the Chief Justice may also have been mindful of the effect that Frankfurter, one of the most celebrated civil libertarians of his generation, would have on his countrymen when he argued in his opinion that the claim of the free exercise of religion protected by the First Amendment should not prevail.

With the support of seven of his colleagues Frankfurter began to draft his *Gobitis* opinion. But the one Court holdout, Justice Stone, so troubled Frankfurter that he attempted anew to persuade the dissenter in a five-page memorandum. "I am not happy that you should entertain doubts that I cannot share or meet," he wrote Stone, "in a domain where constitutional power is on one side and my private notions of liberty and toleration and good sense are on the other." He assured Stone that he was committed to giving "the fullest elbow room to every variety of religious, political and economic view." But here the Court was presented with "the clash of rights, not the clash of wrongs. For resolving such a clash we have no calculus." On balance, Frankfurter was convinced that the responsibility for teaching toleration must come from the people themselves, not the Court. Consider the restrained role that the Court has traditionally played, he wrote Stone, consider the limited effect of his majority opinion and, yes, consider the moment in history in which the Court passes on a patriotic gesture.

But Justice Stone was unmoved by Frankfurter's entreaty. "I am truly sorry not to go along with you," Stone wrote, responding to Frankfurter's memorandum. "The case is peculiarly one of the relative weight of imponderables and I cannot overcome the feeling that the Constitution tips the scales in favor of religion."

With the exception of Stone, Frankfurter's draft opinion won high accolades from his brethren. "You have accomplished most admirably a very difficult and highly important task," Chief Justice Hughes wrote Frankfurter. "The Court is indebted to you." Justice Douglas joined in: "This is a powerful moving document of incalculable contemporary and (I believe) historic value. I congratulate you on a truly statesmanlike job." The concerned Justice Murphy admitted that "this has been a Gethsemane to me. But after all, the institution presupposes a government that will nourish and protect itself and, therefore, I join your beautifully expressed opinion."

Unknown to Frankfurter, his draft opinion had provoked an impulsive and risky reaction from his law clerk, Edward Prichard, Jr. A massive young man with exuberant libertarian loyalties, Prichard was so alarmed by the opinion of his libertarian hero and boss, Justice Frankfurter, that he broke one of the sacrosanct rules of the Court by smuggling a copy of the Frankfurter opinion out of the Supreme Court building. Out of breath and perspiring heavily from Washington's June heat, Prichard arrived at the apartment of his friend, Joseph Rauh, Jr., with the Frankfurter draft opinion. Rauh had served as Frankfurter's first law clerk a year earlier and, at age twenty-nine, was viewed by Prichard as something of an elder statesman.

"Felix has made a terrible mistake," blurted Prichard, waving the Justice's draft opinion in front of Rauh. "You have to speak to him," he said.

Rauh read the opinion and looked up at Prichard. "I'm willing to speak to Felix," said Rauh, "but I will have to tell him I've read the draft opinion. And I'll have to tell him where I got it. Do you still want me to speak to him?"

Prichard quickly weighed the advantage to his country in having Rauh speak to the Justice against the potential disadvantage to his legal career in explaining his transgression to Frankfurter. On second thought, said Pritchard, he did not think Rauh should speak to Frankfurter.

On the morning of June 3, 1940, the Supreme Court was abuzz with word that Justice Frankfurter would break with traditional practice and read his opinion in Court. The *Gobitis* case raised such momentous issues for all Americans that, the rumor had it, Frankfurter wanted to deliver his opinion orally. Having heard of Frankfurter's intentions, Justice Stone, the only dissenter, determined to read his own opinion out loud as well.

To the disappointment of the large crowd that had gathered in the ornate courtroom, Frankfurter chose not to read his majority opinion aloud. But Justice Stone did not follow his example. Hunched forward in his seat, Stone, normally private and undemonstrative, read his opinion with heavy emotion: "History teaches us that there have been but few infringements of personal liberty by the state which have not been justified, as they are here, in the name of righteousness and the public good, and few which have not been directed, as they are now, at politically helpless minorities." He concluded, "This seems to me no less than the surrender of the constitutional protection of the liberty of small minorities to the public will."

The following day the majority opinion of Justice Frankfurter was available for the nation to study. And those who had long admired Frankfurter's extraordinary analytical skills and verbal locutions could find much to appreciate in his *Gobitis* opinion. He had written of the high place of civil liberties in the Constitution's lexicon of values. And he had reminded readers of the carefully circumscribed role of the Court in reviewing an act of a popularly elected branch of government. He also commended patriotism as a positive virtue in a dangerous time. Civil liberties, judicial restraint, patriotism—all laudable values in our American democracy and all given careful attention in the Frankfurter opinion. But many of his most devoted friends were stunned by his conclusion that the claim of the First Amendment's protection of religious liberty must fail.

They did not telephone Frankfurter or drop him a congratulatory note. Those gracious gestures were saved for the Court's lone dissenter, Justice Stone. "When a liberal judge holds out alone against his liberal brethren," Benjamin Cohen, one of Frankfurter's

New Deal protégés, told Stone, "I think he ought to know when he has spoken not for himself alone, but has superbly articulated the thoughts of his contemporaries who believe with him in an effective but tolerant democracy." Frankfurter's close friend, Professor Harold Laski, seconded Cohen. "I want to tell you," he wrote Stone, "how right I think you are in that educational case from Pennsylvania and to my deep regret, how wrong I think Felix is."

Frankfurter had his supporters, not the least being the President of the United States. While he mixed cocktails for Felix and Marion Frankfurter at Hyde Park a few weeks after the decision, FDR approvingly explained Frankfurter's position to a skeptical Eleanor Roosevelt. The Minersville School Board had acted stupidly, FDR said, but not outside its legal authority.

Eleanor Roosevelt listened patiently and did not question the constitutional argument of her husband and Justice Frankfurter. But there was something profoundly unsettling, she said, was there not, with a Supreme Court opinion that made children in public schools salute the flag in violation of their religious beliefs. The First Lady added that such official intolerance could well encourage a cruder variety in the public at large.

Eleanor Roosevelt's fearful speculation came to pass. Vigilante committees formed to enforce respect for the flag. Rampaging mobs attacked Witnesses in Litchfield, Illinois, and Rockville, Maryland, and other beatings and burnings of Jehovah's Witnesses' property were reported in Maine, Texas and California. No one blamed Frankfurter personally for the violent outbursts but a Justice Department study later traced the lawlessness directly to the Court's *Gobitis* decision.

If he was disturbed by the violence, Frankfurter never acknowledged it. He was, however, hurt by the disapproval of friends and angered by the reaction of the overwhelming majority of the nation's newspapers that condemned his *Gobitis* opinion. The editorial in the *St. Louis Post-Dispatch,* one of the earliest and most enthusiastic supporters of Frankfurter's Court appointment, was typical. "We think the decision of the United States Supreme Court is dead wrong," the *Post-Dispatch* declared. "If patriotism depends upon such things as this—upon violation of a fundamental right of religious freedom—then it becomes not a noble emotion of love for country but something to be rammed down our throats by the law."

Curiously enough, the man whose judicial future was perhaps most affected by Frankfurter's *Gobitis* opinion, Justice Hugo Black, offered virtually no comment before it was finally adopted by the Court. When the Justices had first cast preliminary votes in the *Gobitis* case shortly after oral argument, Black was one of only two Justices (Stone was the other) who did not declare his position, although he eventually voted with the majority. Later, when Frankfurter had circulated his draft opinion to his colleagues, and had received laudatory comments from the Chief Justice and several other colleagues, Black did not join in the praise. Frankfurter later wrote that Black had stopped by his chambers the Saturday morning before the decision was announced to say that he "didn't like this kind of law" but saw nothing in the Constitution to justify declaring it unconstitutional.

Frankfurter would write long and learned opinions in every field of constitutional law over the next twenty-two years, but no compendium of his opinions would be complete without reference to *Minersville School District v. Gobitis*. The issues raised in *Gobitis* provided compelling constitutional debate, particularly as they were set in the shadow of World War II. But the Frankfurter opinion would be best remembered not for his clearly articulated position on the law so much as for the fact that Frankfurter, a founding member of the ACLU, would reject one of the most dramatic civil-liberties claims of the modern Court era. His opinion would also prove to be his undoing as leader of the Roosevelt appointees. In a short time he would lose his majority, including Justices William O. Douglas and Frank Murphy, who would with predictable consistency follow the new liberal leader of the Court, Justice Hugo Black.

At the end of the summer of 1940, less than three months after the *Gobitis* decision had been announced, Frankfurter learned from Justice Douglas that Black had changed his mind and would now favor Stone's dissenting position. Frankfurter recorded in his scrapbook his conversation with Douglas:

"Hugo thinks maybe we made a mistake in *Gobitis*," Douglas told Frankfurter.

"Has Hugo been rereading the Constitution?" asked Frankfurter.

"No, he's been reading the newspapers," Douglas replied.

The message was implied: Justice Black lacked intellectual integrity and was now voting his politics, not his principles.

In questioning Black's motives, Frankfurter revealed more about his own angry feelings than about the target of his accusation. He could not accept a defection from the ranks of his leadership as a genuine intellectual disagreement. To Frankfurter, Black was saying that the professor, who had trained and influenced two generations of the nation's brightest young legal minds, could not make his point persuasively where it counted most.

When a second case involving the First Amendment rights of Jehovah's Witnesses, *Jones v. Opelika*, came before the Court two years after *Gobitis*, Black took the opportunity to emphasize how strongly he felt about his initial error. The extraordinary public confession was joined by Justices Douglas and Murphy:

> The opinion of the Court sanctions a device which in our opinion suppresses or tends to suppress the free exercise of religion practiced by a minority group. This is but another step in the direction which *Minersville School District v. Gobitis* took against the same religious minority and is a logical extension of the principles upon which that case rested. Since we joined in the opinion in the *Gobitis* case, we think this is an appropriate occasion to state that we now believe it was also wrongly decided. Certainly our democratic form of government functioning under the historic Bill of Rights has a high responsibility to accommodate itself to the religious views of minorities, however unpopular and unorthodox those views may be. The First Amendment does not put the right freely to exercise religion in a subordinate position. We fear, however, that the opinions in this and the *Gobitis* case do exactly that.

In public, Frankfurter said nothing. But in private, he raged like a wounded animal, attacking his new adversaries with venomous verbal thrusts. He began referring to the trio of Black, Douglas and

Murphy as "the Axis," surely the most treacherous sobriquet imaginable during World War II. And this sensitive human being, who touched so many with his kindnesses and generosity, was now regularly reduced to petty clucking about the perceived weaknesses of his adversaries. Frankfurter told little stories to colleagues, including Stanley Reed and Owen Roberts, that depicted Murphy as slow-witted, Douglas as crassly political, and Black, worst of all, as manipulating each of them for his own transparent strategic advantage.

In Frankfurter's mind Black always stood above the rest, the master puppeteer skillfully controlling the actions of the others. He wrote in his diary in foreboding imagery of Black, Douglas and Murphy as "a solid phalanx," of their "hunting in packs," of an "ominous situation in which Black controls three votes out of nine in all important matters." Every Black initiative was viewed in the most unsavory light. When Black spoke in conference, it became "a harangue worthy of the cheapest soapbox orator." And when his antagonist changed his position, as he did in *Opelika* or *Martin v. Struthers,* another First Amendment case, it was attributed to naked political motives.

An incorrigible proselytizer, Frankfurter stepped up his efforts in the face of the challenge. He had lost three votes he expected to control, so he intensified his attentions with his other colleagues. Ironically, his most conspicuous weapon of persuasion, flattery, was precisely the tactic he accused his adversaries Black and Douglas of using in an unseemly way. Douglas, he said, was "the most systematic exploiter of flattery I have ever encountered in my life" and Black was not far behind.

In fact, no one could rival Frankfurter in flattering colleagues. He was astounded by their insights, dazzled by their learning, generally in direct proportion to their agreement with his own positions.

Frankfurter magisterially welcomed new appointees, Wiley Rutledge, for instance, as if he governed the institution:

> My dear Rutledge: Judges *are* men—and therefore poor and fallible creatures. But there have been three men since the Civil War whose character—their disinterestedness in its subtlest forms and their humility—even more than

pre-eminent intellectual powers, enabled them to tran-
scend men's ordinary limitations. To the fellowship of
Justice Holmes, Brandeis and Cardozo I welcome you.
And no one can possibly do so more warmly than I do.
Yours very sincerely . . .

Rutledge, however, was not impressed. Within a few months of
taking his seat on the Court he concluded that Black, not Frankfurter, was the intellectual leader of the Court.

Law clerks, even those working for the enemy, became accustomed to periodic visits and needling questions from Frankfurter.
Most, like Justice Black's law clerk, Marx Leva, listened politely
but held to their loyalty and support of Justice Black. Rarely, with
a Black clerk, like Max Isenbergh, Frankfurter was successful. The
conversations between Frankfurter and Isenbergh developed into
a rich, lifelong friendship. When Isenbergh joined the academic
ranks, he did so as an avid proponent of Frankfurter's philosophy
of judicial restraint. He even criticized his former boss, Justice
Black, in terms that echoed Frankfurter's. "I thought that Justice
Black conducted himself on the Court as he had in the Senate—as
a politician who voted his political views," Isenbergh said.

Frankfurter had commanded eight votes with his *Gobitis* opinion
but suspected, when the constitutionality of a compulsory flag-
salute exercise in the public schools was again argued in 1943
before the Court in *West Virginia Board of Education v. Barnette,* that
his position would not even win a majority. Black, Douglas and
Murphy would certainly join the original dissenter, Justice Stone,
as they had promised in *Opelika.* Moreover, two new Court appointees had replaced members of the *Gobitis* majority and were
by no means dependable votes for Frankfurter's position. Wiley
Rutledge had taken the seat Frankfurter had hoped would be filled
by his intimate friend and longtime philosophical ally, Judge
Learned Hand, and had already expressed a strong commitment to
individual liberties. And Justice Robert Jackson, FDR's eloquent
Attorney General, was the man who in 1938 had urged the President to appoint Frankfurter to provide *liberal* leadership on the
Court.

Frankfurter prepared for the reversal as a proud but doomed
gunfighter would approach his final shootout. Months before the

Barnette case was argued in the Supreme Court, Frankfurter was already writing his dissent. He jotted down sentences while shaving, then stuffed them into a dresser drawer. Later, at the office he dictated isolated paragraphs to his secretary and placed them in a manila folder. The paragraphs often seemed disjointed to his law clerk, Philip Elman. But Frankfurter did not ask for or accept drafting or research help from his clerk. "I have to do this myself," he told Elman. Later, he invited Elman to his house for dinner and then to his study, where the Justice dictated his opinion to Elman, who dutifully typed out the words.

The vote was 6–3 for reversal in *Barnette* with only Justices Stanley Reed and Owen Roberts supporting Frankfurter in dissent. Robert Jackson wrote the majority opinion and Hugo Black added a concurrence that underscored his growing conviction that when First Amendment liberties were in jeopardy the Court must intervene.

Frankfurter began his dissent with the most wrenchingly personal statement ever recorded in an opinion by a Justice of the Supreme Court. And he did so despite the vigorous arguments of his law clerk that the personal statement was inappropriate. "Phil," Frankfurter told his clerk, "this is my opinion, not yours." And so it was:

> One who belongs to the most vilified and persecuted minority in history is not likely to be insensible to the freedoms guaranteed by our Constitution. Were my purely personal attitude relevant, I should wholeheartedly associate myself with the general libertarian views in the Court's opinion, representing as they do the thought and action of a lifetime. But as judges we are neither Jew nor Gentile, neither Catholic nor agnostic. . . .

With the *Barnette* decision, Frankfurter's leadership of the liberal wing of the Court, so confidently assured only three years earlier, was obliterated. Despite Frankfurter's perception that it was the others who had strayed, in fact it was Frankfurter himself who had drifted from the credible libertarian position. Based on a mixture of philosophical and personal convictions, he had insisted that the Court owed no greater duty to the protection of First Amendment freedoms than a reasonable majority was willing to give. But the constitutional standard was so easily met under Frankfurter's rationale that the First Amendment's protection of belief and expression in wartime was rendered meaningless.

Frankfurter's refusal to change his position provided Black with the opening to assume the reins of liberal leadership on the Court. Black's growing conviction that the First Amendment deserved a preferred position in the constitutional hierarchy guaranteed an impassioned debate with Frankfurter that would extend to the end of their days on the Court together. More importantly, Black's commitment to First Amendment freedoms, which evolved into his insistence on absolute protection, became the centerpiece for his advocacy that would assure his place in judicial history.

The road to Justice Black's complete faith in free expression was significantly more tortuous than the Justice, in his stirring Court opinions of the last two decades of his life, suggested. In fact, his philosophical journey began many years before his judicial appointment. As the junior Senator from Alabama, Black had offered a spirited defense of free speech when he faced his senior colleague in informal but elaborate debate on the meaning of the First Amendment. Senator J. Thomas Heflin, the stereotypical Southern demagogue/buffoon in frock coat and string tie, had spent most of his political career indulging in crude racist cant. One October day in 1929 the Senator claimed different, though not higher, ground. At issue was a proposed amendment to a Senate bill permitting certain literature into the country that would, Heflin declared, contaminate the minds and weaken the moral fiber of all good Americans. Drawing an analogy to an immigration policy of denying entry to "unfit foreigners," Heflin said that he would vote "to keep America from becoming the dumping ground of the obscene, treasonable, and murderous literature of the anarchistic foreigner."

Senator Hugo Black's simple answer was one that he would repeat for decades to come: "I am so firmly convinced that freedom of speech is one of the sacred privileges of a democracy that I cannot vote for any measure or any legislation which tends in

the slightest degree to restrict its inestimable privilege." Black then
noted that one of America's greatest thinkers and patriots, Thomas
Jefferson, had been called an anarchist in England. He recalled that
a price was put on the heads, and the writings proscribed, of "the
great patriots who first dared to assert the principles of human
liberty in the Colonies." And he concluded that "if we take away
from a man the right to think . . . we take away from him the only
privilege that separates the citizen of a democracy from the citizen
of a monarchy and absolute despotism."

Black's views on the First Amendment developed with time and
a prodigious regimen of serious reading—while he was in the
Senate, Black checked out more books from the Library of Congress than anyone else in the Senate or the House of Representatives. Gradually Black arrived at a judicial philosophy of the First
Amendment that, with due deference to the thoughts of Thomas
Jefferson, was unmistakably his own. The pace of his philosophical quest accelerated during his early Court years and, as happened
so often during those years, Felix Frankfurter served as the unwit-
ting provocateur in the intellectual process.

The Black-Frankfurter debates on the essential meaning of the
First Amendment's protection of speech were spread over more
than two decades and produced thousands of words, at times
vituperative, from the two Justices. The disagreement began, however, with a single word and the word was not even of the antagonists' choosing. The word was "reasonable" and it had appeared
several times in the draft opinion of Chief Justice Hughes in 1941
in *Cox v. New Hampshire* that declared constitutional a New Hampshire town ordinance requiring a parade permit. The ordinance
had been challenged by a group of Jehovah's Witnesses who
had been convicted of parading without a permit and argued that
the permit requirement impinged upon their First Amendment
rights to free speech and assembly. Hughes had inserted the
word "reasonable" in an effort to limit the discretion of a government official in granting or denying a permit. If an official denied
a permit because he had already granted one to someone else
for the same time and place, it would surely be a "reasonable"
exercise of discretion. The same official could not deny a permit,
however, to a group because he did not approve of their reli-

gious beliefs or skin color or the cause the paraders wanted to celebrate.

The cautionary modifier suited Frankfurter since it provided a judicial safety valve for the Court's use when the particular facts of a case justified it. But that language did not reassure Justice Black; in fact, he made it clear that he would not join the Chief's opinion unless the word "reasonable" was deleted. For Black, the word invited subjective judgment by the Court as to what was "reasonable." Too often during the New Deal he had seen a conservative Court majority overturn economic and social legislation, justifying their action as an exercise in judicial interpretation. With precious First Amendment liberties at stake, Black was even more determined to prevent judicial trespassing.

Chief Justice Hughes acceded to Justice Black's request, but Frankfurter could not resist cackling privately to the Chief Justice about Black's demand. "Why, of course I agree to the omissions," he wrote Hughes, "even though it amuses me that, as a matter of textual reading, a broader power is now left to the states to make inroads on 'civil liberties' than in your original phrasing." Typically, the former Harvard law professor depicted Black as the poor rube incapable of grasping the subtleties of judicial interpretation. But Black would show here and again and again that his "simple" vision of the First Amendment's protection provided a sturdy bulwark against intrusions by legislatures or the Court itself. As Black's confidence and commitment to First Amendment liberties grew stronger, so did his influence with his colleagues.

Frankfurter firmly believed that he, as the protégé of Holmes and Brandeis, possessed a clearer understanding of the First Amendment protections than any of his colleagues, and that Hugo Black always got it wrong. When two free speech cases, one involving the radical longshoreman Harry Bridges, and the other the shrill editorials of the *Los Angeles Times,* were coupled for Court argument, Frankfurter and Black squared off, each confidently quoting Justice Holmes to bolster their irreconcilable positions.

Bridges had been fined for contempt of court after sending a telegram to the Secretary of Labor (and to several newspapers for publication) criticizing a California judge's decision that did not favor his union; Bridges threatened a strike if the decision remained in effect. The *Los Angeles Times* had also been fined for contempt for publishing three editorials instructing a state court judge in tough language to punish two members of the Teamsters Union. "Probation for Gorillas?" asked the editorial writer and then rejected the possibility in favor of the "assignment to the jute mill."

The two cases presented the Court with one of its most difficult constitutional dilemmas: choosing between guarantees of free press under the First Amendment and fair trial under the Sixth Amendment, each guarantee considered applicable to the states through the due process clause of the Fourteenth Amendment. California judges had attempted to insure that judicial deliberations took place in an atmosphere untainted by a labor leader's threat or a newspaper's verbal harassment. But by issuing the contempt citations the judiciary itself became an intimidating voice, threatening the free flow of information and opinion in the press.

Frankfurter viewed the two cases, as he did so many that came before the Court, as an exercise in careful constitutional balancing in which neither constitutional guarantee necessarily took precedence over the other. Both free press and fair trial protections were important, and it was the task of the Court to weigh the merits of each case, considering carefully the particular facts and circumstances involved. Beyond that analysis, however, Frankfurter considered the whole history of English-speaking peoples, dating back more than half a millennium, and concluded that judicial tradition compelled respect for a court's contempt power. Centuries of British judges had used it to protect the fair administration of justice, and its right and efficacy had properly been transferred to American courts as well. The Court's exercise of the contempt power, Frankfurter argued, represented an unbroken, incontrovertible commitment to the integrity of the judicial process.

An agitated Hugo Black attacked the Frankfurter position with a bolt of intellectual energy reminiscent of his fieriest Senate days. Frankfurter was wrong on first principles, Black charged. The

Court was not bound by the centuries of British judicial history. The starting point for the *U.S.* Supreme Court was the *U.S.* Constitution, and any other reference to the history of English-speaking peoples was irrelevant. American patriots fought the War of Independence to free themselves from British law; to bind American rights of free expression to the British rules was to deny our history. The framers knew British history well, too well, and consciously chose to protect the colonists' right of free expression with the explicit, uncompromising language of the First Amendment. The contempt citations, Black concluded, should be overturned.

Black persuaded only Douglas and Reed, while the remaining five Justices supported Frankfurter's position. Undaunted, Black prepared a scorching dissent. Working from scribbled notes on a scratch pad, he challenged every basic assumption that Frankfurter had promised to defend:

Was the Court to be guided by a concept of ordered liberty or the enforcement of the First Amendment?

"He [Frankfurter] says first. I say latter."

Should First Amendment rights be on a "parity" with other constitutional guarantees?

"I say no, Amendment ranks higher. He says opposite."

Is there an exception to the free speech guarantee when the public discussion involves matters pending in court?

"He says yes. I say no."

Can the Court justify the contempt citations because courts have historically done so?

"He says yes. I say no."

Later in the term, after the Justices had voted in the *Bridges* case, two unrelated events suddenly shook Felix Frankfurter's once-firm majority. Justice James McReynolds, one of the six majority votes, retired, reducing the vote to 5–3. Shortly after the McReynolds announcement, a second member of the Frankfurter majority, Justice Frank Murphy, began to listen with disquieting concern to his law clerk who had argued from the start that the contempt citations should be reversed. The judge in the *Bridges* case had not been intimidated by Harry Bridges's telegram, the clerk contended, and may not have even been aware of it. Murphy reviewed the trial record and ruminated on the larger constitutional issues. Reluctantly he concluded that his earlier vote in judicial conference could no longer be justified.

"The still-new robe never hangs heavier than when my conscience confronts me," Murphy wrote Frankfurter. "Months of reflection and study compel me to give it voice. And so I have advised the Chief Justice and Justice Black that my vote in Numbers 19 and 46 [the *Bridges* cases] must be in reversal."

Significantly, Justice Murphy chose to inform Justice Black of his decision before he told Frankfurter. By this time Frankfurter's early gilded treatment of Murphy had begun to tarnish. His cutting assessments of Murphy's intellectual limitations would soon be no secret, especially to the sensitive Murphy. Justice Black, a consummate politician, could adroitly size up a man's strengths and weaknesses, and his conclusions about Justice Murphy may not have been very different from Frankfurter's. But he kept his opinions to himself and outwardly cultivated Murphy, offering professional respect and personal affection. With his switch in the *Bridges* case, Murphy rejected Frankfurter's leadership for good and accepted that of Hugo Black.

During his struggle over the *Bridges* case Frankfurter indulged in what appeared to be periodic therapeutic exercises in which he privately recorded in his scrapbook his version of conversations with friends. The conversational pattern varied little. Frankfurter would be congratulated by his friend on the soundness of his judicial view. Then he and his friend would lament the shallow and, ultimately, destructive position of Frankfurter's antagonist. His friend during the *Bridges* case was former Justice Brandeis, to whom Frankfurter had sent a copy of his draft opinion.

"That's a very fine opinion of yours," Brandeis told Frankfurter. "I assume you have a unanimous Court."

"Certainly not," Frankfurter replied.

When Frankfurter told Brandeis that he might not even have a majority, and that Black was writing an opinion opposing the Frankfurter position, Brandeis exclaimed, "Black and Company are going mad!"

Whether the conversation with Brandeis took place precisely as Frankfurter recorded it is open to question. Frankfurter's fury in contemplating a stunning defeat, however, cannot be doubted.

On the first Monday in October 1941, Frankfurter and Black

welcomed two new colleagues* who would cast the decisive votes in *Bridges*. They also prepared to hear reargument of the *Bridges* case later in the fall. After oral argument Black discussed the case with his law clerk, Max Isenbergh, in such a way that Isenbergh thought Black had not fully made up his mind.

"How do you think I should vote on this?" Black asked.

"Well, you've always had a strong civil liberties record," Isenbergh said.

"Maybe you're right," Black responded.

Black gave Isenbergh the impression that he was unsure of his philosophical position and was groping for grounds to support his political sympathies. This impression fit in neatly with Justice Frankfurter's image of Black, an image that Frankfurter freely shared with many others, including Isenbergh.

More likely, Justice Black was engaging his young clerk in an intellectual dialogue for the clerk's, not his own, benefit. For Black had already put on paper his exceedingly forceful opinion that First Amendment rights must prevail. When newly appointed Justice Robert Jackson supported that view in conference, Hugo Black had won his majority.

Writing for five members of the Court, Justice Black set aside all of the contempt citations in *Bridges*. In doing so, Black reiterated his theory that the Court must give paramount consideration to the First Amendment, regardless of the instruction of British law. "No purpose in ratifying the Bill of Rights," wrote Black, "was clearer than that of securing for the people of the United States much greater freedom of religion, expression, assembly, and petition than the people of Great Britain had ever enjoyed." Black continued, "The assumption that respect for the judiciary can be won by shielding judges from public criticism wrongly appraises the character of American public opinion. For it is a prized American privilege to speak one's mind, although not always with perfect good taste, on all public institutions."

But that part of Black's opinion was not the worst of it for Justice Frankfurter. Black also introduced an interpretation of Justice

---

* In addition to Justice McReynolds's retirement, Chief Justice Hughes had retired at the end of the previous term. President Roosevelt promoted Justice Stone to Chief Justice and appointed James Byrnes and Robert Jackson to the Court.

Holmes's clear and present danger test that, Frankfurter was certain, distorted his revered mentor's theory. Holmes had written in 1919 that there could be no suppression of free expression unless there was a "clear and present danger" that the expression would create an evil that the government had a right to prevent. Black repeated Holmes's words but infused them with meaning that made First Amendment rights virtually inviolate.

Years later, Black would abandon the clear and present danger test altogether in favor of an absolute protection of speech. But in 1941, when his majority was fragile and his own influence building slowly, he was satisfied to give lip service to Holmes's balancing formula. Even then, Black's interpretation elevated free speech rights above the others in the Bill of Rights.

Felix Frankfurter read his *Bridges* dissent aloud in court the day after Pearl Harbor. Although the nation had focused on the shocking news from the Pacific, the Frankfurter reading carried its own public drama. "Our whole history repels the view that it is an exercise of one of the civil liberties secured by the Bill of Rights for a leader of a large following or for a powerful metropolitan newspaper to attempt to overawe a judge in a matter immediately pending before him." Holmes's test, he suggested, could not be reduced to a mechanistic formula in which First Amendment rights inevitably were protected.

Newly appointed Justice James Byrnes, who had joined Frankfurter's dissent, applauded him in a reassuring note. "What you have done justifies continuance of the practice of announcing decisions," wrote Byrnes. "If you suffered in its delivery, you can be assured its delivery caused suffering to those who differed with you."

But, alas, Justice Frankfurter had fallen one vote short and Stanley Reed's modest attempt at humor did not console him. Frankfurter's dissent was "beautifully done," wrote Reed. "I agree with it all except the conclusion."

With his *Bridges* majority opinion, Black had challenged the former Harvard professor on constitutional theory, and he had prevailed. He had done so by trusting his own reading of constitutional history and concluding that the First Amendment was an original and essential American creation. Notice was given,

as if it were necessary, that the Justice with the paltry legal education and narrow plaintiff's lawyer's experience could operate on
the most ambitious intellectual level. Members of the Alabama bar
had known of Black's brilliance for years, and so had his former
colleagues in the Senate. He had now brought all of the Justices
into the circle—not just Murphy and Douglas, but those like Stone
and Frankfurter, who had so woefully underestimated him a few
short years ago.

The *Bridges* decision came down two years after the Court appointment of Felix Frankfurter, and *Barnette,* the second flag-salute
decision, less than two years later. Within that relatively short span
of time, Frankfurter had not only lost his liberal majority and leadership but had been unceremoniously replaced in that position by
Hugo Black. How, it must be asked, did this happen so quickly?

First, consider Black's and Frankfurter's effectiveness with their
colleagues. Both Black and Frankfurter possessed the powerful in-
tellects to assume leadership roles on the Court, though Frankfurter was slow to recognize that Black's intellect was as
formidable as his own. Others on the Court did so less grudgingly.
When Black began to carve out his own strong position on the
First Amendment, liberal colleagues like Douglas and Murphy
were naturally drawn to his arguments. They listened to Frankfurter's lectures on the balancing of constitutional demands, but
they voted with Hugo Black. They voted with him not only on
principle but also because Black, with his expert political skills,
was better equipped to influence the brethren. True, Frankfurter
had been an adviser to Presidents. But Hugo Black had worked in
the trenches, speaking plainly to lay juries and Alabama voters as
well as U.S. Senators. He knew how to talk persuasively without
lecturing like a Harvard professor. The more Frankfurter lectured,
the less influential he became with his liberal colleagues.

There was also the nasty Frankfurter habit of talking deprecat-
ingly about Justices who did not agree with him. In informal conversations at the Court and with friends, he belittled Frank
Murphy's legal aptitude and castigated Black and Douglas for what
he perceived to be their bald political maneuvering. For his part,

Hugo Black never tired of promoting his view of the First Amendment, but he did so directly and relied on the force of his argument, not on personal insults.

Black's success transcended his ability to persuade his colleagues to adopt his views in individual cases. More significantly, Black responded aggressively to the most important constitutional challenge to the modern Supreme Court—the protection of individual rights. Before their Court appointments, both Black and Frankfurter had condemned Court interference with New Deal legislation; neither, however, suggested that the Court should defer to the legislature on civil liberties issues. Indeed, Frankfurter had made the point in 1938, only a year before his Court appointment, that civil liberties issues came to the Court with a special claim for constitutional protection. But with *Gobitis* and *Barnette,* Frankfurter appeared to forget his own lecture. Black did not.

Frankfurter continued to express concern for civil liberties, but in the final analysis he relied on the legislative branch for guidance. Black rejected that view. For him, the Court's primary role was to protect the individual liberties guaranteed in the Bill of Rights. In this way, Black believed, the people were best defended against overreaching government control. Once Black had identified this basic constitutional need of the American people, he pressed his colleagues to fulfill what he perceived to be their judicial obligation. And he did so through forcefully lucid opinions that projected an unwavering sense of institutional mission.

Still, the battle was only joined, not decisively won. The flag-salute and *Bridges* cases were decided in wartime, but the civil liberties issues raised then would continue to be placed high on the Court's agenda throughout the Cold War. Every step of the way Black and Frankfurter, evangelical in their pursuit of judicial converts, battled each other for souls—and a Court majority.

Their confrontations were not confined to First Amendment issues but were spread throughout the Bill of Rights. Regardless of the civil liberties issues in the forties, however, Justice Black usually could depend on the votes of Douglas, Murphy and Rutledge. These were labeled the Court liberals, with Black commonly acknowledged as their leader.

But four did not make a majority, and Black found it increasingly difficult to capture the crucial fifth vote. For Justice Jackson, the man who had delivered the Court majority opinion rejecting the mandatory flag salute as well as the fifth vote for Black's majority in *Bridges,* would soon desert him. In fact, he would become Felix Frankfurter's best friend and ally on the Court and would, with Frankfurter's encouragement, take up the cudgels against Hugo Black.

Justices at War

ON JANUARY 11, 1943, during a lull in oral argument before the U.S. Supreme Court, Associate Justice Frank Murphy engaged the man next to him, Justice Felix Frankfurter, in informal political conversation. Murphy, a Democrat who had been governor of Michigan before serving in the Roosevelt administration as Attorney General, speculated on the next Democratic nominee for the presidency. Assuming Franklin D. Roosevelt would not run for a fourth term, Murphy was convinced that the Democrats would turn to his and Frankfurter's colleague, Justice William O. Douglas. Douglas would lose the election in 1944, Murphy said, but he would conduct such a strong campaign that he would earn a second nomination in 1948, at which time he would be elected to the presidency.

"I am surprised, Frank, that it doesn't shock you to have this Court made a jumping-off place for politics," Frankfurter replied.

"Well, I don't like it," said Murphy.

"Well, it's much more than a matter of not liking," Frankfurter retorted. "When a priest enters a monastery, he must leave—or ought to leave—all sorts of worldly desires behind him. And this Court has no excuse for being unless it's a monastery. And this isn't idle, high-flown talk. We are all poor human creatures and it's difficult enough to be wholly intellectually and morally disinterested when one has no other motive except that of being a judge according to one's full conscience."

The sacerdotal imagery was not entirely surprising, since Frankfurter, a religious skeptic, had long enshrined two secular institutions, the Harvard Law School and the Supreme Court of the United States. Harvard would always serve as Frankfurter's academic mecca and the Court as its judicial counterpart. Given this reverence for the Court and its work, Frankfurter's disdain for Douglas's suspected political ambitions or Hugo Black's presumed sensitivity to the electorate (after *Gobitis*) seemed understandable. Frankfurter's indictment of the perceived political concerns of his colleagues was hypocritical, however, given his own pervasive involvement in national and international politics while a member of the Court. For Frankfurter remained one of Roosevelt's closest political advisers after his judicial appointment. He spoke to the President often and sent scores of notes and letters to him covering a wide range of major domestic and foreign policy issues. Beyond mere advice, Frankfurter drafted new legislation, delivered advisory opinions on the legality of existing laws, wrote first drafts of campaign speeches for the President and made specific recommendations for Cabinet-level positions, then lobbied for his choices.

While many of Roosevelt's advisers in 1939 had urged caution on the part of the President, even as Nazi troops overran Poland, Frankfurter was building his case for American intervention on the Allies' side. Tyrants throughout world history, he reminded FDR, could not be appeased; bargaining with Hitler would ultimately doom the free world. Frankfurter viewed with complete contempt the attitude of appeasement toward Germany expressed by the U.S. Ambassador to the Court of St. James, Joseph Kennedy. A lifelong anglophile, Frankfurter suggested to the President in a barrage of written and oral presentations in 1939 and 1940 that America's future was inextricably bound with Great Britain. Beyond exhortation, Frankfurter had contributed his knowledge and drafting skills to the task of tilting existing and new legislation toward England's cause.

One of the major obstacles to an enlightened foreign policy in 1940, Frankfurter believed, was the Secretary of War, Harry Woodring. The Secretary's modest administrative talents seemed no match for his Cabinet responsibilities. More importantly, from Frankfurter's perspective, Woodring clung to an isolationist foreign policy, at complete odds with the Justice's view of the world.

After consideration of a number of potential successors to Woodring, Frankfurter settled on his old boss, Henry Stimson. Then seventy-three years old, Stimson possessed the extensive Cabinet-level experience—first as Taft's Secretary of War, later as Hoover's Secretary of State—that Frankfurter deemed essential. Frankfurter also knew that Stimson's foreign-policy sympathies were consistent with his own. In sum, Stimson offered the experience, competence and philosophy to move the War Department in the direction—toward an alliance with Great Britain—that Frankfurter desired.

Frankfurter realized that the President might balk at appointing a septuagenarian to the critical Cabinet post. So the Justice proposed a package to Roosevelt: the experienced Stimson to guide long-range foreign policy, and the much younger Robert Patterson, recently appointed to the U.S. Court of Appeals, Second Circuit, to be Assistant Secretary of War. It was a combination, Frankfurter wrote FDR, that would "click." As to Stimson, "his mind is alert and vigorous and, freed from details, you would have an extraordinarily equipped man for this vital post," Frankfurter wrote. Patterson "is young, he is vigorous, he is able," the Justice continued. "He is the kind of person who combines qualities that made him the first man in his class at the Harvard Law School and also enabled him to have a distinguished war record." Roosevelt followed Frankfurter's advice, appointing both Stimson and Patterson.

It was a happy coincidence, of course, that Frankfurter was well acquainted with Patterson and was probably Henry Stimson's closest friend in the world. Already having easy access to the President, Frankfurter now would, with the appointments of Stimson and Patterson, have the ear and confidence of two more of the most influential men in the country on foreign policy.

With the leadership of the War Department in friendly hands, Frankfurter turned to one of the first and essential pieces of business, legislation that would formalize U.S. support for the Allies. As early as 1939 Frankfurter had urged the President to seek repeal of the Neutrality Act of 1935, which, he argued, effectively "favors the forces of aggression," namely Germany and Italy. By with-holding assistance to both sides of the conflict, the United States was giving substantial help to the Axis powers. Frankfurter, then a newly sitting Justice, had even suggested that the Neutrality Act violated principles of international law.

In 1940 Frankfurter offered his services to the President in con-ceiving and drafting what became the Lend-Lease bill. The legisla-tion enabled the U.S. to supply ships and matériel to Great Britain without requiring immediate payment. The constitutionality of the legislation was never challenged, but the President surely must have been reassured that the legislation was supported by a sitting Justice of the U.S. Supreme Court. Indeed, Frankfurter spent con-siderable time helping Benjamin Cohen draft the legislation for congressional approval and contributed the idea of putting the bill on the congressional docket as Number 1776. To the satisfaction of Frankfurter as well as the President, Lend-Lease became law in the spring of 1941.

At precisely the time that he was urging appointments and leg-islation on the President, Frankfurter was grumbling about the political machinations of his judicial colleagues Justices Black and Douglas. He had already attributed Black's and Douglas's reversal of their position in the first flag-salute case to what he considered a capitulation to the political whims of the electorate. But his own lobbying at the highest political level was acceptable, presumably because he considered that his impartial judgment on the bench remained intact. Not even Frankfurter's greatest admirers, such as his clerk, Philip Elman, found the distinction entirely convincing. On the day after Pearl Harbor, Frankfurter told Elman, "Everything has changed and I am going to war. I am going to need you as no justice has ever needed a law clerk." And so, recalled Elman, "we both went to war." Both on the bench and off, according to Elman, Frankfurter was a patriot first, and his judgment (in *Gobitis,* for example) reflected that priority.

In the early forties, Justices Douglas and Murphy were, like Frankfurter, frequent visitors at the White House, eagerly offering their advice on a variety of political topics. Another member of the Court, Justice James Byrnes, resigned from the Court to serve Roo-sevelt as director of the Office of Economic Stabilization and was replaced by Wiley Rutledge. But not even Byrnes equaled Felix Frankfurter in ardor or influence in the early days of FDR's third presidential term.

> Dear Frank: No one is now so ignorant as not to know that the whole American people are behind you. And one may venture to say, in all humility, that the God of Righteousness is with you—and you are His instrument. Our devoted prayers attend you. Affectionately yours, F.F.

Frankfurter wrote this note to FDR the day Pearl Harbor was bombed; ten days later he laid down in detail his overview of the problem facing his Commander in Chief. The United States, as the Justice saw it, would determine the outcome of the war because this country, among all the major powers in the conflict, had yet to realize its military potential or commit its military might to battle. Study the experiences of the French and the British, Frankfurter suggested to the President, and profit from their mistakes. The critical failure of the Daladier government, the Justice observed, was the inability of the Prime Minister to delegate the implementation of day-to-day administrative decisions to others while he determined broad policy for the nation. The British fared better, he conceded, but were slow to mobilize, too slow to be a model for the immediate American challenge.

In the days to follow, Frankfurter spoke directly to the President about every aspect of the American war effort, from the new wartime government positions to be created and the men to fill them to the plotting of a winning Allied military strategy. And when he was not serving the President directly as administrative consultant, military strategist, legal counselor and cheerleader, Justice Frankfurter held seminars in his Washington home at 1511 Thirtieth Street, N.W., for those in and close to government. Secretary of War Stimson was a frequent guest at the Frankfurters', the earlier mentor-protégé relationship now virtually reversed. Stimson came to Frankfurter to unwind and seek the younger man's counsel on the weighty matters of state. Dean Acheson, appointed in 1941 as Assistant Secretary of State, and Jean Monnet, a Frenchman with close ties to the British and to the French government-in-exile, were also members of Frankfurter's inner cir-

cle. Frankfurter used his former law clerks Joe Rauh, Jr., Ed Prichard, Jr., and Phil Graham as couriers to do his work and bidding in
the middle echelons of the government wartime bureaucracy. Off
the Court, then, his prodigious energy was poured into the task of
achieving "sure victory against the forces of brutal darkness."

Marion was often enlisted in her husband's wartime cause when
Frankfurter presented their joint views to the President, making
clear that his wife was the more sensible member of the partnership. After one of FDR's fireside chats, Frankfurter sent Roosevelt
a note of enthusiastic congratulations. But it was Marion's laudatory opinion of the speech, Frankfurter assured the President, that
gave his own view credibility. "Marion has given the key to its
nobility and its enduring history," Frankfurter wrote FDR. His conversation and correspondence regularly began with the opening
"Marion says. . . ." Frankfurter's clerks publicly spoke admiringly
of Marion Frankfurter and treated her with excessive solicitous-
ness, emulating their boss's behavior. Frankfurter's public adulation for his wife was part of a pattern that he adhered to
throughout their marriage. In that respect, he shared much with
his judicial nemesis, Justice Black.

Throughout their lives, Frankfurter and Black placed their wives,
Marion and Josephine, on pedestals, perhaps in part because both
felt that they had married above their social station. Frankfurter, the small, immigrant Jewish intellectual, married a tall, handsome Congregational minister's daughter whose American roots
were centuries deep. The social gap between Hugo and Josephine
Black was no less dramatic. Black, son of a small-town mer-
chant/dirt farmer in scruffy northeast Alabama, wed the debutante
daughter of Dr. and Mrs. Sterling Foster, whose own Memphis
wedding had prompted a congratulatory telegram from the White
House.

As suitors, Frankfurter and Black had overwhelmed their future
mates, relentlessly wooing them with intense conversation and
lilting paeans of their devotion. Neither man's adoration or court-
ing ever seemed to wane. "Dearest," Frankfurter wrote Marion in
1940, "Here the sun was shining—in the sky, not in my heart. It
never is when you are away from me." Four years later Frankfurter

wrote, "It's awful and wonderful to have such complete identification with you that even the shortest separation feels like a severance from myself." Celebrating their twenty-fifth wedding anniversary he extolled his beloved Marion:

> This is another one of those occasions when I feel with acute poignancy the gulf that separates sensibilities and the power to express them. When two lives have fused as have yours and mine it is not easy to think of one apart from the other even before they came together. Indeed mine was another life before the great happiness came when you took possession. For possession you took of it within a few days of my first sight of you—even though time passed, for me no less than for you wasteful time, before we enjoyed your sovereignty over me. And [illegible] they have been very wonderful years, in good days and cloudy ones—unbelievably few cloudy ones for two people so different in antecedents, education and temperaments. It's all been very unbelievably kind of the Fates—unbelievably fulfilling and vast and deep in the interplay of two lives. You have made me very happy in the only ways in which happiness has other than evanescent significance. And neither the power of your beauty nor the hold of your nature—the penetrating wit and insight and rigorous integrity—have lessened from the day that I first fell under your spell. Well—this is our Day, not only yours for me, and with gay gratitude and happy love I greet you, Your ever devoted, Fixi.

Hugo Black was rarely so effusive in speaking to or of his wife, but no less fervent. Recalling his first meeting with Josephine, Black spoke of her transcendent spiritual qualities. And for all of their days together, Josephine was the perfect wife, the perfect mother, the perfect woman.

Besides the adulation of husband for wife, both marriages shared a second, darker trait. The supreme happiness that Frankfurter and Black proclaimed as theirs in their marriages was not shared by their spouses. Both Marion Frankfurter and Josephine Black were desperately unhappy during many years of their marriages. Both women, in fact, experienced severe emotional problems during much of their adult lives, and their devoted husbands may have been unwittingly responsible. Plagued by doubts of their worth in the world, the wives were forced to cope with immensely successful, self-possessed husbands who could not understand or help them overcome their depressions.

Marion Frankfurter's first defense against her husband's uncontainable ebullience was the droll putdown of Felix's physical and verbal energy. But sarcasm soon turned to despair and, finally, to depression. Marion had put herself under psychiatric care in the early years of her marriage to Frankfurter. The diagnosis was neurasthenia, a debilitating mental condition, which led to a depressive state that deepened as the years passed. By the time the couple had moved to Washington after Frankfurter's Court appointment, Marion was spending increasing amounts of time in her bedroom on the second floor of their northwest Washington residence. She became afflicted with a mysterious disease that caused her to lose the use of her legs. It was never clear to Frankfurter's close friends whether the ailment was physical or psychosomatic, but for all serious purposes, Marion became an invalid confined to bed or a wheelchair.

Throughout Marion's illness, Felix continued to dote on his wife. In public he always deferred to her literary judgment, quoting her views with conspicuous pride. At home he insisted that his friends pay their respects to her, leading them to her bedside for kind words and reports of the world outside. But Felix's friends did not always follow his lead with enthusiasm or conviction. There was complete agreement that Marion was a very bright and handsome woman, but many wondered how, or if, Felix really adored her. For Marion rarely seemed sensitive to her husband's needs or loyalties. Usually the center of attention in his professional and social life, Frankfurter always returned home to the depressed Marion. Sometimes the sadness was not the worst of it. Marion alone could stun Felix Frankfurter into silence as she did one day in the early forties when, in the presence of Frankfurter's young friend, Max Isenbergh, she announced loudly that "I am an invalid because of him," pointing an accusatory finger at her husband.

Marion once confided that she was "a mental invalid" who had chosen to shut the world out of her life. She did not pretend to be happy or pleased with Felix or herself. Indeed, she seemed reconciled to a dreary, bedridden life when she was still in early middle age, a mentally alert and physically very attractive woman.

Some of Felix's friends were sympathetic to Marion, accepting her condition and her husband's feelings for her as genuine. Others were not so charitable. "She was an exquisite monster," said Max Isenbergh, suggesting a wife who berated and bedeviled her husband throughout their marriage.

Even in very public Washington, Senator Hugo Black's wife, Josephine, had kept a low profile. She did not aspire to the social whirl of official Washington, nor did her husband. They preferred, instead, the company of each other, their children and a small circle of friends. Entertainment for the Blacks usually meant small, informal dinner parties in their Alexandria, Virginia, home, with the Senator barbecuing steaks for his guests. To be sure, the occasional formal dinner party had excited young Josephine, as when she and the Senator were invited to Herbert Hoover's White House with Ambassador and Mrs. Charles Dawes and the U.S. Ambassador to Cuba and his wife. "Never have I been so thrilled," Josephine had written her mother. "I almost got sick in my 'tummy' like I used to on Christmas Eve! And it came up to all my expectations! I've never seen anything so absolutely perfect as the table appointments, etc."

Black always spoke of Josephine in the most glowing terms, but the superlatives were by no means his alone. For Josephine Black seemed to touch all who knew her as an almost angelic spirit. It was, however, Justice Black who spoke most movingly of her enduring qualities. "I hope that both of you will grow up to be like my wife," he wrote his first law clerk, Jerome "Buddy" Cooper, and his wife after Josephine's death in 1951. "She was sweet, gentle and kind to everybody. I never heard her speak harshly or angrily to any person in the thirty years we lived together. I believe every person who ever associated with her loved her. She left no enemies in this world—she never had any."

Given her extraordinary personal qualities, Josephine seemed destined to naturally thrive on the exciting life that her husband's public career could have provided. But, like Marion Frankfurter,

Josephine could not make peace with herself, and her husband's dominant personality and relentless public success did not make the task easier. While Hugo was building his confidence and a national reputation in the Senate and later on the Court, Josephine was privately doubting her worth and purpose. She jotted down plaintive pleas to a higher being. Nothing seemed to help.

Hugo's effective work in the Senate led to his Court appointment, but Josephine, already in a tenuous emotional state, could not keep pace. Her private suffering took a turn for the worse, and in the late thirties and early forties Josephine was hospitalized for sustained periods. Black wrote his wife regularly, assuring her that he was taking good care of their three children and that her family "loved her much and missed her more. But we believe you are being benefitted and that is enough." During at least one Court term, Black's clerk, Max Isenbergh, noticed that the Justice seemed distracted because of his wife's illness; uncharacteristically, he delegated to the clerk much of the drafting of opinions. Black apparently was plagued by the thought that he might have been a significant cause of his wife's problems. But Josephine refused to blame him. "All you have done is love me with all your heart and soul—when I am not worthy of that kind of devotion," Josephine told her husband. "But that couldn't possibly be what it is. I just don't know what it is."

If Black was at fault in his relationship with his wife, his shortcomings completely escaped his children. His oldest child, Hugo, Jr., wrote adoringly of his mother and suggested that his father's affections were equally intense. Black's only daughter, Josephine (nicknamed Jo-Jo), remembered her father as loving and unreservedly devoted to his family. Black's letters to his wife while she was hospitalized in the early forties corroborate this picture. With Josephine away, he became a single parent, supervising the children's homework and play, chauffeuring them to school and music lessons. Caring for little Jo-Jo was particularly satisfying to him. "You will be interested to know," he proudly wrote Josephine in the fall of 1941, "that she [Jo-Jo] is absorbed in her school work and is almost as exacting as Sterling [her older brother] in connection with obtaining my assistance. Night and morning she appears with her books. It does not disturb me at all and in fact is sort of recreation."

Jo-Jo herself has recalled that her father was attentive to her every need. Besides driving her to school and her lessons, he was her chief baby-sitter, often at the U.S. Supreme Court. Jo-Jo fondly remembered dashing down the spiral staircase at the Court and running with abandon throughout the building. She also sat in the courtroom while Black and his colleagues heard cases. Jo-Jo's favorite Justice, other than her father, was none other than Felix Frankfurter. "He was the friendliest," she recalled, "and used to write me notes while he was on the bench. They were of no great significance other than to say that he was glad to see me."

When Jo-Jo was nine years old, Frankfurter was describing her father's judicial behavior in his diary in the most deprecating terms. Black was, according to Frankfurter, a politician on the Court without professional integrity, a product of an inferior legal education who did not possess the requisite judicial knowledge to do his job properly. But the same Justice Black was invited on more than one occasion to dine with Frankfurter in his home when the latter played host to important foreign visitors such as the Australian Minister for External Affairs. And Frankfurter extended that cordiality to Black's entire family, inviting all three of the Black children to his house in the early forties, sometimes giving them books he thought they would enjoy. Jo-Jo spent many hours in the Frankfurter home, with Marion upstairs in bed, playing with the daughter of Sylvester Gates, a member of the London bar who had sent his children to the U.S. to stay with the Frankfurters at the height of the bombing of Britain.

Hugo Black was attentive to all his children, but that attentiveness often had a relentless focus that made his two boys, in particular, run for cover. The problem for Hugo, Jr., and Sterling was that their father had learned much about life and success and he was eager, too eager sometimes, to share the lessons about every subject that might touch a young man's life, from toilet habits to Thomas Jefferson. "My father liked to teach; he particularly liked to teach me and my brother," Hugo, Jr., recalled. "By the time Buddy Cooper [Black's first law clerk] came along, we needed some help in allowing him to teach."

Black's oldest child and namesake, Hugo, Jr., struggled throughout his youth to live up to his father's high standards. Always high-spirited and combative, Hugo, Jr., engaged in a prolonged dialogue with his father that, by turns, was touching, hilarious, sad and inspiring. During Hugo, Jr.'s, formative years, his father's long shadow seemed to reach into every corner of the boy's life. "I caused him a lot of disappointment during my grammar school days," Hugo, Jr., recalled. "Like most fathers, he wanted his name-sake to achieve as an extension of himself, I guess, and this pressure was not good for my confidence or self-image. In the first place, he was really one heck of a man. The closer I got, the more apparent this became, and any comparison eroded whatever confidence I might have had in myself."

In the classroom and on the playground, Hugo, Jr., labored to meet his father's lofty expectations. When his grades were high, Hugo, Jr., did not recall hearing any encouragement from his father, but when they dropped, his father yelled, "Why do you have to swoop after you soar?" Nothing Hugo, Jr., did seemed to satisfy either himself or his father. Even a choice piece of fatherly advice to help Hugo, Jr., through a schoolyard crisis ended in disaster. Never be intimidated by bullies, Black had told his older son, and illustrated the point with a story: When he was growing up in Clay County, Alabama, he had one day displayed his best athletic moves to impress the most beautiful girl in his class. Suddenly the school bully crashed into him. Black's first thought was to run, but his girlfriend was watching. So, suppressing a strong survival instinct, he began flailing away at the bully. To his surprise and lifelong satisfaction, he won the fight. The bully was all bluff, father told son, and waited for Hugo, Jr., to report a similarly satisfactory result in his own pugilistic adventures. "This story," Hugo, Jr., recalled, "probably cost me more bruises, cuts and pure humiliation than anything in my life."

There were salutary lessons to be learned as well. One that Black emphasized by word and example was determination in the face of adversity. When Hugo, Jr., was seven years old, he was bedridden with pneumonia. There were no antibiotics at that time and chances for recovery, the doctor said, were not good. Black, Hugo, Jr., remembered, took charge of his recovery like a commanding general poised for the counteroffensive. Father assumed his battle position at Hugo, Jr.'s, side, tending his bedpan, taking his temperature, forcing food into his mouth and supervising every linen and pajama change. Most importantly, the father rejected failure as an unacceptable alternative, on his *and* his son's part. Hugo, Jr., would pull through, he told the doubting physician. And he did.

Hugo, Jr., regularly asked for his father's advice, but occasionally he did not seek it and immediately regretted it. Three months before his graduation from the Florida Military Academy, for example, the sixteen-year-old youth was caught off campus AWOL, and this infraction was reported to Black, who immediately lashed out at his son's misconduct. Black considered his son's behavior inexcusable and suspected that the escapade was prompted by a desire for liquor and the companionship of loose women (both of which the Justice vigorously disapproved).

Black's outrage and accusation prompted an urgent letter from Hugo, Jr., to his mother. "I hope Pop won't mind me writing this to you," Hugo, Jr., began, "but I think possibly you would understand better and explain to him more easily, because you know me better and understand me." The explanation for his absence without leave from the Florida Military Academy was very simple, Hugo, Jr., told his mother. The pressure on him had become unbearable, a result, he suggested, of his good grades and fishbowl existence as the son of a famous Justice of the U.S. Supreme Court. "I could've told Pop all about this in the snap of the finger," he wrote, "should I have been able to get in my two cents worth."

As to his father's charge that he wanted to get drunk, Hugo, Jr., assured his mother that drinking had nothing to do with it. In fact, Hugo, Jr., admitted that he was a little disappointed, not to say shocked, by his father's lack of confidence in him. And thus, he argued to his only sympathetic juror, "In the first place last night I think Pop must have let his imagination run away with him or either he doesn't know me very good. You know that I wouldn't think of drinking, much less getting drunk, and after all you've told me, you know perfectly well that I would not even turn over in my mind going with wild women or doing anything like that until I'm married." Actually, the whole unfortunate episode had caused Hugo, Jr., to worry about his father. "Maybe Pop's worked to [sic] hard or something," he suggested, "but I don't believe he understands kids, because naturally everybody can't be like him."

Black did, of course, forgive his son and soon shifted his concern toward selecting a suitable college for him. He made inquiries at

Dartmouth but later, because of Hugo, Jr.'s, susceptibility to colds, accepted his son's decision to stay in the South.

Hugo, Jr., entered the University of Alabama at Tuscaloosa and seemed to thrive almost immediately. His grades were excellent, though he was not beyond giving his parents a few palpitations ("Mom said you worried about the letter you got concerning my class absences. Daddy, those cuts are not a good thing to have at all. . . ."). He joined a fraternity and felt, perhaps for the first time, fully accepted by his peers. A talent for creative writing was recognized by Mr. Strode of the English faculty, and Hugo, Jr., concentrated on being discovered through the publication of one of his short stories.

There was still time for a little troublemaking, to be sure, as Justice Black was abruptly reminded in August 1942. According to Tom Ward, an old Alabama friend of Black's, Hugo, Jr., and a few friends spoke disrespectfully to an officer of the law and ended up in custody. Ward rescued Hugo, Jr., and wrote the Justice that the episode should not be a cause of serious parental concern.

As a college man, Hugo, Jr., continued to seek the constant approval of his parents, so apparent from his earlier correspondence from the Florida Military Academy. He wrote them often and at length, recording his fraternal activities, academic achievements and romantic interests. But most of all, Hugo, Jr., wanted his parents to know that he loved them and was working hard to earn their love and respect. After asking his father for more spending money, he wrote: "Daddy, do not let this worry you because I promise that you would think more of me right now than you ever have in your life." He gloried in his mother's good looks and charm, reporting with pride the spectacular impression that Josephine had made on his fraternity brothers upon a brief visit to Tuscaloosa. "She simply charmed every one at the house," he wrote. "Nobody there could understand how such a beautiful woman could have such a son as myself."

In his correspondence with his father, Hugo, Jr., had begun tentatively to establish his credentials as a student of constitutional law, admirer of Justice Black and critic of Justice Frankfurter. Commenting on a workman's compensation opinion of his father's, he congratulated him on having "mastered the technique of making what you have to say clear to everybody." He also thought Frankfurter's concurring opinion showed improvement in style though, regrettably, Hugo, Jr., thought both his father "and the little Justice" were wrong in not giving "the poor woman her money" instead of sending the case back to the trial court.*

Later Hugo, Jr., boldly challenged his father's conclusion in an important First Amendment decision, *Martin v. Struthers.* Black had written the majority opinion for the Court striking down a Louisiana ordinance that prohibited door-to-door solicitation by religious and commercial vendors. The ordinance was unconstitutional, Black had declared, because it deprived the vendors of their right of free speech. "I thought your opinion [in *Struthers*] was on the right track," Hugo, Jr., began, "but I did not think it was one of those you can write where the logic is so cold and clear that even those against you could not find any arguments for their side." It seemed to Hugo, Jr., that Thelma Martin, the petitioner in the case, could have exercised her First Amendment rights without disturbing the local residents in their homes. He suggested she could have accomplished her purpose "without waking any one up," perhaps by leaving circulars at the front door. Hugo, Jr., thought that the ordinance preserved Thelma Martin's free speech while it justifiably eliminated annoyance to residents. "Ringing doorbells to distribute handbills," he wrote his father, "usually brings nothing but animosity to the cause the person is trying to help."

While respectfully disagreeing with his father, Hugo, Jr., was incensed by Frankfurter's opinion in *Struthers,* though he was not entirely clear on the position Frankfurter had taken. "Also I did not understand what Frankfurter was driving at or what side he was on, and I would like to slug him for getting smart and saucy in his opinion," Hugo, Jr., wrote. "That little guy really has a nerve talking about your opinion wanting in explicitness when he probably has trouble understanding what he himself writes. No one else understands what he writes, even if he does."

By the time Hugo, Jr., was a college junior, many of his friends had been drafted and were fighting in Europe and the Pacific. Hugo, Jr., wanted to enlist and set his sights on officers' candidate

---

* Justice Black responded by noting that the trial judge had not permitted a jury trial, as required by law, so the Supreme Court was obligated to return the case to the trial court.

school, which made his father extremely proud. In the fall of 1943, young Hugo arrived at Camp Davis, North Carolina, for his military training, beginning a new phase in his life—and a spate of advisories from Black on how to cope with army life and the petty tyrannies of commanding officers. Be sensitive, Black counseled his son, to career military men who had not enjoyed the privileges of a college education and a middle-class life-style. "The best way to assure your success is to prove to them that you can be completely obedient in connection with every order—even though you may think inwardly that it is whimsical and its execution wholly unnecessary," Black wrote. A week later he warned Hugo, Jr., not to complain about the food. "However bad it is, I venture the assertion that it is better than 75 percent of the people in the United States have now or ever have had."

Naturally, Hugo, Jr., turned to his father when confronted with a crisis at the very beginning of his career as a military man. "Daddy, today has been disastrous to me," he wrote. "I know it now, and the realization of it hurts me. I haven't got the guts. I have the mental equipment and the physical coordination. I just don't have the guts."

Hugo, Jr.'s, distraught letter followed an assignment to lead his company through its paces under the watchful eye of his commanding officer. Inexplicably, he had marched his men into a pool of water. The commanding officer shouted to Hugo, Jr., to give orders that would take the men out of the water. "I stammered, stuttered and marched them by the right flank, which simply put them in deeper water!" Hugo, Jr., wrote. "The lieutenant [illegible] his hair and had a talk with me. He was very nice and encouraging but he said at the moment I stunk."

Several times in his eight-page handwritten letter Hugo, Jr., pleaded with his father to give advice to his "spineless" son. The Justice responded with a two-page typewritten letter that was supportive, comforting and, as requested, full of paternal advice. Hugo, Jr.'s, letter triggered a twenty-five-year-old memory, Black wrote his son, taking him back to his own military-training days. There was a brilliant architect named Smith, Black recalled, who could design skyscrapers with great skill but could not give the simplest military command. Smith marched his company forward well enough at the beginning of a drill, but when the company seemed headed for a collision with the mess hall, the architect became completely tongue-tied. The soldiers dutifully marched into the side of the building, and the architect was certain that his military career had thereby ended in abject failure. But Smith was wrong, Justice Black noted, and, in fact, served honorably throughout the war.

"You at least did better than Smith, who was unable to stammer or stutter any command," the Justice wrote his son. "One mistake is not now and never has been synonymous with failure," he assured Hugo, Jr. Neither he nor his son would be disgraced, he added, if he failed to receive a commission. "Nothing is really disgraceful except that which is dishonorable and it is never dishonorable to fail to achieve something if the person does the best he can," he wrote. Privates also serve, the Justice reminded his son, and as long as Hugo, Jr., worked to reach his potential as a soldier and a person, his father would be proud: "So long as you do your duty in the Army, live so as to keep your self-respect, and keep your head in the midst of temporary disappointments, I shall be just as proud of you as though you occupied the shoes of General Eisenhower, himself."

During the war, both Black and Frankfurter faced extraordinary family problems. Josephine Black and Marion Frankfurter were ill, and their suffering caused their husbands worry and pain of their own. The circumstances also placed additional responsibilities on the two men to make adjustments in their private lives. Felix, in effect, became a caretaker for Marion, serving as her nurse as well as her intellectual link to the outside world. For Black, Josephine's illnesses meant that he assumed additional responsibilities—helping Jo-Jo with her homework and counseling her two brothers on the perils and opportunities of adolescence and young manhood. In those difficult times, Black and Frankfurter revealed the same indomitable will to succeed that had characterized their professional careers. They refused to accept setbacks passively, either in their personal lives or on the Court.

While Felix Frankfurter had operated a military-command post from his northwest Washington home during World War II, Hugo Black had concentrated on the Court's work and the time-consuming affairs of his family. But he, like Frankfurter, was intensely patriotic, and his feelings, and ultimately his judicial actions, demonstrated that fact.

The bombing of Pearl Harbor had jolted Black as it had every other loyal American: "We have gone back to work but it seems difficult to concentrate on individual disputes between Americans at a time when the entire country is participating in a world dispute," he wrote Josephine on December 8, 1941. "The atmosphere at the joint session was grim and determined. Japan has done something Roosevelt could not—it has brought about a greater spirit of unity than ever before existed when this country went to war. And since war has seemed inevitable for quite a time our loss of lives brought about by the surprise attack can be considered as the contribution of some to this country's welfare—a tragic price to pay, but perhaps a necessary one."

Former Artillery Captain Black served vicariously through battle reports in the newspapers and in letters from those like his former law clerk, Marx Leva, who saw action in Italy. He also participated through correspondence with his two sons, who were experiencing the traumas of basic military training. Although Black had never soldiered outside of the United States during World War I, he spoke as if he had fought "the Hun" in the trenches at Château-Thierry and eagerly passed on the accumulated wartime wisdom to his sons. His pride in military service had been instantly rekindled when in 1943 Hugo, Jr., had announced his intention to enlist. "I think I can fully understand your desire to get into combat service as soon as you can," he wrote his son. "My experience in the last War leads me to believe that I should feel exactly as you do if I were in your shoes today." And he congratulated his younger son, Sterling, on the good fortune of having "a hardboiled first Sergeant and a hard pushing Adjutant."

On the Court, Justice Black proved to be "hardboiled" in his own right, particularly when the Court confronted constitutional challenges to the military's treatment of Japanese-Americans on the West Coast. Under orders from General J. F. DeWitt, more than 100,000 Japanese-American citizens and aliens had been herded into assembly centers and then relocated in internment camps from the California desert to the hills of Arkansas. General DeWitt had claimed that the harsh policies were necessary because of the threats of espionage and sabotage by Japanese-Americans on the West Coast.

The trouble with that argument was that there was no credible evidence that Japanese-Americans, as a group, were any more guilty of espionage and sabotage than any other group. The orders, therefore, smacked of racism and presented, at the very least, acute civil liberty issues that would seem to have pricked Black's liberal conscience.

But Captain Black, the military man, completely dominated the debate with Justice Black, the civil libertarian. So resolute was Black in defending the military policy of General DeWitt that he found himself positioned a significant distance in his thinking from his familiar libertarian companions, Justices Douglas and Murphy. Indeed, Justice Black's closest philosophical ally in two critical Japanese-American cases that came to the Court in 1943 and 1944 was a colleague who consistently placed patriotism in wartime above individual liberties—Justice Frankfurter.

The Supreme Court first reviewed General DeWitt's policies after Gordon Hirabayashi, an American citizen of Japanese descent completing his senior year at the University of Washington, ignored a military curfew and order to report to a "Civil Control Station" as a preliminary step to evacuation from the Seattle area. As a result of his defiance, Hirabayashi was arrested and sentenced to two three-month prison terms. Later, Hirabayashi challenged his arrest and imprisonment in court, claiming that the military had exceeded its constitutional authority and deprived him of his rights as an American citizen. Both the federal district and appellate courts upheld the military orders, and in the spring of 1943 the Supreme Court agreed to hear arguments in the *Hirabayashi* case.

At the judicial conference following oral argument Black opened the discussion by declaring his support for the government's position and admonishing his brethren to decide the case on the narrowest possible constitutional grounds. That meant, according to Black, that the Court should confine itself to the issue of the constitutionality of the curfew and not extend the ruling to the evacuation order, even though Hirabayashi had been convicted of violating both the curfew and evacuation orders. Frankfurter, apparently stunned by Black's sudden advocacy of judicial restraint, sat in uncharacteristic silence.

Chief Justice Stone, drawing on the full measure of his persuasive powers as well as the prestige of his office, dominated the discussion and strongly supported the government's position. He raised Black's point first, insisting that the Court need only decide the single issue of the constitutionality of the curfew without addressing the legality of the evacuation order. To justify the curfew, Stone invoked the general war powers provisions of the Constitution,* saying that the Japanese-Americans could inflict "grave damage" through espionage and sabotage activities. He did not, however, refer to specific documentation to support his statement; by conference's end, the Chief Justice could count every member of the Court in his majority, save Frank Murphy, who had not yet made up his mind.

On May 30, 1943, Stone circulated the first draft of his opinion, which presented a reading of the government's war powers that was awesome in scope. Those powers, he wrote, were not restricted to victories on the battlefield but must embrace the national defense and all "evils that attend the rise and progress of the war." The military's curfew order would properly come within the Constitution's war powers if it could be shown that the measure was necessary to meet the threat of espionage and sabotage. On the basis of unsubstantiated allegations submitted by government attorneys, the Chief Justice concluded that "the nature and extent of the racial attachments of our Japanese inhabitants to the Japanese enemy" were justifiably matters of grave concern to the nation.

Ironically, the Court's bitter antagonists on most civil liberties issues, Black and Frankfurter, stood together as the Chief's most loyal supporters, staving off threatened defections from their colleagues. Frankfurter's support of Stone was readily explicable on both philosophical and personal grounds. Stone's position was, after all, a classic example of judicial restraint, since he insisted on deciding no more than was necessary for constitutional resolution. Moreover, the Chief's conclusion—that the military should be

---

* The President's war powers are derived from Article II, Section 2, which makes him the Commander in Chief of the armed forces. Congress's war powers reside in Article I, Section 8, which give it the power to declare war and support the armed forces.

given virtual carte blanche power in time of war—was perfectly compatible with Frankfurter's superpatriotism.

Black's position was more difficult to comprehend. To be sure, his patriotism was as deeply rooted in his background and experience as Frankfurter's. But his commitment to civil liberties, freshly declared during the same term as *Hirabayashi,* in his concurrence in the second flag-salute decision, fell by the wayside. In his steadfast support for the military's policy, Black risked outright rebellion by his closest ally on the Court, Justice Douglas.

Although Black had no trouble supporting the Stone draft, Justice Douglas expressed serious reservations about the opinion. Having grown up in the Northwest with several Japanese-American friends, Douglas challenged Stone's position that Japanese-Americans had maintained racial solidarity that had "encouraged their attachment to Japan and Japanese institutions." That statement, Douglas wrote in a letter to Stone, was not true. " 'Racial solidarity' and 'lack of assimilation,' " Douglas wrote, "do not show lack of loyalty as I see it."

A second Douglas criticism of Stone's opinion centered on the Chief's failure to indicate that the Court might later question the necessity of long-term evacuation and internment. "Is it not necessary," Douglas asked, "to provide an opportunity at some stage (although not necessarily in lieu of obedience to the military order) for an individual member of the group to show that he has been improperly classified?"

Following his earlier questioning of the Chief Justice's position, Douglas wrote a concurring opinion that at once endorsed the military's policy and doubted the constitutionality of certain aspects of that policy. Both portions of the bifurcated view angered Frankfurter, who termed the first part of the opinion "cheap oratory." The last part Frankfurter saw as pandering to libertarianism that could throw the doors of the courts open to thousands of unwelcome challenges from Japanese-Americans who wanted judicial confirmation of their loyalty.

Black reacted to the Douglas opinion in a less waspish but equally disapproving manner. First, said Black in a judicial conference on June 5, it was elementary that someone had to exercise authority in wartime, and, for him, that authority was the military. The courts, he asserted, had no business undermining that authority. Secondly, he attacked language in the Douglas opinion that seemed to invite Japanese-Americans to file suits in federal courts to prove their loyalty. Finally, Black reiterated his broad support for the military. If he were commanding general, he told his colleagues, he would not let the evacuated Japanese come back to the West Coast even if the Court directed that it be done.

Justice Murphy had exceeded even Douglas in disagreeing with Stone's draft majority opinion, circulating a lone dissent among the Justices. Priding himself on his sensitivity to racial discrimination, Murphy bluntly disputed the Chief's assumption that there was sufficient evidence of disloyalty among Japanese-Americans. The conclusion was inescapable to Murphy that tens of thousands of Americans, including Hirabayashi, had been deprived of their liberty because of a particular racial inheritance. "This is so utterly inconsistent with our ideals and traditions, and in any judgment so contrary to constitutional sanctions," he concluded, "that I cannot lend my assent."

As was his wont, Frankfurter took it upon himself to lead the lost judicial soul back to the flock. His memorandum to Murphy began with a disclaimer: He had no intention of trying to persuade Murphy to change his position, which he assumed was "immovable." By memo's end, however, Frankfurter had made a heavy-handed appeal to Murphy's institutional and national loyalties in an effort to talk Murphy out of his dissent. Is it, he asked Murphy, "conducive to the things you care about, including the great reputation of this Court, to suggest that everybody is out of step but Johnny and more particularly that the Chief Justice and seven other Justices of this Court are behaving like the enemy and thereby are playing into the hands of the enemy?"

With the conspicious support of Black and Frankfurter, Chief Justice Stone was able to forge uneasy unanimity among the Justices. Douglas's concurring opinion was softened considerably so that it did not invite further litigation from Japanese-Americans, as Black had feared. And Murphy apparently succumbed to Frankfurter's pressure, withdrawing his dissent at the last minute. But Douglas and Murphy had been pulled along reluctantly, and they stood ready to renew their challenges when the next constitutional test of the military's orders came before the Court. Sixteen months after *Hirabayashi,* the Justices heard oral argument on behalf of another Japanese-American, a San Leandro welder named Fred Korematsu, who had been arrested after he refused to follow military orders excluding him from his home and directing him to go to an assembly center to prepare for relocation away from the West Coast.

When he opened the judicial conference in the *Korematsu* case, the Chief Justice knew that the discussion among his colleagues was likely to be acrimonious. Both Douglas and Murphy had virtually announced their future dissents with their severe comments during the *Hirabayashi* deliberations. Wiley Rutledge had also expressed serious reservations about the constitutionality of the military orders. And now Korematsu's attorneys had made the task significantly more burdensome for the Chief Justice, since they had attacked the entire military policy—not just the West Coast curfews but the detention of Japanese-American citizens in assembly centers and their relocation in camps outside the coastal area. It would be difficult, therefore, for Stone to confine the Court's focus to legal technicalities—but that is precisely what the Chief Justice attempted to do.

The issue before the Court in *Korematsu,* the Chief Justice suggested, was of a very narrow compass. Fred Korematsu had been arrested after he had violated the military's order excluding Japanese-Americans from critical West Coast centers. The Justices were only obligated, Stone said, to decide whether the military order of exclusion was constitutional. The Chief asserted that it would be mere speculation on the Court's part to assume that the military's exclusion, and detention, would inevitably lead to relocation. Accepting this premise, Stone suggested that the Court need only follow the narrow reasoning of *Hirabayashi.*

The first Associate Justice to speak, Owen Roberts, shattered the Chief's plan to finesse the relocation issue. The notion that Korematsu could be sent to an assembly center with any realistic hope of avoiding relocation was chimerical, Roberts argued. Both Korematsu and the Justices knew that Korematsu faced only two choices: defy the military's exclusion order and face imprisonment, or be transported to one of the assembly centers and face the inevitable prospect of relocation. Government attorneys had, in fact, conceded the basic point that military authorities had planned to relocate Japanese-Americans like Korematsu once they had been excluded from their homes and sent to assembly centers.

After Roberts, Hugo Black spoke, voicing his unequivocal support for the Chief Justice's position, as did the next two Justices to present their views, Stanley Reed and Felix Frankfurter. Although their comments at conference were not recorded, both Douglas and Murphy later challenged in writing Stone's formulation of the legal issues before the Court. If Douglas's and Murphy's objections could have been anticipated, those of Justice Robert Jackson could not. In heated disagreement with the Chief, Jackson charged that there was no compelling reason for the military orders. "I stop at *Hirabayashi*," Jackson said defiantly. Only the cautious acquiescence of Justice Wiley Rutledge delivered a fragile 5–4 majority to Stone.

Conference discussion underscored the obvious: Duplication of the Chief Justice's feat of unanimity in *Hirabayashi* would be impossible. Indeed, Stone would have to struggle to retain a bare majority in *Korematsu*. In a calculated move to hold his majority, the Chief assigned the Court's opinion to Hugo Black. Without articulating his purpose in the assignment, Stone must have been counting on Black to exercise his manifest political skills to keep the one wavering member of the liberal wing, Rutledge, in line and, perhaps, persuade one of his dissenting liberal colleagues to cross over to the majority.

From the moment that he began to write his opinion, Black resolutely held to the narrow legal position that the Chief Justice had advocated in conference. As Black saw it, the Court was asked to decide only whether the military-exclusion order was constitutional, and need not venture into the more problematic areas of detention and relocation. To accomplish his task, Black simply followed Stone's reasoning in *Hirabayashi*, reading the war powers provisions of the Constitution broadly and accepting the military's argument that exclusion of Japanese-Americans, like the curfew, was necessary to protect the security interests of the nation.

Frankfurter was the first to congratulate Black on the first draft of his opinion. "I am ready to join in your opinion without the change of a word," he wrote Black. Frankfurter could not resist, however, advising Black to minimize the Court's role in reviewing military policy or congressional action. The Court was doing no more than affirming Congress's authority to make a violation of a military order a criminal offense, he suggested. The elimination of a single offending sentence in Black's draft satisfied Frankfurter, and he enthusiastically joined Black's opinion.

Other members of the Court were not so easily placated. Black's most serious problems were posed, predictably, by his usually congenial colleagues, Douglas and Murphy. In a draft dissent Douglas wrote that the Court could not legitimately separate the exclusion and detention/relocation issues, as Black had done. Justice Murphy, who had been brooding since *Hirabayashi,* also circulated a dissent. In his opinion he unleashed an impassioned attack on the military order as racist, presenting an unanswerable argument that there was no credible evidence to back the military's claim that Japanese-Americans, as a group, posed a security risk to the West Coast of the United States. Finally, Black had to contend with Justice Jackson's dissent, condemning the entire judicial exercise. The military's policy was based on highly improbable assumptions, Jackson wrote, and the Court majority had chosen to overlook the shaky military presuppositions at the risk of condoning military dominance that would "approximate Lenin's definition of a dictatorship."

Surveying the raw emotions laid bare by *Korematsu,* Justice Murphy wrote his clerk, "The Court has blown up over the Jap case—just as I expected it would."

Drawing on the cold determination that had served him so well in earlier professional crises, Black stuck to his original position. He would accept minor revisions of language to assure that Frankfurter would not write separately. And he would include a statement that the Court had not decided the detention and relocation issues, suggesting that other Justices might wish to do so. This brought Justice Douglas into the majority, making the vote 6–3. Beyond those relatively insignificant concessions, Black would not budge. Fred Korematsu was excluded from his home, Black wrote, not because of hostility to him or his race, but "because we are at war with the Japanese Empire." Seemingly unconcerned that the government had produced no hard evidence of Japanese-American disloyalty, Black relied on more general "investigations" of disloyalty that were, in fact, no more persuasive in result. "We conclude," Black wrote, "that the government's action was predicated not on racial prejudice, but upon the compelling urgencies of national defense."

Korematsu was the worst judicial opinion that Justice Hugo Black wrote in his thirty-four years on the Court. It was devoid of meaningful analysis of the underpinnings of military policy. It was deceptive in its strained narrowing of the constitutional issues that had been presented by Korematsu's attorneys. And it was a philosophically incoherent defense of broad government power by one of the most influential civil libertarians in the Court's history.

Shortly after Black's *Korematsu* decision was announced, knowledgeable commentators condemned it for all of the right reasons. Although Black did not say so, he had given the military a license to trample on individual rights at will during wartime. Black's suggestion that the policy was justified by military necessity was ludicrous. It could not be documented in the government's brief at the time, and was thoroughly discredited in later years when the full record on the military orders was made public.

Curiously, Black never revealed the slightest tremor of remorse. Wave after wave of criticism of his opinion did not move him. In fact, it only caused him to justify his opinion, and the military orders, in bolder terms. "There's a difference between peace and war," he said later. "You can't fight a war with the courts in control." Had he been the President, Black said, twenty years after *Korematsu,* he would have done "precisely the same thing." That Japanese-Americans were the object of the discriminatory policy did not trouble him. "They all look alike to a person not a Jap," Black said. "Had they [the Japanese] attacked our shores you'd have a large number fighting with the Japanese troops. And a lot of innocent Japanese-Americans would have been shot in the panic. Under these circumstances I saw nothing wrong in moving them away from the danger area."

American political thought during World War II was dominated by the war effort. The war also affected the Supreme Court calendar—and the judicial decisions of Justices Black and Frankfurter. Both men willingly conceded the broadest constitutional power to the executive and legislative branches of the federal government, even though those concessions undermined the individual rights of American citizens of Japanese descent. To serve the cause of the U.S. government in wartime, Black and Frankfurter demonstrated that they were prepared to shelve their long-standing concerns for civil liberties.

FELIX FRANKFURTER, age 12, the year he immigrated with his family to the United States from his native Austria. When he arrived at Ellis Island, Felix did not speak a word of English.

EMMA FRANKFURTER in 1898, four years after her family settled in an apartment on New York's lower East Side. Her husband, Leopold, sold linens door to door, but Emma held the reins of power in the family.

PORTRAIT OF HUGO BLACK as a young man. At an early age, Black expressed an avid interest in both law and politics.

THE WILLIAM L. BLACK family on the front porch of their home in Ashland, Alabama, in 1892. Six-year-old Hugo is fourth from the left, standing between his father and his mother, Martha.

Faculty of the
Harvard Law School
May 1927

SUPREME COURT nominee Felix Frankfurter, *opposite page,* with his counsel, Dean Acheson, testifying before the Senate Judiciary Subcommittee in 1939. Frankfurter answered questions about his leadership role in the American Civil Liberties Union and other matters that the senators thought relevant to his fitness to serve.

PROFESSOR FELIX FRANKFURTER (back row, second from right) with other members of the Harvard Law School Faculty in 1927. Dean Roscoe Pound is in the front row, left.

MARION FRANKFURTER with Eleanor Roosevelt in 1937. By the time the Frankfurters moved to Washington, Marion was spending increasing amounts of time in her bedroom, a victim of a condition diagnosed earlier as neurasthenia.

FRANKFURTER served FDR as confidant and advisor both before and after his appointment to the Supreme Court in 1939. Here, in 1940, Justice Frankfurter administers the oath of office to Frank Knox, incoming Secretary of the Navy, with the President looking on.

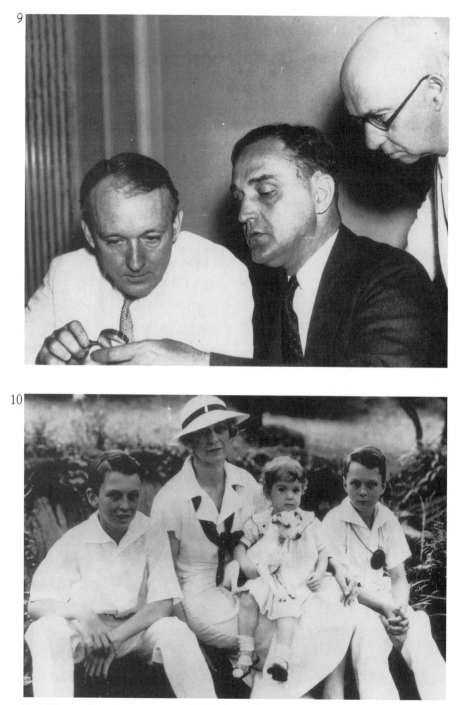

THE HUGO BLACK FAMILY in 1937 after Black was nominated by Roosevelt to be his first appointee to the Supreme Court. From left to right, Hugo, Jr., Josephine Black, Jo-Jo, and Sterling.

CHAIRMAN HUGO BLACK, *opposite page,* and other members of the Senate Lobbying Investigating Committee reviewing evidence before a 1935 hearing. Black used his trial lawyer's skills to become one of the Senate's most feared and effective legislators.

A TENSE SUPREME COURT nominee Hugo Black during a national radio address to explain his former membership in the Ku Klux Klan. "It did the trick," Roosevelt declared privately after the address. "You just wait and see."

11

12

HUGO AND JOSEPHINE BLACK were all smiles as they were surrounded by Senate supporters following Black's Court confirmation by the Senate, 63 to 16.

THE JUSTICES of the U.S. Supreme Court in 1939, the year that Frankfurter joined Black on the Court; the Justices are (front row from left): Harlan F. Stone, James McReynolds, Chief Justice Charles Evans Hughes, Pierce Butler, Owen J. Roberts; (back row from left): Frankfurter, Black, Stanley Reed, and William O. Douglas.

THE ANTAGONISTS in one of their rare light moments together at a bar association lunch in 1943.

15

MR. JUSTICE FRANKFURTER, the Court's eloquent spokesman for judicial restraint.

16

MR. JUSTICE BLACK, the liberal leader and libertarian hero of the modern Supreme Court.

Everyman and the Devil

FIELD MARSHAL HERMANN GOERING sat in the corner seat of the defendants' dock, alert and defiant, stalking the American prosecutor's every move and thought. He wore the light-gray double-breasted military uniform of his own design, stripped by the victorious allies of all insignia and decorations. A brown army rug was tucked loosely around his legs, a sign that the defendant was suffering from a slight cold. But Goering did not invite pity in the crowded Nuremberg courtroom that March day in 1946. Indeed, Goering himself, though considerably thinner than during his days of triumph, appeared strangely robust, his face animated, the brutish grin on display at the least provocation of his interrogator.

The international press corps was poised for the Goering cross-examination, anticipating the dramatic highlight of the five-month-old trial of twenty-two Nazi leaders accused of crimes against humanity. Hermann Goering was the highest-ranking Nazi leader on trial, the one defendant who had proudly plotted with Adolf Hitler from the beginnings of the Nazi party and of the Third Reich.

Now the American prosecutor, Associate Justice Robert H. Jackson of the U.S. Supreme Court, confronted Goering with the horror and responsibility of it all. For Jackson, the Nuremberg trial posed the greatest challenge of his professional career, a challenge he had readily accepted at the invitation of the new U.S. President, Harry S. Truman, only one week after the death of Franklin D.

Roosevelt. For the first time in all of human history, Jackson told the international tribunal at Nuremberg, those "flushed with victory and stung with injury, stay the hand of vengeance and voluntarily submit their captive enemies to the judgment of the law." The trial, Jackson assured the court in his eloquent opening statement, represented "one of the most significant tributes that Power has ever paid to Reason."

Chief Justice Harlan F. Stone did not share Jackson's lofty view of the proceedings. "Jackson is away conducting his high-grade lynching party in Nuremberg," the Chief groused. "I don't mind what he does to the Nazis, but I hate to see the pretense that he is running a court and proceeding according to common law. This is a little too sanctimonious a fraud to meet my old-fashioned ideas."

Skepticism about the integrity of the trial at Nuremberg was only one reason that Stone disapproved of Jackson's decision to serve as chief U.S. prosecutor of the Nazi leaders. The Chief Justice had long been on record as opposed to leaves of absence for members of the Court. Such leaves, Stone feared, suggested to the public that the Court's work was of secondary importance. Moreover, the Chief resented the additional work that absences left to the eight remaining Justices. In Jackson's case, the absence also increased the likelihood of deadlock on the Court, already severely split on close constitutional issues.

Stone's criticism of Jackson's views was primarily based on institutional grounds. That of Justice William O. Douglas was of a more personal nature. From Douglas's perspective, Jackson's Nuremberg prosecution was no more than a grandstand play for public glory. Jackson, for his part, admitted privately that his motives were not entirely altruistic. He was, in fact, eager to escape the seemingly interminable fractiousness among the Justices. Hugo Black, in Jackson's opinion, was the root of the problem; in that assessment, he was joined by Felix Frankfurter.

At the end of the 1944 Court term, Associate Justice Owen Roberts had resigned, bitter and cynical about his colleagues. He considered Justice Murphy insufferably self-righteous, labeling him "The Saint." And to Roberts, Hugo Black, once his close friend, had become the worst of all: a rank bully who intimidated his

colleagues in judicial conference. Frankfurter had patiently cultivated Roberts's friendship; he also encouraged Roberts's growing
antipathy toward Black, freely discussing with Roberts in his
chambers Black's "vehemence" and "ruthlessness." By the time of
his resignation, Roberts had stopped eating lunch with his colleagues and had even refused to participate in the informal ritual
of shaking hands with the other Justices before each Court session.

Further insult was added to injury when the Justices could not
agree upon a formal note of regret over Roberts's resignation. The
Chief Justice had tried his hand at the gracious farewell but Hugo
Black had vetoed it, scratching out Stone's line that Roberts made
"fidelity to principle your guide to decision," and curtly informing
Stone that he would not sign a statement including that sentence.
Douglas joined Black's cause, while Frankfurter and Jackson rallied
behind Stone's original statement. In the end, no letter was sent to
Roberts.

By 1945 Hugo Black had become the most feared member of the
Court, ready and able to challenge his colleagues on both philosophical and personal issues with a toughness that some Justices
found threatening. Frankfurter had been complaining to his colleagues for years about Black's crude directness. Now Roberts had
withdrawn entirely as a result, Frankfurter and Jackson were convinced, of Black's rough tactics.

Justice Jackson had attempted to take Black's measure, always
with Frankfurter in the wings subtly goading him toward confrontation. Even while Jackson had disagreed in print with Frankfurter,
as he did in the second flag-salute case, the two had remained
close personal friends. One of their common pastimes was de-
spairing over what they perceived to be Black's hopelessly inappropriate judicial behavior. Frankfurter's diary entry for January 30,
1943, for example, recorded the following:

> Attended Mary Acheson's wedding and later the recep-
> tion at the Dean Acheson house. There I ran into Bob
> Jackson looking none too happy. He took me off into a
> corner and said "Do you feel as depressed as I do after
> these Saturday conferences?" I replied that I certainly do
> not come away normally happy and certainly did not do
> so today because every time we have that which should
> merely be an intellectual difference gets into a champion-

> ship by Black of justice and right and decency and every-
> thing and those who take the other view are impliedly
> supporters of some exploiting interest.

Jackson, over time, came to despise Black. In June 1945, he found reason beyond the usual gossiping with Frankfurter to rage against his adversary. Black had, Jackson believed, violated a basic canon of judicial ethics by hearing oral argument in a case in which his former law partner, Crampton Harris, had participated. Harris had appeared before the Court on behalf of a local chapter of the United Mine Workers, arguing that the Fair Labor Standards Act allowed miners' pay to be calculated from the time they entered the portal of the mine rather than from the time that they actually began extracting the coal.

The Court voted 5–4 in favor of the UMW, with Black support- ing a majority opinion that made Harris's client victorious. In dis- sent, Jackson not only disputed the majority's legal analysis, but attacked Black personally, suggesting that he had taken an unprin- cipled position that undercut his earlier proclamations in the Sen- ate on the purpose of the Fair Labor Standards Act. Black had vigorously objected to the personal reference ("If the dissent goes down as now printed, it will not be a fair representation of the true facts"), but Jackson refused to withdraw it. That had not been the end of the matter. The losing litigant, the Jewell Ridge Corpo- ration, had petitioned the Court for a rehearing on the grounds that Hugo Black should have disqualified himself and, therefore, that the Court's decision was tainted. The Justices denied the pe- tition.

Hugo Black was not the first Justice to have heard argument by an attorney with whom he had earlier been affiliated. Both Justices Holmes and Brandeis, paragons of integrity, had done so, as had Chief Justice Stone. The decision on disqualification had tradition- ally been left to the individual Justice with no formal reason ordi- narily given by the Court for a Justice's decision on the issue. It was a surprise to the brethren, therefore, when Stone proposed a statement noting the well-established fact that the Court did not rule on the question of disqualification to accompany the unsigned opinion rejecting the petition. All four dissenters from the original decision, including Jackson and Frankfurter, agreed to the statement.

Reading Stone's statement as a personal attack on his integrity, Black reacted with predictable fury. If such a statement was sent to the printer, Black wrote Stone, it should only be signed by those who endorsed it. And Black, for one, refused to do so. The four other Justices who, with Black, had formed the majority in *Jewell Ridge* supported Black and also refused to sign the statement. This left the Chief with yet another embarrassing schism on the Court.

The judicial conference in which the issue was discussed only exacerbated an already ugly situation. Black declared that *any* statement would serve as "a declaration of war," and all of the Justices knew that Hugo Black did not bluff. The Chief retreated, withdrawing his proposed statement. But Jackson, joined by Frankfurter, insisted on introducing his own statement that publicly called Black's participation in the case into question. In a letter to Black, Frankfurter pleaded innocence, explaining that he "had no share in creating the situation whereby Bob felt it to be his duty to make clear the issue of qualification. But since he had done so, I could withhold joining him only by suppressing my belief in the truth. I do not propose to do that—and that is the sole reason why I join him. Needless to say, I greatly regret the whole incident." With Frankfurter's backing, Jackson had, thereby, launched the first attack of the war that Black had promised. Shortly after the confrontation, Jackson left the Court to prosecute Nazi defendants at Nuremberg.

Robert Jackson had prepared meticulously for his opening statement to the Nuremberg tribunal. Although his skills as an advocate had been well established in his native New York state and in Washington, D.C., where he had served under Roosevelt as solicitor general and Attorney General, Jackson's assignment in Nuremberg was of an entirely different order: He planned to amass credible evidence to prove the incredible events of the Nazi master plan. To accomplish the task, Jackson and the other prosecutors and their staffs sifted through 25,000 photographs, 100,000 German documents and millions of feet of captured film.

On the day of his opening statement, Jackson had been determined to overcome his natural tendency to speak quickly, an understandable temptation at Nuremberg given the voluminous
materials he would attempt to cover. Before speaking, he placed a
slip of paper in front of him at the podium with the word "slowly"
handwritten on it. And he adhered to his own advice, delivering
every phrase with measured weight. His opening statement consumed almost an entire day, but by session's end Jackson had
accomplished his purpose. He had traced the atrocities of the Third
Reich from the meek beginnings of the Nazi party, and skillfully
built toward his general theme of premeditated, organized crimi-
nality that had culminated in the worst war the world had ever
known. At the conclusion of his presentation, Jackson's colleagues
had clustered around him, congratulating him on a superb performance.

That opening day's statement would be the highlight of the 216-
day trial for Robert Jackson. His cross-examination of Hermann
Goering would be the nadir, although the scene had seemed perfectly set for another Jackson triumph. Goering had, with little
prodding from his counsel, proudly narrated the story of the rise
of the Third Reich and had not disguised his prominent role in that
rise. While his co-defendants had dashed for cover from responsibility, Field Marshal Goering had not only admitted his critical role
in the success of the Third Reich but had flaunted it. He had
seemed, therefore, perfectly primed for a searing cross-examination by Robert Jackson.

The prosecutor had planned that his cross-examination track
with his opening statement, attempting to establish the basic ten-
ets of Nazism with the expectation of building toward the final
atrocities. But almost immediately Jackson lost control of the pace
and substance of the questioning; Field Marshal Goering refused
to cooperate.

Jackson opened his interrogation with a question about the Nazi
leadership principle, and Goering immediately seized the opportunity to remind the prosecutor that after World War I Germany
had been "on the verge of ruin" and needed absolute control from
the top. He even quoted Franklin D. Roosevelt to make the point
that certain governments in Europe had forsaken a democratic

form of government because "democracy had brought forth men who were too weak to give their people work and bread and to satisfy them."

Jackson asked the tribunal to limit the witness's answers to "yes" or "no," but, to the prosecutor's chagrin, the presiding judge, Lord Justice Lawrence, allowed Goering to respond more expansively. Throughout the day Goering took his cue from the Lord Justice, expounding on virtually every question asked. The effect on Jackson was devastating. He seemed confused and defensive, so much so that Goering and the prosecutor appeared to reverse positions. Almost routinely, the witness took Jackson's questions and turned them to his own advantage.

When Jackson asked Goering about a system of detention by the police, Goering responded by lecturing Jackson on the difference between the Nazi regime's political police, which detained political prisoners, and the regular police which, Goering said, did not.

"Let's omit that," snapped Jackson. "I have not asked for that."

But the Lord Justice gently admonished Jackson, not Goering. "Mr. Jackson," he said, "the Tribunal thinks the witness ought to be allowed to make what explanation he thinks right in answer to the question."

With obvious irritation, Jackson addressed the witness. "The Tribunal thinks you should be permitted to explain your answer now," he said to Goering, "and *it* will listen to your answers."

During the cross-examination that followed, Goering played the role of schoolmaster to Jackson's recalcitrant schoolboy. When Jackson suggested that in January 1945 Field Marshal Goering had ordered more air attacks on England, Goering replied bluntly, "I believe you are mistaken."

Remarkably, Jackson had no documentation to substantiate this or many of his other lines of inquiry. Once challenged by Goering, Jackson shifted his inquiry abruptly, leaving the impression that he was both disorganized and unprepared.

Had not Goering been responsible for the fire that destroyed the Reichstag on the eve of the Nazi party's rise to power?

That was impossible, Goering replied, since he had no motive or reason. The witness could not resist a further burst of self-congratulation. "But the fact was that I almost perished in the flames, which would have been very unfortunate for the German people, but very fortunate for their enemies."

Jackson switched to another subject. "So, as I understand you," he said, "from the very beginning, publicly and notoriously, it was the position of the Nazi party that the Versailles Treaty must be set aside and that protest was important for that purpose?"

Goering shot back, "From the beginning it was the aim of Adolf Hitler and his movement to free Germany from the oppressive fetters of Versailles, that is, not from the whole Treaty of Versailles, but from those terms which were strangling Germany's future."

When Jackson suggested that Goering had never expected the United States to enter the war, Goering labeled the suggestion "nonsense." He explained, "Such nonsense—I hope you will excuse me—as to say that America would not come into the war even if she were attacked, you will understand that I could never have uttered, because, if a country is attacked, it defends itself."

Finally Jackson's cross-examination totally collapsed when he insisted that Goering had met with the Reich Defense Council to plan the annexation of the Rhineland in 1938. "Oh, no," exclaimed Goering, "here you have made a great mistake." First, said Goering, Jackson had incorrectly translated a Reich Defense Council document. It was not the *Rhineland* the Council was considering but the mobilization of the *Rhine* region. Secondly, he, Goering, was not present at the meeting and the fact that the Field Marshal was listed as a member of the Council only verified his formal position, and Jackson's embarrassing misunderstanding of the situation.

Jackson pressed. Weren't these preparations for armed occupation of the Rhineland?

Goering: "No, that is altogether wrong."

Jackson: "But weren't they of a character which had to be kept entirely secret from foreign powers?"

Goering: "I do not think I can recall reading beforehand the publication of the mobilization preparations of the United States."

Jackson exploded, tearing off his headphones and throwing a sheaf of notes onto the counsel's table. His face flushed with anger, he shouted at the Tribunal, "I respectfully submit to the Tribunal that this witness is not being responsive. It is perfectly futile to spend our time if we cannot have responsive answers to our questions. This witness, it seems to me, is adopting and has adopted in the witness stand and in the dock, an arrogant and contemptuous attitude toward the Tribunal which is giving him the trial which he never gave a living soul nor dead ones either. . . ."

In the Nuremberg courtroom that day, Jackson had presented a real-life portrayal of *The Caine Mutiny*'s Captain Queeg, at first confident, then unnerved, and finally losing control entirely.

Mercifully, the Lord Justice adjourned the session for the day.

> *There was an upstart called Jackson*
> *Who went to Germany for action,*
> *Not to bring men to justice,*
> *But to feather his nestice,*
> *And finally fell flat on his asston.*

Everyone did not agree with the opinion of Jackson's general performance at Nuremberg as set out in Justice Douglas's limerick. But there was widespread disappointment and criticism of Jackson's cross-examination of Goering. One newspaper, for example, compared Jackson to a punched-out prizefighter who was saved from a KO "by the gong."

Jackson defended himself in a letter to Frankfurter, blaming the debacle on the Lord Justice's failure to restrain Goering. The Goering cross-examination was only one of many concerns that seemed to have put Jackson on edge. He felt increasingly uneasy about his extended leave from the Court, mindful that the Chief Justice disapproved. His letters to Frankfurter justifying his decision to come to Nuremberg were strained, as if Jackson constantly had to reassure himself of the correctness of his decision. Far from Washington, Jackson also experienced a deep sense of isolation. On June 9, 1946, visibly under stress, Jackson threw a public tantrum that profoundly altered his place in Supreme Court history and drew both Hugo Black and Felix Frankfurter into the web of the controversy.

The dramatic sequence of events leading to Jackson's outburst began with news of the death of Chief Justice Stone on April 22,

1946. Rumors began circulating immediately that Jackson would be Stone's successor. For several years it had been common knowledge among Washington insiders that Jackson had been Roosevelt's first choice for Chief Justice after Charles Evans Hughes had announced his retirement in 1941. Only Roosevelt's desire to maintain a bipartisan front with America on the brink of entry into World War II had persuaded the President to appoint Stone. The man who had made the argument for Stone most forcefully in 1941 was Felix Frankfurter. Putting aside his personal affection for Bob Jackson, a Democrat, Frankfurter had argued that the choice of Stone, a Republican, would be in the nation's best interest.

With the war won, it was natural, in 1946, for the new President, Harry S. Truman, to reconsider Jackson. But there were also substantial reasons offered by Jackson's opponents to deny him the promotion. The deep divisions on the Court were a matter of scholarly commentary and Washington gossip. The fact that Jackson had taken a leading role in the battles, such as *Jewell Ridge,* while not known to the general public, was not entirely a secret either. In sum, Jackson's ability to unify the Court was seriously questioned.

In Nuremberg, Jackson was aware that his name was being mentioned for the Chief Justiceship. He also had heard that there was strong opposition to his candidacy, particularly from those sympathetic to Hugo Black and, Jackson believed, from Black himself. His suspicions about Black's determination to deny him the Chief Justiceship were fanned on May 16, 1946, with the publication of a column in the *Washington Star* by Doris Fleeson. The columnist reported on the Black-Jackson confrontation in *Jewell Ridge* and also that President Truman had been told that if he appointed Jackson as Chief Justice Justices Black and Douglas would resign. Fleeson did not say who had told the President about the resignation threats but did write that the information came from "inside the Court."

Already feeling isolated, Jackson assumed the worst: Hugo Black had gone to the President with the threat of resignation. As in *Jewell Ridge,* Black was using rough tactics to get his way, and his way confounded the professional destiny of Robert Jackson. Less than a month after the publication of the Fleeson column, Fred Vinson, Truman's Secretary of the Treasury, was nominated by the President to be the Chief Justice of the United States. Truman later admitted that the feuding on the Court had been a factor in his decision to appoint Vinson, who he hoped would be able to unify the Justices.

One day after the announcement of the Vinson nomination, the President received a transatlantic cable from Jackson in Nuremberg. The cable contained the message that he planned to make public the following day from Nuremberg that would set the record straight, as Jackson saw it, on a number of matters that affected the integrity of the Supreme Court. Unleashing a blistering attack on Hugo Black, Jackson recounted his version of the *Jewell Ridge* controversy and, with undisguised bitterness, accused Black of meddling with the President's choice of a Chief Justice.

Truman asked Jackson to delay releasing his statement for twenty-four hours so that he might talk directly with him about the contents. Jackson refused. The next day in Nuremberg he made public the letter that he had sent to the chairmen of the House and Senate Judiciary Committees.

Jackson's attack was the most personal and virulent ever delivered publicly by a member of the Court against a colleague. He accused Hugo Black of bullying tactics and unprincipled decision-making in the *Jewell Ridge* case, breaking tradition and confidentiality by quoting Black's "declaration of war" threat in judicial conference. He also pointedly suggested that Black himself had threatened the President with resignation if Jackson were appointed Chief Justice.

"It is high time that these stories of 'feuds' cease to be mysteriously and irresponsibly fed out and that Congress have the facts," Jackson told reporters. "If war is declared on me, I propose to wage it with the weapons of the open warrior, not those of the stealthy assassin." He concluded with a promise of renewed resolve to fight Black on the issue raised in *Jewell Ridge*. "If it [the disqualification issue] is ever repeated while I am on the Bench, I will make my *Jewell Ridge* opinion look like a letter of recommendation by comparison."

The attack stirred a public furor. *The New York Times* condemned Jackson for "an error of taste" and Black "for the worse offense of lowering judicial standards." The *Knoxville* (Tennessee) *Journal* called for Black's impeachment, if he did not resign, but the *New*

York Post saluted Black's "sterling liberalism" and criticized Jackson's "personal pique." The *Washington Post* demanded the resignations of both Black and Jackson. So did Senator Scott Lucas of Illinois. "There can't be any confidence in the Court as long as the feud goes on," Lucas told reporters. "For the good of themselves, for the good of the Court, and for the good of the country, both Justices should resign."

Felix Frankfurter sent a letter of encouragement to Jackson, packaging his support in the form of a colloquy with his wife, Marion:

Felix: "I suppose this is the first time in American history that a man failed of the Chief Justiceship because he showed character when character needed to be shown."

Marion: "I am glad for Bob's sake that he doesn't have to take on this awful situation."

Felix: "Yes, and he felt that way himself when he discovered the situation in the Court—that it didn't come his way when Stone was appointed. But it is not comfortable to have skulduggery succeed."

Marion: "Heavens, no!"

In the same letter, Frankfurter urged Jackson to dismiss any thought of resignation, again putting his thoughts in the form of a recollected conversation with his wife.

"I do hope that Bob doesn't resign," Marion Frankfurter said, according to her husband. And that wishful statement provoked the following reply from Felix. "I can't imagine that he will. The situation reminds me of the situation when Lowell issued the adverse report in the Sacco-Vanzetti case. You will remember the reporters came around and asked me if I was going to resign from Harvard. And you remember my reply, printed at the time: 'Why should I resign? Let Mr. Lowell resign!' Not only is Bob a fighter but he is no fool."

Frankfurter concluded his letter to Jackson with the reassurance "that the facts as you set them forth in your Nuremberg statement give an accurate account in every detail of what actually took place."

Despite Frankfurter's encouragement, Jackson was not sure that he should remain on the Court. In his response to Frankfurter he questioned "whether this is a good use of one's life. I am certain that the position on the Bench would have been intolerable if I had not taken this audacious and desperate step. I am not sure that it will be tolerable after it." But he further argued that to resign and leave Hugo Black in charge was the most intolerable thought of all: "Black is now rid of the Chief, whose reputation as a liberal made his opposition particularly effective and irritating. Black, as you and I know, has driven Roberts off the Bench and pursued him after his retirement. Now if he can have it understood that he has a veto over the promotion of any Associate, he would have things about where he wants them."

Shortly after Jackson had issued his statement from Nuremberg the President called Black. "Don't get in a pismire with Bob Jackson," he told him.

Truman needn't have worried. With the cool public detachment that had served him so well during prior controversies, Black remained both unflappable and silent (though privately he denied that he had ever talked with Truman about resigning). When a United Press reporter thrust the Jackson statement in front of Black the day after Jackson's Nuremberg news conference, Black barely glanced at it, then folded it under his arm and said that he had more important business than responding to the Jackson attack. He was late for a tennis game with his son, Hugo, Jr., just back from military service, and he had to be on his way.

Four years later, the authors of the book *The Truman Merry-Go-Round* charged that Felix Frankfurter had instigated Jackson's attack by sending word to him in Nuremberg that Black had threatened the President with resignation if Jackson were appointed Chief Justice. After he learned of the charge, Frankfurter wrote Black denying any part in the controversy and telling him that he was very tempted to sue the authors for libel. Black responded with a gracious note assuring Frankfurter that he was not at all disturbed and leaving the impression that the thought of Felix Frankfurter's making such trouble never entered his mind.

That was not the case. In fact, Black had told Hugo, Jr., that he was certain that Frankfurter had done exactly what he later denied.

The Supreme Court term ended shortly after Jackson's blast from Nuremberg. In the aftermath, all members of the Court found themselves uncomfortably in the spotlight. Still, Jackson and

Black refused to give ground, neither submitting the resignations called for by Senator Lucas and the *Washington Post.*

In his chambers Justice Frankfurter offered a depressing assessment of the work accomplished by the Court over the previous nine months. He wrote Frank Murphy that the Justices had made judicial history in the worst possible way, writing more opinions that were politically motivated, unprincipled and below minimum professional standards than any previous Court. He did not name names, but Frankfurter's diary entries from the period suggest that he held Black primarily responsible, assisted by Douglas and Murphy, for the record he so deplored. "Having been endowed by nature with zestful vitality," Frankfurter concluded, "I still look forward hopefully to the era which will open on the first Monday of October next."

There was considerable anxiety among the Justices in October 1946 when Robert Jackson returned to the Court's work for the first time in more than a year. Would there be another angry scene between Jackson and Black? Could there possibly be an atmosphere of civility after so much rancorous feeling had been expressed? The answer came on October 10, 1946, when Hugo Black entered the judicial conference room and quickly walked over to a seated Robert Jackson to shake his hand. "Good morning, Hugo," said Jackson, and the dreaded moment of awkwardness was averted. The two joined in the conference discussion with controlled geniality, giving no hint of their earlier hostilities. That correct, but distant, posture would be maintained until Jackson's death in 1954.

Frankfurter was undoubtedly encouraged by the return of Jackson. The optimism about the 1946 Court term that he had earlier expressed to Justice Murphy was further buoyed by the promise of a new Chief Justice, for Frankfurter had become increasingly disenchanted with Chief Justice Stone. But Frankfurter's initial enthusiasm for the Vinson appointment soon dissipated. After Vinson's first judicial conference Frankfurter wrote: "The way Vinson dealt with them [the argued cases] gives further evidence that he is likely to deal with complicated matters on a surface basis. He is confident and easy-going and sure and shallow."

If Vinson performed below Frankfurter's expectations, at least one of his colleagues, Hugo Black, was true to form. Black had become, according to Frankfurter, the epitomical demonic judge, sly, sinister, and bent on wholesale destruction of the law.

In his diary, Frankfurter staged the judicial conference as a morality play with himself as Everyman and Black as the devil, appearing in various disguises to hide his singularly malevolent goals. In the first meetings of the fall term Black "has appeared to be all sweetness," Frankfurter observed. But Frankfurter was certain that it could not last. When the Justices considered the constitutionality of the Hatch Act, a law which curtailed political activity by government employees, Black's true character, as Frankfurter perceived it, was exposed. Black "let loose for the first time," Frankfurter wrote, indulging in what he considered an unseemly demagogic defense of the government employee's right to engage in political activity in a democratic society. "It led me to say to myself," wrote Frankfurter, " 'Oh, Democracy, what flapdoodle is delivered in thy name.' Not the less so because it was all said in Black's irascible and snarling tone of voice."

Frankfurter's hostility was so consuming that it often prevented him from recognizing that Hugo Black, snarls and all, presented the most serious philosophical challenge to accepted constitutional doctrine in the twentieth century. The prevalent view, long advocated by Frankfurter, designated the Court, in Alexander Hamilton's phrase, "as the least dangerous branch." Possessing neither the power of the purse nor the sword, the Court relied exclusively on reason and political savvy to maintain its high prestige and clout in the constitutional system. It spent much of its time parceling out responsibility to the other federal branches of government and to the states, leaving only the most narrowly defined and judicially manageable issues for itself. That was the essence of judicial restraint as preached by James Bradley Thayer and his disciple Felix Frankfurter.

A large part of Frankfurter's antagonism toward Black was based on the fact that Hugo Black ignored his lessons of judicial restraint. The Black-Frankfurter philosophical disagreement reached its contentious peak over the interpretation of the due process clause of the Fourteenth Amendment.* Ironically, the two began the debate

---

* The clause reads: "No State shall . . . deprive any person of life, liberty, or property, without due process of law. . . ."

in perfect agreement on their premise. Both believed that the due process clause of the Fourteenth Amendment had been used by the Court in the past to impose its conservative economic values on popularly elected representatives and that use was a flagrant violation of constitutional trust.

While on the Harvard faculty, Frankfurter had condemned the veto power the Court had willingly exercised over social-economic legislation. Hugo Black, too, worried about an ambitious Court abusing its role in interpreting the Fourteenth Amendment. As a Senator, he had railed against the conservative majority that had twisted the meaning of the due process clause of the Fourteenth Amendment to affirm their conservative views. "No one has ever defined it," declared Senator Black. "No one has ever marked its boundaries. It is as elastic as rubber."

Their common complaint led both Frankfurter and Black to pose the crucial constitutional question: how could the Justices give meaning to the due process clause without indulging in subjective decision making? For Frankfurter, the Justices were obliged to seek the answer through their study of constitutional history, drawing on the knowledge of their predecessors and their own sense of fairness and decency. Despite the vagaries of the language, Frank-furter was confident that the collective wisdom of the Court—and the Justices' commitment to judicial restraint—could produce a rational and just result.

Black became increasingly impatient with what he considered Frankfurter's "natural law" framework, which did not tie the Court to an explicit set of constitutional rules. The Court should not make law, as the anti–New Deal Court had done, but seek to anchor the Fourteenth Amendment* to the wording of earlier sections of the Constitution. Specifically, Black wanted the Justices to read the language of the Fourteenth Amendment as a mandate to enforce the Bill of Rights against violations of the states.

It was a view that had been successfully and almost effortlessly ignored by the U.S. Supreme Court since the Fourteenth Amendment was adopted in 1868. The issue had been first raised only a

---

* Black did not confine his study to the due process clause alone but considered the entire Fourteenth Amendment.

few years after the Amendment became law. The Court had discussed and then dismissed the argument that the individual liberties of the Bill of Rights should be enforced against the states under the Fourteenth Amendment. That decision conveyed a finality which subsequent courts embraced as a matter of course. Later courts, nonetheless, accepted the argument by corporations that the due process clause of the Fourteenth Amendment could be put to good use to protect property rights.

The Court did not give up completely on the argument that the due process clause should protect some individual liberties of citizens against infringements by the states. In 1938, in *Palko v. Connecticut,* Associate Justice Benjamin Cardozo formally announced for the Court that certain concepts in the Bill of Rights were so basic to a constitutional scheme of "ordered liberty" that the Court was required to provide protection. In deciding whether the due process clause of the Fourteenth Amendment was violated, Cardozo offered two criteria: a right must be a "principle of justice so rooted in the traditions of our people as to rank as fundamental" or a violation "so acute and shocking that our polity will not bear it."

Although Frankfurter was not yet on the Court when the Cardozo opinion was written, he later supported it. For *Palko* clung largely to Frankfurter's approach that, at its core, focused on procedural fairness in the state courts. Most importantly for Frankfurter, *Palko* stood for cautious intervention so that the Justices would not be bound by rigid adherence to the sweeping guarantees of the entire Bill of Rights.

In his first full year on the Court, Hugo Black had joined the Cardozo opinion. But later he moved away from the Court's position, convinced by his reading of the history of the Fourteenth Amendment that its *Palko* decision was wrong. The Court had not given sufficient weight to the views of Senator John A. Bingham, whom Black called the "James Madison of the Fourteenth Amendment." Bingham and other key framers of the Amendment, Black concluded, intended that the Amendment incorporate all of the Bill of Rights and make them applicable to the states. In addition to this historical argument, Black asserted that the *Palko* approach invited the Justices to impose their personal values on the nation.

That had happened in the mid-thirties with the conservative majority endorsing substantive due process for the benefit of the propertied classes. Even with the best of intentions, this promised to occur again when the Justices began to separate the "fundamental" liberties from the less crucial ones. Who decides? Upon reflection, Black was not willing to let even the great Justice Benjamin Cardozo do so. He preferred the explicit language of the Bill of Rights as the Court's guide.

Felix Frankfurter relished the philosophical debate with Black, even as he was denouncing him elsewhere for his evil ways. In this debate, neither politics nor personal ambition was relevant, as he believed them to be in other arguments with Black. Their dispute over the Fourteenth Amendment could be fought on the more familiar terrain of Supreme Court history and wisdom.

Frankfurter's correspondence with Black on the subject was cordial, scholarly and insistent. He was deferential at first, begging Black's indulgence as he tried to understand Black's position. Before asking Black a series of probing questions in 1943, Frankfurter had presented his own perspective on the Fourteenth Amendment, refined, as he told Black, over twenty years of scholarly study. "Once you go beyond a procedural content [to the Fourteenth Amendment] and pour into the generality of the language substantive guarantees," he wrote Black, "it is to me inconceivable that any kind of definition of the substantive rights of the guarantee will not repeat in the future the history of the past, namely will according to the makeup of the Court give varying scope to the substantive rights that are protected." He then offered a mini-seminar on the need for judicial restraint so that the popular will would be realized and the Court, the undemocratic feature in the constitutional system, restricted to its narrowest limits. That did not mean that the Court was rendered superfluous, not with men like Holmes, Brandeis and Cardozo serving. "I appreciate the frailties of men, but the War is for me meaningless and Hitler becomes the true prophet if there is no such thing as Law different from and beyond the individuals who give it expression."

Frankfurter assured Black that he would be happy to subscribe to his theory of "incorporation" of the Bill of Rights under the Fourteenth Amendment if the Alabamian could lead him to the historical truths that he espoused:

I am truly eager for understanding this matter, and therefore should be grateful to you if you will refer me to the
materials which justify one in saying that the general language of the Fourteenth Amendment was in fact a com-
pendious statement of some or all of the earlier nine
Amendments. Are all nine so incorporated? Did the Fourteenth Amendment establish uniform systems of judicial
procedure in all the states and freeze them for the future,
both in criminal and civil cases, to the extent that the
Constitution does for federal courts? Is it conceivable that
an amendment bringing about such a result would either
have been submitted to the states, or, if submitted, would
have been ratified by them? And if not all the nine
Amendments, which of the prior nine Amendments are
to be deemed incorporated and which left out? . . . Believe
me that in writing this nothing is farther from my purpose
than contention. I am merely trying to get light on a subject which has absorbed as much thought and energy of
my mature life as anything that has concerned me.

There is no recorded response by Black to Frankfurter's elaborate
entreaty. It is safe to report, however, that neither Frankfurter's
boast of twenty years of study of the issue nor his provocative
questions caused Black to retreat. As time passed, it was clear that
Frankfurter's studied patience would not reap the rewards that he
hoped for. Frankfurter held fast to his position that the history of
the Amendment obligated the Court only to impose standards of
procedural fairness on state courts through the due process clause,
and not the full substantive guarantees of the Bill of Rights. And
Black was just as insistent that his reading of the history of the
Amendment dictated a contrary conclusion.

Whenever Frankfurter lectured on the due process clause of the
Fourteenth Amendment, Black rejoined. This happened after
Frankfurter wrote a concurring opinion in 1945 when the Court
ruled that the due process clause was violated because state action
failed to meet "civilized standards." Black responded:

This [Frankfurter's opinion] seems to me to be a restora-
tion of the natural law concept whereby the supreme constitutional law becomes this Court's view of "civilization"
at a given moment. Five members of the Court, including

Mr. Justice Frankfurter, have expressed their assent to this interpretation of the Due Process Clause. I disagree with that interpretation. Due Process, thus construed, seems to me to make the remainder of the Constitution mere surplusage. This Due Process interpretation permits the Court to reject all of those provisions of the Bill of Rights, and to substitute its own ideas of what legislatures can and cannot do. In the past, this broad judicial power has been used, as I see it, to preserve the economic status quo and to block legislative efforts to cure its existing evils. At the same time, the Court has only grudgingly read into "civilized standards" the safeguards to individual liberty set out in the Bill of Rights. . . .

Black promised to explain his views in comprehensive detail in a later opinion, and the opportunity arose less than a year later in the case of *Adamson v. California.* In *Adamson* a Court majority of five once again supported the Frankfurter position. But *Adamson* would best be known to future generations of law students for Hugo Black's dissent and the groundwork that it laid for later courts to move cautiously toward his incorporation theory.

The most impressive official fact about Admiral Dewey Adamson was his name. Otherwise he did not seem very different from other poor, ignorant blacks whose records revealed too many run-ins with the law. Adamson had twice served time, first for burglary in 1920 and then for robbery seven years later. He had been out of prison for seventeen years when the police arrested him for the murder of Stella Blauvelt, a sixty-four-year-old widow, who was white.

Mrs. Blauvelt's body had been found on the floor of her Los Angeles apartment with a lamp cord wrapped tightly around her neck. The only evidence connecting Adamson to the crime were six fingerprints on the door leading to a garbage container in the dead woman's kitchen. Police witnesses at the trial testified that the fingerprints were Adamson's.

On advice of his counsel, Adamson did not take the witness stand in his own defense. Had he taken the stand, the prosecutor could have impeached his testimony with questions about his prior record. The defendant's attorney, a veteran in the criminal courts of Los Angeles, was convinced that the jury's knowledge of

Adamson's criminal record would result in almost certain conviction. But when Adamson failed to testify, the prosecutor suggested to the jury that this was definitive proof of his guilt. If he was innocent, the prosecutor harangued the jury in his summation, it would have taken "twenty or fifty horses" to keep him off the witness stand. Shortly after the summation, Admiral Dewey Adamson was found guilty by the jury and sentenced to death.

Under California statute the prosecutor was permitted to comment on the defendant's failure to take the witness stand in his own behalf. But as part of the legal strategy to save Adamson's life, the defendant's attorney challenged the California statute as a violation of Adamson's constitutional right under the U.S. Constitution's Fourteenth Amendment. Comment on a defendant's failure to testify was as bad as forcing a defendant to take the stand, and either, Adamson's attorney argued on appeal, undermined his client's constitutional right to due process.

Adamson's attorney presented his argument to the U.S. Supreme Court during two days in January 1947, pleading with the Justices to overturn his client's conviction. As was his habit, Frankfurter was vocal during the oral argument, asking many questions of counsel about both the technical detail and implications of the state law.

Black was also vocal during oral argument, unusually vocal. But unlike Frankfurter, Black did not focus on the law's technicalities, insisting instead that counsel answer his questions on the broad constitutional issues that the case raised. By carefully framing the issues, Black forced both defense and state attorneys to concede that the Court could rule on the basis of the Court's traditional due process standard of fairness or, as he preferred, on the explicit Fifth Amendment guarantee against self-incrimination, incorporated under the Fourteenth.

At judicial conference Frankfurter told his colleagues that the answer to the *Adamson* challenge was obvious and had, in fact, been decided four decades earlier when the Court had faced precisely the issue raised in *Adamson*. In 1908 the Court had ruled in *Twining v. New Jersey* that a state statute providing for comment on a defendant's failure to testify was constitutionally permissible since it did not violate basic notions of fairness protected by the Fourteenth Amendment. It was significant, Frankfurter noted, that in *Twining* the Court majority had expressly rejected the argument that the self-incrimination clause of the Fifth Amendment was the relevant constitutional standard to be applied to the states under the Fourteenth Amendment's due process clause.

This Court should honor the *Twining* precedent, Frankfurter argued, and reject Black's incorporation theory. He was successful. Though not assigned the majority opinion, Frankfurter wrote a concurrence challenging Black's reading of the history of the Fourteenth Amendment and reiterating his view that the Court could maintain the correct constitutional perspective only by holding states to general standards of fairness and decency as understood by English-speaking peoples.

Hugo Black had, in effect, been preparing for his *Adamson* dissent for years, collecting voluminous materials and polishing phrases in drafts here and there that would present his theory in the most forceful way. Anticipating the *Adamson* case, he had devoted his summer vacation of 1946 to additional research on the history of the Fourteenth Amendment. And when the time came to write the opinion, Black was ready with the bold, passionate and demanding arguments that had become his judicial hallmark:

> I cannot consider the Bill of Rights to be an outworn 18th Century "strait jacket" as the *Twining* opinion did. Its provisions may be thought outdated abstractions by some. And it is true that they were designed to meet ancient evils. But they are the same kind of human evils that have emerged from century to century whenever excessive power is sought by the few at the expense of the many. In my judgment the people of no nation can lose their liberty so long as a Bill of Rights like ours survives and its basic purposes are conscientiously interpreted, enforced and respected so as to afford continuous protection against old, as well as new, devices and practices which might thwart those purposes. I fear to see the consequences of the Court's practice of substituting its own concepts of decency and fundamental justice for the language of the Bill of Rights. If the choice must be made between the selective process of the *Palko* decision applying some of the Bill of Rights to the States, or the *Twining* rule applying none of them, I would choose the *Palko* selective process. But rather than accept either of these

> choices, I would follow what I believe was the original
> purpose of the Fourteenth Amendment—to extend to all
> the people of the nation the complete protection of the
> Bill of Rights. To hold that this Court can determine what,
> if any, provisions of the Bill of Rights will be enforced,
> and if so to what degree, is to frustrate the great design of
> a written Constitution.

In the heat of their debate both judges, ironically, lost sight of
the fact that they had strayed from their original intention of elim-
inating subjective decision making. Black had effectively exposed
the weakness in Frankfurter's "natural law" approach that relied
on the Justices' sense of fairness and decency. In later cases Frankfurter would decide whether police conduct violated the Fourteenth Amendment if it "shocked the conscience." Whose
conscience? asked Hugo Black. But Frankfurter would counter that
Black's theory that the Fourteenth Amendment incorporated all of
the Bill of Rights and made them applicable to the states, in addition to being historically flawed, delivered an awesome amount of
power to the Justices. Much of the language of the Bill of Rights
did not insure judicial objectivity. Could the Justices agree, for
example, on what was an "unreasonable" search and seizure
under the Fourth Amendment? Black and Frankfurter's many disagreements on the Fourth Amendment's protection would prove
the point.

The Court majority never fully accepted Black's theory, but his
strong advocacy did, in fact, push the Justices toward incorporating
more and more of the Bill of Rights on a selective basis. With
Adamson, Black's reputation as the intellectual leader of the liberal
wing of the Court was further strengthened. His allegiance to the
individual liberties of the Bill of Rights was now complete and a
matter of impressive public record. At the same time, Frankfurter's
opposition to the incorporation theory was seen as further evidence of his anti-libertarian sympathies. Black supporters made
scathing reference to Frankfurter—outspoken critic of the post–
World War I Palmer raids and defender of Sacco and Vanzetti—as
the Court's conservative.

Black's civil libertarian mantle was a source of constant frustration and anger to Frankfurter. For it was Frankfurter, much more

than Black, who scrupulously protected defendants' rights under the Fourth Amendment. Frankfurter's reading of the history of that Amendment and the value of privacy that it preserved compelled him to protect the Fourth's liberties with special vigilance. Black, on the other hand, took a narrower view of the scope of the Amendment, often showing a willingness to countenance intrusive police behavior (for example, wiretapping) that did not violate his constitutional interpretation of "unreasonable" searches and seizures.

Black's and Frankfurter's interpretations of other provisions of the Bill of Rights could be equally confusing to those who automatically placed Black in the liberal camp and labeled Frankfurter the Court conservative. Those accustomed to Black's literal interpretation of the First Amendment were perplexed, for example, by his reading of that Amendment's clause prohibiting the establishment of religion.* The case in point, *Everson v. Board of Education,* was a challenge to a New Jersey law providing state subsidies for school bus transportation to both Catholic and public schools. The revered Thomas Jefferson, high in Black's American hagiology, had insisted that the First Amendment erected a "wall of separation" between church and state. The New Jersey statute appeared to undermine the Jeffersonian doctrine.

But when the Justices discussed the constitutionality of the New Jersey law, Black, avid student of Jefferson though he was, seemed strangely ambivalent. He conceded that the state made payments to help defer costs of Catholic school students. Moreover, those payments were not available to other sectarian students or private, nonsectarian students. Yet Black saw no constitutional violation, and he cast the decisive fifth vote at conference upholding the law.

It was left to Felix Frankfurter, the Court "conservative" and spokesman for judicial restraint, to lead the spirited opposition that voted to strike the law down. Frankfurter insisted that the New Jersey law could not be reconciled with Jefferson's principle of separation. Separation means separation, and the framers of the First Amendment contemplated no compromises, he argued.

---

* The First Amendment states that "Congress shall make no law respecting an establishment of religion, or prohibiting the free exercise thereof." The religion clauses were later made applicable to the states through the Fourteenth Amendment.

He was joined in dissent by Justices Jackson and Rutledge and the newest Court appointee, Harold Burton, the former Republican Senator from Ohio who had replaced Owen Roberts. Needing only one vote to swing the majority to his position, Frankfurter focused his persuasive energies on Frank Murphy, the most consistent and emotional civil libertarian on the bench. In a "Dear Frank" letter, Frankfurter first warned Murphy of the danger of his false friends (read Black and Douglas) "who flatter you and play on you for *their* purposes, not for your good." Write your own opinion, Frankfurter urged, but uphold the "great American doctrine" of separation of church and state. Frankfurter closed with an impassioned appeal to Murphy's patriotism and loyalty to the Catholic Church: "You have a chance to do for your country and your church such as never has come to you before—and may never come again. The things we most regret—at least such is my experience—are the opportunities missed. For the sake of history, for the sake of inner peace, don't miss. No one knows better than you what *Everson* is about. Tell the world—and shame the devil. . . ."

Frankfurter overplayed his hand with his heavy rhetoric. Murphy stayed with Black's majority. But Frankfurter's intense lobbying did have a significant effect—on Hugo Black's opinion for the Court majority. Aware of the pressure being exerted by Frankfurter on his colleagues, Black wrote draft after draft (eight in all), gradually building his own high wall of separation between church and state. By his eighth and last draft, Black had traced the history of the establishment clause in inspiring detail and declared anew the Court's dedication to the separation principle. But his conclusion ranked as one of the great anticlimaxes of modern constitutional jurisprudence. Having crafted a stirring narrative on the necessity of the separation of church and state, Black maintained, nonetheless, that New Jersey's bus payments were for the general welfare, not religion. The state had, according to Black, preserved the requisite neutrality toward religion. The wall between church and state "must be kept high and impregnable," Black insisted. "We could not approve the slightest breach. New Jersey has not breached it here."

The Black opinion infuriated Frankfurter, who noted privately that it was characteristic of Black "to utter noble sentiments and depart from them in practice—a tactic of which the *Everson* opinion is a beautiful example." As a Jew, Frankfurter was sensitive to the controversy that might arise if he wrote an opinion in opposition to state support for parochial-school transportation. He therefore confined his efforts to encouraging two dissenters, Jackson and Rutledge, as they took turns attacking the Black opinion. The firm embrace of the separation principle in the Black opinion, and then the immediate abandonment of that principle, reminded Jackson of Byron's Julia, who whispered, " 'I will ne'er consent'—and then consented." Rutledge was less caustic than Jackson, but equally critical. He began his dissent by quoting the First Amendment's religion clauses followed by Jefferson's words before the General Assembly of Virginia on religious freedom. "I cannot believe that the great author of those words, or the men who made them law, could have joined in this decision," wrote Rutledge. Because of Black's Court opinion, Rutledge charged, the wall between church and state is "neither so high nor so impregnable today as yesterday."

Failing to win a majority in *Everson,* Frankfurter was determined to diminish its long-range effects. His opportunity came only a year after *Everson* when the Court dealt with another case, *McCollum v. Board of Education,* that presented an establishment clause issue. In *McCollum* a religious instruction program in Champaign, Illinois, conducted in public school buildings during school hours was challenged as a violation of the establishment clause. This time eight members of the Court, including Frankfurter *and* Black, found a constitutional violation.

When Hugo Black was assigned the majority opinion, Frankfurter seized the moment to demand, as the price for joining a Black Court opinion, that Black eliminate all references to his *Everson* opinion. To strengthen his bargaining position, Frankfurter called a meeting of the four *Everson* dissenters in his office to plot strategy and harden resolve, particularly that of Rutledge and the newest and most vulnerable Justice, Harold Burton. But Burton balked at Frankfurter's intransigence. Instead, he proposed a compromise in a memorandum that he hoped would satisfy both Black and Frankfurter.

Once again, Black showed his expert political skills and proved that he, rather than Frankfurter, was the better negotiator. First, he met Frankfurter's primary challenge head-on: "I have just been handed a memorandum from Justice Frankfurter to the effect that he will not agree to any opinion in the *McCollum* case which makes reference to our decision in the *Everson* case. I will not agree to any opinion in the *McCollum* case which does not make reference to the *Everson* case." Having thus marked the parameters of the discussion, Black privately expressed his willingness to omit certain especially offending references to *Everson* to gain support for his *McCollum* opinion. That was good enough for Burton and Rutledge, who agreed to join Black's *McCollum* opinion for the Court.

Frankfurter was foiled yet another time in his attempt to bend Hugo Black to his judicial will. And his failure obscured what should have been a heartening victory. Frankfurter had, after all, pushed Black in his *Everson* opinion toward his own position of a clearly delineated separation between church and state, much more so than Black had originally intended. Moreover he could count eight of the nine members of the Court with him in *McCollum* (including Black and Murphy), four more than in *Everson*.

But that was no cause for celebration or even satisfaction for Felix Frankfurter. He still brooded about Hugo Black's hold on his brethren. He was particularly angered by Justice Burton, whom he had counted on to stand firm against Black in *McCollum*: ". . . Burton is one of these men who thinks you can put evil out of the world by trying to shut your eyes to it. It literally hurts him to have me make a remark that brings to the surface behavior or motives that are not nice or sweet. He hasn't the remotest idea how malignant men like Black and Douglas not only can be, but are."

Frankfurter stuck to that damning assessment of Justice Douglas for the rest of his life. His view of Hugo Black, however, changed dramatically for the better soon after *McCollum*. Indeed, Frankfurter began to show increasing respect, and affection, for the man who for a decade had symbolized all that was evil in his judicial world.

Different Lenses

WILLIAM ORVILLE DOUGLAS GREW up in Yakima, Washington, at the turn of the century, more than three thousand miles from Hugo Black's Clay County, Alabama. Serving as the central Washington headquarters for the Northern Pacific Railway, Yakima was in those days a prosperous town. On one side of the railroad tracks, a thriving middle class lived in large homes, cultivated beautiful lawns and gardens and enjoyed shade trees on all sides. But there was another side of the railroad tracks, where most of Yakima's less affluent citizens resided, and it was on this side that William O. Douglas and his older sister and younger brother were raised by their mother.

Julia Fisk Douglas was widowed by the death of the Reverend William Douglas when her older son, William, was five years old. Left with the proceeds of a $600 life insurance policy and very little else of monetary value, Julia Douglas bought a modest clapboard house on North Fifth Avenue in Yakima and began to take in washing from neighbors to make meager ends meet. "We never felt poor," said Martha Douglas, Bill Douglas's older sister. "We just didn't have money." But the Douglas children did have intelligence and pride and driving ambition, thanks to their mother, who nurtured dreams of their worldly success. Martha became the personnel director for several large department stores at a time when very few women achieved such status in the business world. Arthur Douglas, the youngest child, rose to the presidency of the

Statler Hotel chain. And Orville, as his mother preferred to call Bill Douglas, seemed to hold the most promise of all. As an infant, he was nicknamed "Treasure," and he remained his mother's favorite child, sensitive, high-strung, conscientious—in every way just like her.

Bill Douglas worked hard to earn his mother's approval. To bolster the family's finances, he took odd jobs when he was in grade school, delivering the *Yakima Republic,* washing store windows, sweeping floors and, as a teenager, picking fruit in the Yakima Valley with itinerant laborers from California and Mexico. Born with a facile and brilliant mind, he made top grades in the Yakima public schools, gave the valedictory address at his high school graduation and was named the most distinguished member of his class. He attended Whitman College in nearby Walla Walla on full tuition scholarship and compiled a comparably outstanding record as champion debater and honor student.

After graduation from Whitman, Douglas served briefly on the faculty of his old high school, then tended a herd of two thousand sheep in freight cars headed east before enrolling in the Columbia Law School. He finished second in the class of 1924; Douglas's classmate Simon Rifkind recalled that Douglas was unquestionably the brightest man in their class. "Others may have been more urbane and sophisticated," said Rifkind, "but for sheer intellectual talent, Douglas was at the top of the class."

Like other select Columbia graduates, Douglas was offered a job at one of Wall Street's blue chip law firms, Cravath, Henderson and de Gersdorff. At Cravath he shared an office with John J. McCloy, another young associate destined for important government work in Washington. Douglas spent his days, and many, many nights, drafting intricate legal documents on behalf of the Chicago, Milwaukee and St. Paul Railroad, which suddenly had found itself bankrupt and in need of sustained legal advice and representation. Corporate bankruptcy and reorganization, as well as securities regulation, became William O. Douglas's legal specialties, and his expertise led to teaching jobs at Columbia and the Yale Law School and later to the chairmanship of the Securities and Exchange Commission.

At first glance, the backgrounds of Douglas and Hugo Black do not suggest a natural affinity of interests, experiences or basic values. The scruff-hard red clay of Black's rural northern Alabama did not invite a love of nature as did the fertile Yakima Valley and the always visible and magnificent Cascade Mountains. William O. Douglas developed a lifelong love affair with the wilderness, hiking, horseback riding and fishing in the Northwest's Cascades and Wallowa Mountains well into his seventies. Hugo Black, thirteen years his senior, played tennis. And, while Douglas earned a reputation as one of the nation's most innovative teachers and scholars in the corporate field, Black built his as Alabama's premier personal injury lawyer who could coax a healthy defendant's verdict out of the most reluctant jury.

But below the obvious surface differences, Black and Douglas had much in common. Both were sons of overtly ambitious mothers who were determined that their sons would have better lives than their own. Their extraordinary intellect and intense drive created a combustible formula for success—and Hugo Black and Bill Douglas were never satisfied with anything less than success throughout their lives.

Growing up, both Black and Douglas felt that their families were outsiders, treated coldly by those who served as the establishment in tiny Ashland and Yakima. The local Baptist church fathers in Ashland condemned William Black's drinking, and the small gentry of Yakima were indifferent, at best, to the widow Douglas and her three children.

As a teenager and into adulthood, Bill Douglas harbored resentment against Yakima's establishment. "I was hardly fourteen," Douglas later recalled, "but I knew the Rich were pillars of Yakima. They treated labor as scum, they controlled the police; some of them even had investments in Yakima's brothels. They went to church and were 'godly' men but I had nothing in common with them."

Although young Hugo Black was never so vocally hostile to the vested interests of Clay County, his law practice in Birmingham and his later political campaigns were built on his proudly proclaimed bond with the underdog. The enemy was always the powerful corporate interests, the haves among all of Black's have-not clients and constituents. The populism of Clay County was not, in the end, very different from that of the Yakima Valley, and

both Black and Douglas were receptive to early and lasting indoc-
trination.

After they arrived in Washington, both Senator Black and SEC
Chairman Douglas openly displayed their sentiments in public
forums. Black's interrogations of corporate executives in the shipping and airline industries propelled him to prominence in the
Congress and a coveted place among President Franklin Roosevelt's political advisers. Douglas was no less effective at the SEC,
where he enforced new government securities regulations against
some of Wall Street's most prominent bankers and securities trad-
ers. Like Senator Black on the Hill, SEC Chairman Douglas did not
balk at confrontation, even when it involved powerful officers of
the New York Stock Exchange itself. Douglas's SEC issued a devastating report cataloguing the excesses of the Exchange and its
officers, which resulted in important institutional reforms.

The goals and accomplishments of Douglas, like those of Black,
fitted neatly into FDR's political view of the world, where the
common man would get a New Deal and arrogant, selfish corporate bigwigs would ignore the public interest at great peril. During
Roosevelt's second term, Douglas joined the President's inner circle of economic advisers as well as his poker parties. In 1939, two
years after Black's appointment to the Court, Roosevelt nominated
Douglas. At forty, Douglas became the second youngest man to
serve in the Court's history.

During the next thirty-two years, Black and Douglas became
inextricably bound in judicial causes, so much so that the phrase
"Black and Douglas" melded into a single declaration of liberal
idealism. Their early populism was regularly translated into support for the "little guy," whether the injured blue-collar worker,
the poor criminal defendant or the offbeat religious zealot exercising First Amendment rights. They also shared a common opponent: Justice Frankfurter.

Douglas took his seat on the Court only three months after
Frankfurter, whom he had known for more than a decade. In the
twenties, Douglas had joined thousands of others in applauding
Frankfurter's defense of Sacco and Vanzetti. And Frankfurter had
been one of the first to congratulate Douglas on his SEC investigation into securities violations and the report that followed. Each

respected the other's scholarship, though Frankfurter's fields of constitutional and administrative law were very different from Douglas's commercial specialties. When Douglas joined the Court, he was greeted by Frankfurter as a valued, though junior, colleague.

Justice Frankfurter viewed Douglas as a promising student in need of instruction and drafted his memorandums accordingly. "I am bound to say," Frankfurter wrote Douglas about an early Douglas opinion, "that it is bad for both of us that we are no longer professors. Because if you were still a professor, you would have written a different elaboration and if I were still a professor, I would get several lectures out of what you have written." And in another case Frankfurter criticized Douglas for not disclosing "what you are really doing. As you know, I am no poker player and naturally, therefore, I do not believe in poker playing in the disposition of cases."

The patronizing jibes rankled Douglas, but not enough to rebel. In the first flag-salute decision, the first test of Frankfurter's leadership of the Roosevelt appointees, Douglas deferred to the older man's judgment, as did fellow FDR appointees Black, Murphy and Reed. But the trio of Black, Douglas and Murphy recanted a short time later in their *Jones v. Opelika* apologia, which served as a stunning personal and philosophical rebuke to Frankfurter.

Frankfurter dismissed Frank Murphy as a second-rater whose passions overwhelmed good sense. Black and Douglas were different. Both were considered by him to be very bright, shrewd, but ultimately morally corrupt. Black was the acknowledged leader of "the Axis" and Frankfurter privately indulged in a vocabulary of vituperation to denounce him. His opinion of Douglas was even worse. Douglas was one of "the two completely evil men" that Frankfurter had ever met.

The Frankfurter-Douglas estrangement had to do with personality as much as judicial principle. To be sure, Douglas abandoned Frankfurter's school of judicial restraint early in his Court career. But aside from philosophy, he was temperamentally unsuited for a prolonged apprenticeship under the Harvard professor. If Frankfurter wove elegantly intricate verbal tapestries, Douglas unfurled bolts of raw cloth, dazzlingly brilliant in color. Frankfurter craved intellectual company and erudite conversation, but Douglas was not his man. Douglas's lightning-quick mind was impatient with collegial deliberation; he was a loner and a doer. To exacerbate matters, Douglas owned a sometimes crude and always mischievous sense of humor that he delighted in directing toward Frankfurter. He once told Frankfurter that he and Black viewed him as a nut to be cracked. Frankfurter didn't laugh. "Douglas was a Westerner," said his friend Abe Fortas. "He either worked or played. Felix never played and he never understood Douglas, who did. It caused him to underestimate Douglas."

Hugo Black was a country boy and a fine politician who naturally enjoyed Douglas's company. He also respected his colleague's need for intellectual space. He did not try to cultivate Douglas's friendship with the cloying attention displayed by Frankfurter. But he did not ignore their shared backgrounds and values either, their difficult, productive youths, their suspicions of concentrated power and their egalitarian ideals. Both the friendship and judicial partnership were close and enduring, with Douglas accepting Black's leadership in the relationships.

Usually shy and taciturn, Douglas admired Black enormously and was eager to tell him so. After Stone was appointed Chief Justice to succeed Charles Evans Hughes, Douglas immediately reported his disappointment to Black. "I am sorry it did not go to you," he wrote Black. "I thought you deserved it. And I know it would strengthen the Court greatly if you were the Chief."

Black became a father figure as well as a colleague to Douglas, who not only confided in the older man but frequently sought his attention and approval. One obvious method was to invoke the name of Felix Frankfurter in an unfavorable context. Douglas was certain that Frankfurter had been behind the Stone appointment (and therefore against the nomination of Black) and duly reported his suspicions to Black. "I said to Mildred [his wife], 'Felix has done it again.' And there is no question in my mind that he was responsible."

When Douglas faced a tough professional decision, as he did in 1941 when he reported that President Roosevelt wanted him to supervise the country's defense efforts, he turned to Black for advice. "He [FDR] wants me to be the top guy in the defense work —take it off his neck; to be his 'alter ego,' " he wrote Black. According to Douglas, the President was putting pressure on him to

take the job—and resign from the Court. He had no enthusiasm
for it, Douglas told Black, because there were too many "fat cats"
still entrenched and too many others "dedicated to the task of
ruining me. As you know, I greatly enjoy the work of the Court.
Furthermore, I think that as a member of the Court I can knock
out a base hit once in awhile. In the defense job I would go to bat
with 2½ strikes on me."

As if further reason were needed to turn down the President,
Douglas raised the specter of a conniving Felix Frankfurter. "I am
quite sure that F.F. has inspired this offer—at least that he has
been influential. It has come to me 'straight' that he thinks I am
the only man. If he could get me there and you back in the Senate
I am sure he would be happy." He would do nothing before discussing the offer with Black, Douglas assured him.

"The prospect that you might leave the Court disturbs me
greatly," Black, who was in Colorado, wrote Douglas. Black had
no doubt that Douglas could best serve his country on the Court:
"You and I know that the Court has the last word on questions of
law which are determinative of questions of public policy upon
which the course of our republic depends."

Douglas quickly responded to Black, assuring him that he fully
agreed with his views and was prepared to turn the President
down. "I have not seen the President as yet," Douglas wrote. "I
expect to have it out with him the first of the week. My only
embarrassment is in saying 'no' to him. But I think I can wiggle
out this time. I will keep in touch with you."

Douglas did not leave the Court in 1941 or for the next thirty-
four years, even though rumors floated around Washington period-
ically that he was seeking national political office. Frankfurter was
convinced that Douglas had presidential aspirations in 1944 and
1948, and the very idea of a Justice of the U.S. Supreme Court
considering such an office, as he told Frank Murphy and others,
sullied the reputation of the institution. Douglas never actively
sought the presidential nomination, though he did not exert pressure on his friends to drop their campaign on his behalf. If the draft
had come, Douglas undoubtedly would have accepted. It did not,
which did not seem to disturb him, but it deprived Frankfurter of
a final, satisfying harumph.

During his thirty-six years on the Supreme Court, William O.

Douglas's many publicized outside activities often overshadowed his judicial work. His presumed political ambitions were talked about, not just by Frankfurter, but by Democratic party regulars and reporters as well. He traveled widely and wrote volumes about his adventures. He continued his varied outdoor activities and served enthusiastically as a rallying figure for environmental causes. And he took four wives, each younger than the last, and this seemed to infuriate or embarrass just about everyone but William O. Douglas.

Despite the attention given to his nonjudicial activities, Douglas will best be remembered for his unique contributions to the Court. True, he followed Hugo Black's lead—but he was no lapdog. His support for Black was drawn from independent and creative channels of judicial thought that coincided, with remarkable consistency, with Black's own conclusions. But his was an original judicial mind, capable and willing to break new ground, declaring a right to privacy, for example, that sometimes demanded a greater leap of constitutional faith than his best judicial friend, Hugo Black, was willing to take.

Douglas served as Black's dependable lieutenant throughout the forties, in *Jones v. Opelika* and the Japanese-American exclusion cases, in *Jewell Ridge* and *Adamson, Everson* and *McCollum*. And he hunkered down with Black during the Cold War when the two, sometimes alone, reminded a frenzied America that even Communists (and suspected Communists) possessed constitutional rights. At the beginning of that dismal political era, Douglas reported to Black that President Truman had telephoned to say that he wanted to meet with Douglas to discuss a "more active" job. As in the past, Douglas assured Black that he was not interested. "I am very happy right here [on the Court]," he wrote Black. "And I want nothing but the opportunity to slug away alongside of you for the next 30 years" (the underlining is Douglas's).

The breach between Douglas and Frankfurter was permanent; the two not only disagreed in judicial opinions but refused to speak to each other for extended periods of time. Their clerks and other allies emulated their mentors' animosity. Yale professors Alexander Bickel, a former Frankfurter clerk, and Fred Rodell, a Douglas

loyalist, first debated Frankfurter's and Black's opposing schools of
constitutional thought. Then they, too, broke off personal relations
as well as professional dialogue. After Frankfurter died in 1965,
only Justice Douglas among members of the Court did not attend
the funeral.

Unlike the progressively painful Frankfurter-Douglas break,
Frankfurter's relations with Hugo Black, which had disintegrated
hopelessly during the forties, brightened at the beginning of the
next decade. Their bonds of friendship grew stronger throughout
the fifties and into the sixties, even as they fought on the Court.
How could Frankfurter, brimming with rage toward Black during
their first decade together on the Court, travel toward that happy
end? And how could Hugo Black, with the stealthy instincts of the
assassin (according to Bob Jackson), forgive his sworn judicial
enemy?

Two tragic events, one personal, the other political, drew the
two antagonists toward each other. The personal tragedy was the
untimely death of Black's wife, Josephine, who had battled coura-
geously throughout her life to overcome mental as well as physical
problems. "I myself as a small girl was early worried by the problems of injustice and poverty and cruelty," she once explained to
Hugo, Jr. "I seem always to have been conscious of tremendous
forces operating on all the planes of manifestation—physical,
mental and spiritual. Life was never a simple thing for me. . . ." As
a thinking and caring adult, Josephine had seemed to suffer exces-
sively over the human condition, though she worked hard to overcome her anxieties. Religion was a comfort to her. So was her
family. And in her last years she discovered a new channel for
expression—oil painting—which gave her satisfaction and recognition (Grand Prize in Washington's Famous Artists contest).

Hugo was constantly aware that his wife's condition remained
fragile, though he continued to be optimistic. Writing to Hugo, Jr.,
in April 1951, only seven months before Josephine's death, Hugo
reported that she was well. Five months later he again wrote his
older son that "your mother is really better than she has been for
years." Three months later Josephine Foster Black was dead at the
age of fifty. "She ought to be the last of her generation to die,"
mourned her husband, "not one of the first. Life is wrong—it's
just wrong."

Official Washington grieved with the Black family. "My thoughts have been constantly of you ever since Bess phoned me of the sorrow which has come to you and yours with sudden and crushing force," wired President Truman. Hundreds of other telegrams, notes and letters poured in, none more touching than that of Felix Frankfurter.

> Dear Hugo:
>
> One has no words for such an event as Josephine's death. It chokes one with silence for it must be received, if not accepted, with awe. And so, nothing is farther from my thought and no thought would be more impertinent than to attempt any consolatory words. There are none such.
>
> But I venture to intrude on your grief for I think I can claim Josephine as a friend and can come to you with my own sense of grief in her going.
>
> She was a loving spirit and conveyed that spirit with exquisiteness. She touched life with tenderness of considered compassion in a world inherently difficult and harsh. Hers was the instinctive tenderness and the healing warmth of loving kindness. And the ring of her laughter will vividly keep ringing in my memory.
>
> Strength to you and the children to bear the awful emptiness that she has left.
>
> Yours very sincerely,
> Felix Frankfurter

This was not the familiar message of Frankfurter the incorrigible flatterer or Court conspirator. This was the heartfelt feeling of a sensitive human being who instinctively reached out to a fallen friend. Frankfurter had always reserved a special place of tenderness for the three Black children and their mother. Those soft, personal feelings were allowed to flourish, even as the two Justices warred at the Court. And now, in Black's worst moment, Frankfurter was with him, and it was important then and for the rest of their lives together.

The foreboding political atmosphere in the early fifties also created a centripetal force in the Black-Frankfurter relationship. When the Cold War hysteria had begun to invade this country, both Black and Frankfurter feared its consequence for the nation they served and loved. Each gave expression to his convictions. Hugo Black's concerns were most effectively expressed in his libertarian judicial opinions. But during the political scourge, he also stated his strong views privately, and in one instance those views directly affected Frankfurter, though Frankfurter did not know it.

The incident involved one of Black's former law clerks, John P. Frank, who, while on the faculty of the Yale Law School, had been asked to review a book on the constitutional work of Justice Frankfurter by Samuel Konefsky. In his review, Frank criticized Frankfurter's philosophy of judicial restraint, but also included a few personal references about the Justice (" . . . he has a widely rumored capacity for exasperating his colleagues with conference room lectures"). Frank sent a draft of the review to Black for comment. The response was not encouraging; Black did not like the negative tone of the review. "I am compelled to state that if left up to me," Black wrote Frank, "I should prefer that it not be published." He admitted, however, that he was not the best judge and, in any case, that Frank had "a quasi-public duty" to discuss subjects in his field of constitutional law. Black concluded his comment on the Frank review with a plea to eliminate all personal references to Frankfurter. "New situations are developing which I think you should bear in mind in connection with the publication," he wrote Frank. "There are ominous signs that Justice Frankfurter is about to be made the target of powerful forces gathering strength from the present national hysteria. Should these forces not be arrested, I have no doubt that you would be 100% on the side of the Justice."

Black did not elaborate on the "ominous signs" or "powerful forces." But at the time of his letter Frankfurter, a Jew, an immigrant and a vocal supporter of liberal causes all of his life, seemed particularly vulnerable to attack. And Frankfurter had not made life easier for himself by vouching for the integrity of Alger Hiss, who had been accused by the House Un-American Activities Committee of membership in and work for the Communist party. At Hiss's perjury trial that followed, Justice Frankfurter had volunteered to be a character witness for the defendant. Frankfurter had, in fact, recommended Hiss, a superb Harvard Law School student, to be law secretary to Justice Holmes and had watched young Hiss rise in the State Department hierarchy, culminating in his important role as aide to Roosevelt at Yalta and assisting in the organization of the United Nations.

J. Edgar Hoover's FBI kept a thick dossier on Frankfurter that ranged from crank letters to serious investigative reports. An FBI informant from Philadelphia told a Bureau man in 1950 that Secretary of State Dean Acheson and Frankfurter were the "Number One and Number Two Communists, respectively," in the country, and that the two "weaken the fibre in the United States." Though there was no documentation to support the claim, the FBI dutifully recorded the charge and kept it in their active files. A field agent informed J. Edgar Hoover that he had it on the word of General Douglas MacArthur, no less, that Frankfurter was the brains behind the Communist conspiracy in the U.S. And Hollywood producer Cecil B. De Mille reported to the FBI that Frankfurter was a radical to be watched carefully. As proof, De Mille offered a copy of Theodore Roosevelt's letter to Frankfurter in *1917,* accusing Frankfurter of Trotskyite leanings after the young lawyer had submitted his report on labor unrest in the West. "It is felt that this [De Mille's report] will be of considerable interest to the Bureau at this time," the FBI report stated.

The FBI and the Immigration and Naturalization Service received many inquiries in those scary days questioning the authenticity of Justice Frankfurter's U.S. citizenship. Was the Justice really a naturalized citizen, as he had contended at his confirmation hearings in 1939? Senator McCarran had questioned Frankfurter then, and now others wondered if the Justice had given false testimony.

The FBI perused all of the hundreds of items referring to Frankfurter in their files to determine whether Leopold Frankfurter, his father, had become a naturalized citizen, thereby validating Justice Frankfurter's own citizenship claim. The report that followed noted that after Frankfurter's brother, Otto, had been appointed to the Economic Cooperation Administration in Paris in 1948, the FBI had conducted an investigation of Leopold Frankfurter's citizenship. That investigation, an FBI report stated, also "involved a

serious question as to the citizenship status of Justice Frankfurter."
FBI Director Hoover was aware of the investigation and had instructed investigators to "go thoroughly into this and get all the
facts." The result of the extensive investigation, however, only
confirmed what Justice Frankfurter had always claimed; his father
had become a naturalized U.S. citizen in 1898.

Frankfurter did not advertise his scorn for the Red-hunters of the
era with inspired judicial opinions, as did Hugo Black. But Frankfurter, in his way, was just as wary and courageous, and both
Justices seemed to sense, early on, that they were on the same side
in this historic struggle.

Black attacked the attackers, brandishing the First and Fifth
Amendments to back up his conviction that all U.S. citizens, including Communists, were entitled to the constitutional rights of
free speech and association and the protection against governmental pressure for self-incrimination. Frankfurter never spoke so
boldly, but through private commentary, public gesture and a variety of ingenious judicial means, he seemed to repossess his old
liberal's conscience.

The key element in Frankfurter's thinking during the period was
his commitment to the integrity of the constitutional system, always at the root of his jurisprudence. A fair judicial process was
the last best defense against tyranny, Frankfurter always preached,
and the lesson was never needed more than during the Cold War.
The mounting evidence suggesting that Alger Hiss had lied to the
House Un-American Activities Committee had not prevented Justice Frankfurter from voluntarily testifying as a character witness
for the defendant at the first Hiss perjury trial. Deciding Hiss's guilt
or innocence was not Frankfurter's responsibility, but bringing to
the Court all credible evidence bearing on the issue clearly was, in
his view. And the fact that he faced cameras and further scrutiny
by those who suspected darker purposes did nothing to deter him.

In private Frankfurter expressed his worst fears for the nation,
as powerful people in and out of government searched for short-
cuts to rid the country of subversives. A national paranoia had
spread and ideas no longer flowed freely. Critical First Amendment
liberties were compromised—not just free speech but also the
right to free association. No one, it seemed, wanted to be associated with those advocating unorthodox ideas. The fear reached

absurd heights. "If Communists like apple pie and I do, I see no reason why I should stop eating it," one federal employee told social psychologists Stuart W. Cook and Marie Jahoda. "But I would," he added. The Cook-Jahoda study of the social and psychological effects of the anti-Communist crusade on government employees reported a shocking concern for conformity.

The legal profession itself, sworn to protect individual constitutional liberties, bent to the pressure, a phenomenon that was acknowledged, and deplored, by Justice Frankfurter. When Henry Wallace was scheduled to appear before the McCarran Committee to discuss the Communist victory in China, Frankfurter noted that nobody in his profession seemed willing to sit at the former Cabinet member's side. "It is hard to believe but it is a fact that at least a dozen reputable lawyers have refused to appear with him," Frankfurter wrote his colleague Justice Jackson. "Some of them gave silly excuses but a few of them had at least the candor to say they do not want to get mixed up in this Communist business."

Frankfurter's particular purpose in writing Jackson was to lobby in the case of *Sacher et al. v. U.S.,* in which the criminal contempt convictions of lawyers representing eleven Communist defendants had been challenged. Sacher and the other lawyers defending their American Communist clients against charges of subversive activity under the Smith Act had treated the trial as political theater. They had constantly ridiculed the proceedings and the trial judge, Harold Medina, and the judge had risen perfectly to the bait. Provoked and, finally, uncontrollably angry, Judge Medina reacted in kind, heaping his own abuse upon the defense attorneys, then citing them for contempt and sentencing them to prison.

Frankfurter had no sympathy for the antics of the Communist defendants, their attorneys or Judge Medina. But he felt that there was an urgent need for the Court to stand squarely behind the legal process itself and to remind Judge Medina and the nation that lawyers, even obstreperous ones who represented Communists, were important to the integrity of the system. If Sacher and his ilk could be intimidated by the contempt citations and prison sentences of an intemperate judge, then no lawyer was safe, and the system itself was in jeopardy. The Court majority, however, did not share Frankfurter's outrage at the contempt citations and prison sentences and upheld the lower court's rulings.

Two members of the Court, Black and Frankfurter, wrote dissenting opinions in *Sacher*. But Frankfurter was not satisfied merely to register his disagreement with the majority. He also wanted to influence the majority, particularly Justice Jackson, whose opinion he hoped would also serve as a lesson in civic responsibility. State your conclusions, Frankfurter counseled Jackson, but educate the public to the high duty of the legal profession. "I repeat, because I believe it so strongly . . . an opinion by you in this case would be a powerful lifter of fear, a dissipator of a good deal of nonsense, and an instiller of traditional manliness in our profession."

The Court, Frankfurter believed, must represent the dispassionate voice of reason in dangerous, emotional times: "There is a special claim upon those of us whom the accidents of life have placed upon this Court at this time to help reduce the fever of fear and hysteria and infuse the atmosphere with what we like to think of as traditional American sturdiness and fair dealing." He suggested to Jackson that the Court should "radiate examples of a self-contained, calm, and austere attitude toward the anxious situation confronting the country." And he quoted Brandeis approvingly for the proposition that the Court served, foremost, as teacher to the nation.

But that desire to project an image of cool, detached judgment could work, paradoxically, to take the Court completely out of the controversy. And when that happened, as it did in *Dennis v. U.S.,* Frankfurter's advocacy of the Court as national teacher seemed curiously impotent. Eugene Dennis and the ten other Communist defendants had been convicted under the Smith Act on the charge of conspiracy to advocate the overthrow of the government by force. They had contended that they were guilty of nothing more than teaching Marxist-Leninist doctrine, and that teaching alone could not be elevated to outlawed subversive activity. In any case, their teaching presented no clear and present danger to the national security, they had argued. If the Smith Act covered their conduct, their argument continued, then the Smith Act itself must fall as a violation of the First Amendment's free speech provision. That was the defendants' legal position and the constitutional challenge before the U.S. Supreme Court in 1951.

While the Justices deliberated in *Dennis,* organized efforts were made by partisans on both sides to influence their decision. A statement broadcast nationally on the radio and attributed to the Communist party threatened protest demonstrations across the country if the Justices did not rule in favor of the Communist defendants. At the same time the American Bar Association condemned the conduct of the attorneys for Eugene Dennis and his co-defendants and called for their disbarment.

Felix Frankfurter was appalled by both actions and informed his brethren in a memorandum that if he could act as a single judge he would be tempted to cite the Communist party *and* the American Bar Association for contempt. He could not do that, of course, but he wanted to impress his colleagues with his strong view that the Court must always exercise detached judgment, regardless of outside pressures.

Despite the gravity of the constitutional issues presented in *Dennis,* the Justices spent precious little time in conference discussion. "Those wanting to affirm [the convictions] had their minds closed to argument or persuasion," Justice Douglas observed, adding, "The discussion was largely *pro forma.*" Chief Justice Vinson, who led the discussion, announced his vote to affirm the convictions with "practically no discussion," Douglas noted.

Only Justice Frankfurter, among those who voted to affirm, appeared more than marginally interested in debating the constitutional questions raised. First, he escorted his colleagues through an intellectual tour of the history of the clear and present danger test, then posed essential questions for the Court. How imminent must the danger be? Can the Court take judicial notice of the danger of communism?

Chief Justice Vinson, who wrote the Court opinion, indicated that he was not disturbed by Frankfurter's questions or those raised by the defendants. He spoke forcefully about the dangers of communism, and then committed all members of the Communist party, including the defendants, to the party's most violent and subversive design. It did not matter that the prosecutor in *Dennis* had proved nothing more than that the defendants had *taught* Communist doctrine. The Vinson opinion made a mockery of the clear and present danger test. Under the Chief Justice's test, once the danger was recognized—communism in this case—the government could do whatever it considered necessary to control it.

Frankfurter's concurring opinion was more sophisticated but no more persuasive. He did show more respect than Vinson for the First Amendment issue raised, attempting in his application of the clear and present danger test to balance First Amendment values and Congress's need to protect the national security. But Frankfurter's scale tipped inexorably toward national security and the legitimacy of the Smith Act. Finally, Frankfurter hinted at the essential reason behind his conclusion. "History teaches," he warned, "that the independence of the judiciary is jeopardized when courts become embroiled in the passions of the day and assume primary responsibility in choosing between competing political, economic and social pressures."

It was another lesson in judicial restraint by the Court's most distinguished proponent of that philosophy. Frankfurter had put his faith in the political branch of government, the legislature, as the institution best equipped to make political judgments. This had been his consistent view since *Gobitis* in 1940. His philosophical conviction that the Court must remain above the gale-force political winds carried special meaning during the heyday of Senator Joseph McCarthy.

But something vital was lost in Frankfurter's constitutional lecture. The safeguards of the First Amendment were relegated to minor importance in *Dennis,* and the Court's role as the nation's teacher of elemental democratic values was effectively abandoned —at least, by the majority. By default, the role of national educator was assumed by the only dissenters in *Dennis,* Justices Black and Douglas.

Hugo Black was so disgusted by the majority's position that he squiggled his frustrations in notes on a draft of Chief Justice Vinson's Court opinion. The Chief Justice had asserted that "armed internal attack" (presumably, including the defendant's activities) justified restriction on speech. "Now puts speech and armed attack in same category," wrote Black. Vinson attempted to distinguish early applications of the clear and present danger test from what he considered the decisively greater danger posed by communism. Black retorted sarcastically, "The goblin'll get you." When Vinson declared his emaciated version of the clear and present danger test, Black concluded, "In other words, courts can approve suppression of free speech at will and despite First Amendment."

Black's and Douglas's strong words of dissent reverberated for decades. Douglas recalled the exalted place of the First Amendment envisioned by Jefferson, and lamented that Communists, "miserable merchants of unwanted ideas," had now provoked a Court majority to forsake Jefferson's ideals. In his dissent Black wrote that he hoped the travesty of judgment, so apparent in *Dennis,* would be temporary. "Public opinion being what it is now, few will protest the conviction of these Communist petitioners," wrote Black. "There is hope, however, that in calmer times, when present pressures, passions and fears subside, this or some later Court will restore the First Amendment liberties to the high preferred place where they belong in a free society."

Despite their disagreement in *Dennis,* Black and Frankfurter compiled an impressive record of agreement during the Cold War on a broad range of pressing civil liberties issues. In the area of constitutional rights directly affected by the terrorism of the McCarthy era, the two stood together in *Sacher,* insisting that an overzealous judge had breached his institutional duty. And they were together again, though on different grounds, when several New York City public school teachers challenged New York's Feinberg Law, which authorized a listing of subversive organizations and made membership by a public school teacher in one of the listed organizations grounds for dismissal. The Court majority found no constitutional violation, concluding that New York public school teachers had a free choice: Either work in the public school system under the terms of the Feinberg Law or "retain their beliefs and associations and go elsewhere."

Black, in dissent, said this was an untenable choice under our constitutional system of free speech and association. Frankfurter did not join Black but dissented on separate jurisdictional grounds. The Court majority had been wrong to reach the constitutional issue at all, wrote Frankfurter, and should not have given its imprimatur to the statute. No one had been fired yet, and therefore, in Frankfurter's view, there was no tangible case for the Court to decide.

Frankfurter's argument hinged, typically, on a technical point of constitutional law; he had, after all, taught federal jurisdiction at Harvard for two decades. But he took "considerable satisfaction," he wrote Black, in finding himself on the same side as his libertarian colleague. In fact, his letter to Black at the end of the term noted their agreement in both *Sacher* and the Feinberg Law case, among others, though the two old antagonists did not always see the issues "through the same lenses."

In another decision that term, *Zorach v. Clauson,* Black and Frankfurter again joined in dissent when the Court majority ruled that religious exercises held for public school students during school hours, but not on school premises, were not a violation of the First Amendment's clause prohibiting the establishment of religion. Frankfurter wrote to Black with obvious pride in their common position and the attacks on their position that followed. They were charged with "obtuse reasoning," he reported. "And for good measure there is added some rancid Billy Graham stuff whereby we shall be reviled as atheists. But then, it wouldn't be the first time that you and I are reviled." The note was signed "Ever yours."

Black, too, found this new Black-Frankfurter alliance, wholly unpredictable only a few short terms ago, a matter worthy of benign comment. "As you probably have noted," he wrote his former clerk, John Frank, in 1952, "our general direction in re civil liberties is very much the same, although I continue to think (as I tell him) that he tries to go by the wrong route and stops so short that he defeats his own purpose." Black further noted in his letter to Frank that he and "F.F." were on "a very friendly basis," an unnecessary observation given the warmth with which he spoke of Frankfurter.

Frankfurter's correspondence with Black during the period was conspicuously cordial, collegial and affectionate in tone, showing no trace of the earlier hostility. After listing their agreement on many important cases during the 1951 term, Frankfurter good-naturedly admonished Black that the members of this newly discovered judicial partnership could not "rest on our oars."

On a more personal note in the same letter, Frankfurter apologized for having missed Black during his "rounds of summer goodbyes." Undoubtedly Frankfurter was mindful that this would be Black's first summer in thirty years without his beloved Josephine. He wished Hugo "lots of enjoyable tennis" but could not resist a gentle sermonette on moderation—"remember that the Greeks were right, if not in all things, certainly in tennis!"

Shortly after Ethel and Julius Rosenberg had been convicted and sentenced to die in 1951 for conspiring to pass atomic secrets to the Russians, the Rosenbergs' attorneys petitioned the Supreme Court to review the legal proceedings, the most controversial of the entire Cold War period. On five separate occasions the Justices were asked to review various aspects of the litigation. Only two members of the Court—Justices Black and Frankfurter—voted in each instance to hear the Rosenbergs' attorneys' arguments. The story of the solidarity of the two Court leaders on this issue is one of the most intriguing episodes in their twenty-three years on the Court together.

During a twelve-month period beginning in June 1952, the Rosenbergs appealed their convictions to the Supreme Court on several constitutional grounds. One of the most troubling was that they had been charged with a conspiracy to commit espionage, not treason, but throughout their trial they had been branded as "traitors"; under the Constitution one could be convicted of treason only on the testimony of two witnesses for each overt act. Much of the evidence against the Rosenbergs, their attorneys argued, had been provided by a single witness on the uncorroborated evidence of an accomplice. The Rosenbergs also argued that the death penalty violated the Eighth Amendment's prohibition against cruel and unusual punishment, since the Rosenbergs were, in effect, sentenced to death for treason without being accorded the constitutional safeguards for those accused of the crime. Two additional issues were raised by the Rosenbergs in June 1952. First, they charged that the prosecution violated the federal criminal code by not providing the defense with a list of witnesses three days before trial. Second, U.S. District Judge Irving Kaufman had consistently shown hostility toward the Rosenbergs, their attorneys contended, and deprived them of a fair trial.

The U.S. Court of Appeals for the Second Circuit had rejected the Rosenbergs' initial appeal on all grounds but had indicated a split on the legal issues and suggested that the appellate rulings deserved further review by the U.S. Supreme Court. When, however, the Supreme Court considered review of the Rosenberg litigation for the first time in June 1952, only three Justices voted to grant the review.

Justices Black and Frankfurter voiced concern about the imposi-

tion of the death penalty without Supreme Court review. Black
was also troubled by the Rosenbergs' first argument—that they
had been sentenced to death for treason, in effect, without the
required constitutional safeguards. Justice Burton, the third Justice
voting for review, admitted that his vote was cast in part because
of the strong views expressed by Black and Frankfurter.

The same three Justices again voted to hear oral argument five
months later when the Rosenberg attorneys petitioned for a rehearing. But again the Rosenbergs fell one vote short of review.
According to Frankfurter's notes, Black again argued that the am-
biguous nature of the prosecution was sufficient cause for the
Court to review the case. For his part, Frankfurter had become
increasingly concerned that the Rosenbergs' convictions had become a *cause célèbre*—and a divisive political influence in the country. It was important, he believed, that the Justices review the case
to assure all Americans that justice was done. Privately, Frankfurter
was furious that Justice Douglas, who enjoyed a national reputation for liberalism, refused to contribute the fourth vote for review.

The Rosenbergs' attorneys later added two new arguments that
they hoped would persuade the Justices to review their case. First
they offered to present evidence that one prosecution witness had
perjured himself on the witness stand. Second, they charged that
the prosecutor, Irving Saypol, had prejudiced their case by out-of-
court statements to the press during the trial, which he failed to
prove in court. In April 1953, this third attempt at Supreme Court
review also failed. Only Justices Black and Frankfurter voted to
hear argument. Justice Burton did not consider the new arguments
substantial enough for Court review.

The third refusal of the Court to review the Rosenberg case
further distressed Frankfurter because he had become convinced
that the trial presented serious questions about the integrity of the
whole process. He was so agitated, in fact, that he decided to take
the unusual step of writing a dissenting opinion to the Court's
denial of certiorari. Later, however, he reconsidered his decision,
fearing that his dissent might embroil the Court in controversy and
be a basis for further disunity in the nation over the Rosenbergs'
fate. Following discussion, both Frankfurter and Black decided to
limit their written comment to a single sentence: "Mr. Justice Black

and Mr. Justice Frankfurter, referring to the positions they took . . . last November, adhere to them."*

In announcing that decision to his brethren in a written memorandum, Frankfurter vented his deep feelings about the entire Rosenberg proceeding. "My brethren may well be bored to have me repeat that the Court's failure to take the case of the Rosenbergs has presented for us the most anguishing situation since I have been on the Court," he began. He was not convinced that the Rosenbergs' convictions should be overturned, he emphasized. But enough substantial procedural questions had been raised on appeal, Frankfurter insisted, so that the Supreme Court was obligated to review the case. It was important that the public arena not be left to Senator McCarthy and his kind, wrote Frankfurter, but that others "who are as fiercely hostile to the Communist danger" show their concern for American traditions of fairness. Frankfurter, naturally, included himself—and the Court—in that category. "I am one of those who deems it ignominious to be awed by fear of the puny force of Communist influence in this country," he wrote. "I am, however, concerned about men and women as high-minded as any of us, though with less understanding of law and its workings, who feel as I do that it is a concession to Communism, not a safeguard against it, to retreat from reason and to compromise those cherished traditions which one likes to think of as the peculiar characteristics of an Anglo-American justice."

On June 15, 1953, three days before the scheduled electrocution of Ethel and Julius Rosenberg, the Court formally rejected the Rosenbergs' motion for a stay of execution. Both Black and Frankfurter had voted to hear oral argument on the motion, but again they were unsuccessful. The same day the Justices also turned down an application for habeas corpus based on allegations that the Rosenbergs' prosecutor, Irving Saypol, had knowingly used perjured testimony. Black wanted to grant the application and Frankfurter argued for what he called an "open hearing" on the question. But the Court majority refused.

A final dramatic appeal followed the Court's formal action on June 15. A day later, after the Court had recessed for the summer,

* Later Justice Douglas added his vote to Black's and Frankfurter's to grant certiorari.

Justice Douglas heard argument in his chambers from two attorneys who did not formally represent the Rosenbergs. The Rosenbergs' indictment, trial and sentence had been secured under the wrong law, they argued. The defendants should have been brought to trial under the Atomic Energy Act of 1946, rather than the older Espionage Act, since the conspiracy in which the Rosenbergs allegedly participated took place from 1944 to 1950. And under the Atomic Energy Act, a judge could only impose the death penalty on the recommendation of the jury and only with the showing that the offense had been committed with the intent to injure the United States. Neither condition had been met in the Rosenberg case.

Douglas was convinced that the attorneys had presented a substantial constitutional argument that required full oral argument before the Court. Since the Court was in summer recess, Douglas exercised his authority to grant the Rosenbergs a stay of execution pending that argument. An annoyed Chief Justice Vinson quickly scheduled oral argument on the issue for the very next day. Two questions were to be addressed. First, did the full Court have the authority to vacate Douglas's stay? Second, did the apparent conflict between the penalty provisions of the Espionage Act and the Atomic Energy Act present a "substantial" question requiring further study and litigation?

At two volatile conferences after the oral argument, Black bitterly criticized the Chief Justice for his hasty convening of the special session. It was wrong, he charged, to act so precipitously, undercutting the legitimate authority of one Justice to issue a stay. Frankfurter supported Black's position, questioning whether the Court could properly countermand Douglas's stay. Burton joined Black, Frankfurter and Douglas in the argument. The Court should not overrule Douglas, Burton said. "Let it take due course," he argued. "There is a substantial question. That's all we should pass on now."

It was a lost cause. The other five members of the Court voted to vacate the stay. When it was clear that a majority would not uphold the stay under any conditions, Burton switched his vote, making the vote 6–3. An angry Felix Frankfurter wrote a note on the page proof of the Chief Justice's opinion for the Court: "The fact is that all minds were made up as soon as we left the Bench—indeed, I have no doubt . . . before we met on it!"

On Friday, June 19, the Justices entered the courtroom looking unusually somber. The Chief Justice read the Court's brief, unsigned opinion vacating Douglas's stay with a calmness that belied the bitter internal dispute among them. It was the Court's responsibility to supervise the administration of justice, Vinson said, and it was the majority's view that the stay should be vacated. As to the legal issue that caused Justice Douglas to issue the stay, the Chief Justice brushed it aside as if it were a routine administrative matter. "We think the question is not substantial," he said. "We think further proceedings to litigate it are unwarranted."

Julius Rosenberg, thirty-five years old, received the first shock of 2,000 volts of electricity in Sing Sing prison at 8:04 P.M. on June 19. He was pronounced dead two minutes later. His wife, Ethel, was electrocuted and died ten minutes later. The couple were the only Americans in the nation's history to die for the crime of espionage.

Although their effort was obviously futile, both Black and Frankfurter wrote dissenting opinions to the Court's *Rosenberg* decision. In vacating the stay, Black argued that the Court had misread judicial precedent, federal statute and the Constitution. "It is not amiss to point out that this Court has never reviewed this record and has never affirmed the fairness of the trial below," he wrote. "Without an affirmance of the fairness of the trial by the highest court of the land there may always be questions as to whether these executions were legally and rightfully carried out."

Frankfurter did not write his dissent until three days after the executions, but his words were still alive with meaning. "To be writing an opinion in a case affecting two lives after the curtain has been rung down upon them has the appearance of pathetic futility, but history also has its claims." Convinced that the Rosenbergs were entitled to a full review by the Court, Frankfurter suggested that errors had been made. "Perfection may not be demanded by law," he wrote, "but the capacity to counteract inevitable, though rare, frailties is the mark of a civilized legal mechanism."

Hugo Black and Felix Frankfurter thought of America first, but their ardent anticommunism, unlike that of the McCarthys of the day, did not pander to Americans' lowest instincts and worst fears. Both placed their faith in the American system of justice, though they did not interpret the system "through the same lenses."

Black had always defended outsiders, as a populist Senator from Alabama, and later as a Justice who believed implicitly in the Court's obligation to protect minority rights. His concerns during the McCarthy era were consistent with his broad constitutional commitment to the rights of the lowliest U.S. citizens and, in the *Rosenberg* case, the most vilified.

Frankfurter's central concern for three decades had been the integrity of the judicial system. He warned judges in the fifties, as he had in the twenties, that they could not succumb to external political pressures and, at the same time, fulfill their institutional responsibilities. In the *Rosenberg* case, he could be true to his deepest philosophical convictions and still demand that the Court be actively involved. For in this case the integrity of the very judicial system he so revered had been called into question.

Black and Frankfurter would never live in complete harmony on the Court. Their divergent judicial philosophies and indomitable wills made that impossible. But for that critical moment in the nation's history, they stood together to teach their countrymen, in the best Court tradition, the deepest meaning of our constitutional democracy.

CHAPTER VII

Fever Patients

IN *AN AMERICAN DILEMMA,* the massive work dissecting the problem of racial injustice in a white-dominated America, social scientist Gunnar Myrdal wrote of the ambivalence of the liberal white Southerner. His ideals demanded that he condemn the injustices surrounding him. At the same time, his allegiance to his region severely limited his enthusiasm, and ability, to effect change. The handful of Southern liberals in Washington—Senator Claude Pepper of Florida and Senator Lister Hill of Alabama, for example —seemed to have had an easier time winning their seats, Myrdal noted, than being "really influential at home." Another example of the phenomenon, Myrdal suggested, was the former Senator from Alabama, Justice Hugo Black.

Before his appointment to the Court, Hugo Black had demonstrated his public color blindness time and again in performing his official duties. As a police judge, Black had consistently applied the same high standard of fairness to the black defendant as to the white. As county prosecutor, Black had condemned the abominable conditions in the Jefferson County jail, where an overwhelming number of prisoners were black. Prosecutor Black had also ordered a thorough investigation and written the report excoriating white police officers in Bessemer, Alabama, who had tortured their black prisoners.

But this same liberal Southerner had joined the Ku Klux Klan and spoken of "Anglo-Saxon courage" for years after his resignation from the organization. Black read Southern history avidly, never lost his soft Alabama accent, and believed deeply in many of the traditions of the white South. As a Senate liberal, he had worked tirelessly for FDR's New Deal and the benefits to the poor, both black and white, that New Deal legislation produced. But as a white Southern politician, he had been very protective of his region and his white constituents. He opposed the federal anti-lynching bill on the floor of the Senate and expressed doubts about giving blacks the vote. Once he advised four women students from Vassar and Wellesley colleges, who had questioned the fairness of the trial of the four black Scottsboro defendants convicted of raping two white girls, to turn their reformist energies away from the South and toward injustices in the North.

After the furor over his Klan membership had subsided and Black had taken his seat on the Supreme Court, there was still widespread skepticism about Black's commitment to civil rights and liberties. Chief Justice Charles Evans Hughes, undoubtedly sensitive to the situation, offered Black a unique opportunity to put the rumors of his latent prejudice to rest by assigning him the majority opinion in *Chambers v. Florida.*

Four young, ignorant black tenant farmers in rural southeast Florida, including Chambers, had been rounded up and interrogated for six days without interruption by white police officers relentlessly pursuing a confession for the murder of an elderly white man. Police had arrested the young black men without warrants. Once in custody, the suspects were not allowed to speak to an attorney or a relative. Finally, after an all-night session, Chambers and three others confessed; they were later convicted of murder and sentenced to death.

Justice Black reviewed the facts of the case with rising indignation. "From virtually the moment of their arrest until their eventual confessions," he wrote, "they never knew when just any one would be called back to the fourth floor room, and there, surrounded by their accusers and others, interrogated by men who held their very lives—so far as these ignorant petitioners could know—in the balance." Declaring that the defendants had been denied their due process rights under the Fourteenth Amendment, Black concluded: "Under our constitutional system, courts stand against any winds that blow as havens of refuge for those who might otherwise suffer because they are helpless, weak, outnumbered, or because they are non-conforming victims of prejudice and public excitement."

Black's admirers frequently cited the *Chambers* opinion, written in 1940, as eloquent testimony to his liberal creed. And with the notable exception of his judicial positions condoning the exclusion of Japanese-Americans from the West Coast during World War II, Justice Black displayed an exemplary voting record of protection of the civil rights and liberties of minorities. He joined the Court majority that outlawed the white primary in Texas, racially restrictive covenants in Missouri and segregated graduate education in Oklahoma. But he wrote no opinion in any of those important decisions advancing the cause of equal rights for blacks. And when he did write opinions in civil rights cases, those opinions, typically, hewed closely to the facts of the case without offering inflammatory rhetoric.

Although everyone knew where Hugo Black stood on the issue of racial prejudice, the Justice did not preach to the white South, even in his famous *Chambers* opinion. He emphasized fairness for all without singling out any group for protection or criticism. He remained a white liberal Southerner on the Court, sure of the correctness of his beliefs, but careful not to disturb unnecessarily the sensibilities of his white Southern friends who did not share his strong views.

That special mixture of idealism and pragmatism helps explain Justice Black's position in the school desegregation cases, beginning with challenges to segregated graduate schools in 1950 and culminating in *Brown v. Board of Education.* Black never wavered in his support for the principle of desegregation of the public schools under the equal protection clause of the Fourteenth Amendment. At the same time, he counseled caution in implementation, once the constitutional principle had been announced. In this respect, Black's approach was similar to that of Justice Frankfurter.

The young Felix Frankfurter left it to others to attach labels to his liberal views and activities. For Professor Frankfurter of Harvard, political labels were irrelevant. He did not lecture on tolerance of religious and racial minorities in a democracy; he lived it.

As the only Jew on the Harvard law faculty, he earned the respect of his colleagues through his works. And when the president of Harvard insisted on a Jewish quota at the university, Frankfurter attacked the president's policy, as an American Jew fighting irrational, destructive prejudice. He offered his legal services to groups that furthered his causes in a progressive democracy and those groups included the National Association for the Advancement of Colored People.

Frankfurter inspired and helped guide the careers of three of this century's most prominent black attorneys—Charles Houston, William Hastie and William Coleman, Jr. All three men played important roles in the legal fight against school segregation. In his mentoring role, Frankfurter made no point of his protégés' race, but made much of their talent.

Charles Houston was drawn to the personality and teaching of Frankfurter after he entered the Harvard Law School in 1919. At Harvard, Houston was elected to the *Law Review* and stayed an additional year to work with Frankfurter on a graduate degree. Later Houston became the chief strategist in the NAACP's legal fight against segregation and was described by William Hastie as "our Moses," who "led us through the wilderness of second class citizenship toward the dimly perceived promised land of legal equality."

Hastie followed Charles Houston to Harvard where he, like Houston, served on the *Law Review* and became one of Frankfurter's favored students. Several years after graduation, Professor Frankfurter recommended Hastie for the NAACP legal staff. A generation later, Justice Frankfurter selected William Coleman, Jr., an honors graduate of the Harvard Law School, to be his clerk in 1949, the first black law clerk in the history of the Supreme Court. Later Coleman worked with the NAACP's team of lawyers challenging school segregation before the Court. The NAACP prepared arguments in *Brown* soon after Coleman's clerkship ended; he served unofficially and invaluably as a consultant on Justice Frankfurter's philosophy of judicial restraint.

Despite his personal commitment to liberal political causes, Frankfurter balked at forcing them upon the electorate by judicial fiat. Decades before Justice Frankfurter was counseling judicial restraint, a younger Professor Frankfurter was making the same point in articles in *The New Republic*. In a 1925 piece entitled "Can the Supreme Court Guarantee Toleration?" Frankfurter concluded that the answer to the question was no. He applauded the liberal result of Supreme Court decisions that struck down illiberal state laws, but he concluded that the Court should not force its value judgments, however wise, on an unwilling citizenry—unless constitutional principle had been violated. Only grass-roots education and cultivation of a liberal spirit by enlightened national leadership could, Frankfurter suggested, ensure tolerance in America's democracy.

When the NAACP began its legal battle to eradicate segregation from the public schools, Frankfurter's heart and head were squarely on the side of the challengers. He opposed racial segregation. He also believed implicitly in the value of education for all Americans, black and white. Set against these beliefs, Frankfurter's philosophy of judicial restraint braked his rush toward the desired result. Should the Supreme Court impose its will on a large, reluctant segment of the electorate? What if the Court attempted to do so and its mandate met sustained political opposition? Would the Court then become mired in a protracted struggle that sapped its energy and undermined its prestige? These were the large institutional questions that Justice Frankfurter pondered as the school-segregation cases wound their way to the Supreme Court.

By 1952, the year that *Brown v. Board of Education* was first argued before the U.S. Supreme Court, the slow dismantling of racially segregated public facilities in the southern United States had assumed an uneasy inevitability. Two decades earlier NAACP attorneys had conceived a broad-based strategy to uproot segregation in schools and other public facilities. They knew, intuitively and by experience, that the "separate but equal" doctrine was a ruse created by whites to subjugate blacks. But they also were aware that each of the three branches of the federal government had consistently condoned the practice. The most injurious institutional offender, ironically enough, was the U.S. Supreme Court, which had ruled in 1896 in *Plessy v. Ferguson* that the equal protection clause of the Fourteenth Amendment was not violated by a Louisiana law enforcing segregation in its public-transportation facilities. Every southern and border state, encouraged by the Court's endorsement of the "separate but equal" doctrine, strengthened its own system of segregation, and no one, not the President or Congress or the Supreme Court of the United States, disturbed the status quo.

The rumblings of discontent, faint at first, finally intruded upon the national consciousness. White America felt the jolt to the political process with black migration from the farms of the South to the urban centers of the North and Midwest after World War I. The population shifts created a new black political voice, directed at candidates of the overwhelming choice of American blacks, the Democratic party. The most popular President of the century, Franklin D. Roosevelt, responded, introducing the New Deal's vocabulary of aspirations for black Americans as well as white. World War II accelerated the demand for equality, intensified by the strengthened economic might of blacks suddenly thrust into well-paying jobs in the war-production industries. "Thank God for Hitler," one black production worker in Detroit said, not entirely facetiously.

The war against Hitler also provoked America's propaganda machine to rail against the racist enemy. But that propaganda ricocheted, returning a haunting message to a white America that had done little to rid itself of racism at home. "The treatment of the Negro is America's greatest and most conspicuous scandal," Myrdal wrote. But he also pointed out that white Americans genuinely desired, while discriminating against blacks, to honor their basic egalitarian creed. "They [Americans] stand warmheartedly against oppression in the world," Myrdal observed. "When they are reluctantly forced into war, they are compelled to justify their participation to their own conscience by insisting that they are fighting against aggression and for liberty and equality."

In the late thirties and early forties, attorneys at the NAACP had quietly prepared the legal antidote to official racism. Using the equal protection clause of the Fourteenth Amendment as the instrument for change, they posed the argument that had no serious rejoinder: the claim that blacks enjoyed public facilities equal to whites was patently false, and the inequality was built upon the invidious premise that blacks were inferior to whites.

Legal advances had been shrewdly plotted by the NAACP lawyers, who focused much of their energy on the elimination of racial discrimination in public schools. Progress in public education, they calculated, was a crucial step toward the first-class citizenship that had eluded blacks since the founding of the Republic. The problem of government-sponsored racism was pervasive, however, and elimination of segregation in the public schools threatened white Southerners at a basic emotional level. If little black first-graders sat at desks next to little white first-graders, socializing could not be far behind and that would lead to . . .

Rather than dredge up the worst racist nightmares, NAACP lawyers initially chose to fight against school segregation at the margins. They didn't challenge segregation in the primary and secondary schools; instead, they attacked the system at the graduate level. The NAACP's litigator, Thurgood Marshall, wryly explained: "Those racial supremacy boys somehow think that little kids of six or seven are going to get funny ideas about sex or marriage just from going to school together, but for some equally funny reason youngsters in law school aren't supposed to feel that way. We didn't get it but we decided that if that was what the South believed, then the best thing for the moment was to go along."

In 1950 two NAACP challenges, one from Texas and the other from Oklahoma, forced the Court to face the reality of so-called "equal" education for blacks. The Texas suit was brought by a black Houston mail carrier named Heman Sweatt who had been denied admission to the all-white law school at the University of Texas in Austin and had, with NAACP support, sued the university. In an attempt to deflect the suit, state officials hastily approved the establishment of a second law school, which the petitioner and other blacks were eligible to attend. The second, all-black institution did not offer even a semblance of equality, in library, faculty or prestige.

Oklahoma's claim in the companion case, *McLaurin v. Oklahoma*, similarly taxed the credulity of the judicial branch. The state argued that the black petitioner had been granted an equal education to his white colleagues at the University of Oklahoma graduate school. As a student at the university, George McLaurin had been required to study and eat apart from whites. He had also been forced to sit at a table outside the classroom, customized for his special status as a black with a rope and a sign, "For colored only," separating McLaurin from his white classmates.

In the late forties Frankfurter had opened a file on school segregation for his personal use, but on April 11, 1950, he decided to share his materials with Black. Frankfurter's gesture was prompted by the Court's deliberations in *Sweatt v. Painter* and *McLaurin v. Oklahoma.* In both cases the Court majority had voted to strike down state-imposed graduate school segregation and Black, as the senior Justice in the majority, had assigned the Court's opinion to himself.

"You may find the data on school segregation of use," Frankfurter wrote Black. The data that Frankfurter sent included statistics that showed segregation in graduate schools less prevalent than at the secondary and undergraduate levels. Frankfurter attached a note to his materials, suggesting to Black that his opinion for the Court stick closely to the facts in *Sweatt* and *McLaurin.* "Let me take this occasion to say that if you write as narrowly as you talked [in conference], you will or ought to have a unanimous Court or almost," he wrote. "That would be most fortunate."

At the earlier judicial conference in which the Justices had discussed *Sweatt* and *McLaurin,* Black and Frankfurter had spoken at length and found themselves in agreement on the facts. Neither Sweatt nor McLaurin, they had concluded, had been offered an education equal to that offered white students. But both Justices had expressed concern about the scope of a majority opinion ruling in favor of the black petitioners. Black had told his colleagues that the Court faced a critical choice. The Justices could rule on the facts alone, saying no more than that the educations offered to Sweatt and McLaurin were not equal to those offered white students. Or they could go further, announcing a broader constitutional edict that segregation in graduate school was prohibitively "unreasonable." The latter course would have sent a chilling message to the South that the "separate but equal" doctrine, comfortably accepted for fifty-four years, was no longer tenable constitutional law. Black had said that he favored the more conservative approach, reversing the lower courts in each case on narrow factual grounds without questioning the underpinnings of the "separate but equal" doctrine.

Frankfurter had also voted to reverse in both cases and did so on precisely the grounds articulated by Black. There was no doubt in Frankfurter's mind as to what the outcome in *Sweatt* and *McLaurin* should have been. But just as important, Frankfurter believed that the Court "should not go beyond what is necessary." There was no need to "go out and meet problems," he had told his colleagues. On the facts, the educations for Sweatt and McLaurin were not equal to those for whites, Frankfurter stated, and that was all that it was prudent for the Court to decide.

Less than a week after Frankfurter had written his encouraging note to Black in the *Sweatt* and *McLaurin* cases, Black relinquished the assignment of writing the majority opinions in favor of Chief Justice Fred Vinson, who, apparently belatedly, had joined the majority. Vinson worked assiduously to achieve a unanimous court in *Sweatt* and *McLaurin,* soliciting advice from his colleagues and then drafting an opinion that confined the Court's holding to the particular facts in the cases without suggesting that segregation per se was unconstitutional.

Both Black and Frankfurter were pleased with the Chief Justice's effort and result. For Frankfurter, the Vinson opinion contained exactly the tone and content necessary for the occasion. Black agreed. "This is written in beautiful style," Black congratulated Vinson, "and I sincerely hope it can obtain a unanimous approval."

The other Justices responded to the Chief Justice's opinion just as Frankfurter and Black had hoped. The vote was unanimous. But the ultimate challenge, the Justices knew, still awaited them.

From the beginning, Frankfurter asserted himself in the school-segregation cases, persistently counseling reason and restraint. His anxiety level, already high, swelled with the realization that unanimity, so recently achieved in *Sweatt* and *McLaurin,* was clearly unattainable in the five cases argued before the Court in 1952 as *Brown v. Board of Education.* Even with his most optimistic tabulation, Frankfurter could only count five votes in favor of striking down laws that mandated segregated facilities in primary and secondary schools in four states and the District of Columbia.

The problem started with the Chief Justice, who had worked effectively to achieve the unanimous decisions in *Sweatt* and *McLaurin*. It was proper for the Court to decide that the educations offered to the black petitioners at the graduate school level had violated their personal constitutional rights. It was quite another matter, as far as Chief Justice Vinson was concerned, to declare segregated facilities at the primary and secondary levels unconstitutional. The remedy for large numbers of blacks and whites in existing segregated systems went far beyond any measures that the Chief, a Kentuckian, was prepared to contemplate.

Two other Justices from border states, Stanley Reed of Kentucky and Tom Clark of Texas, shared Vinson's concerns and opposed overruling *Plessy*. Robert Jackson also expressed reservations about overturning *Plessy* but did so on independent grounds. He questioned the Court's power to enforce desegregation, asserting that the constitutional authority properly resided with Congress, not the Court. Jackson recommended that the Justices send the problem to the elected representatives for resolution.

Those close to Frankfurter at the time that *Brown* first appeared on the Court docket, such as his former clerk, William Coleman, Jr., said that the Justice's commitment to desegregation was never in doubt. Still, Frankfurter did not announce that position in the Court's early deliberations in *Brown*. In fact, Douglas interpreted the comments expressed by Frankfurter in conference to mean that he would have upheld *Plessy*. But Frankfurter later insisted that his guarded stance was taken to protect overriding institutional interests. The main task, he believed, was to preserve the integrity of the Court. Rather than declaring his own position and possibly forcing a formal vote that would reveal a divided Court, Frankfurter played for time until a consensus among the Justices could develop.

To Frankfurter, the four members of the Court who had announced their willingness to overrule *Plessy*—Black, Douglas, Burton and Minton—were as wrongheaded as those who had taken the opposite position. The primary goal, according to Frankfurter, was to avoid any premature declaration by the Court that would indicate disagreement on the issue.

"If the 'great libertarians' had had their way," Frankfurter later wrote his close friend Judge Learned Hand, "we would have been in the soup." The reference was apparently to Black and Douglas. To Frankfurter, Douglas had been a lost cause for years. But what about Hugo Black, his colleague and friend in the early fifties? Black had seemed to soften the edges of his aggressive, activist jurisprudence in those years, even in the constitutional area at issue, school desegregation. Just two terms earlier Black had echoed Frankfurter's argument for judicial restraint in both words and action in the *Sweatt* and *McLaurin* decisions.

When the Court faced the challenges in *Brown,* Frankfurter suspected that Black was reverting to his old intransigence. In January 1952, he counseled the other Justices in *Briggs v. Elliott,* later consolidated in *Brown,* to return the case to the district court for further deliberation. To Frankfurter's chagrin, Black dissented. He did so, Frankfurter believed, to make a political point: Black wanted the Court to decide *Briggs,* so that he could write a vigorous dissent appealing to his liberal political constituency.

But if Frankfurter's theory depicted the "old" Black, the theorist revealed the "old" Frankfurter—quick to ascribe a malevolent motive to his colleague. There was an equally plausible, if more benign, explanation for Black's vote in *Briggs.* Consistent with his attitude and votes in *Sweatt* and *McLaurin,* Black may have wanted the Court to decide the South Carolina case narrowly and urged the Justices to confine the holding to the particular facts in the case. In this way the Court could have outlawed the specifically challenged segregated education in South Carolina without forcing broad action across the South. It was just such an approach that Black later advocated in *Brown* when the Court discussed an appropriate remedy.

In December 1952, the Justices again considered *Briggs* as well as four other cases challenging school segregation argued before the Court as *Brown v. Board of Education.* Frankfurter was no more sanguine that a Court consensus could be achieved in judicial conference in the spring of 1953 than he had been during the previous term. His strategy, therefore, was to continue urging delay in the ultimate decision on school segregation. To help carry that strategy out, he enlisted the services of his young clerk, Alexander Bickel.

Together, Bickel and Frankfurter prepared a series of five pene-

trating questions on the constitutionality of public school segregation that focused on legislative history, Court authority to decide
the issue and possible remedies. On May 27, 1953, Frankfurter
circulated the list of questions among his colleagues with a memorandum suggesting that the Court schedule reargument of *Brown*
in the fall of 1953 when attorneys for both sides could address the
issues raised by the Bickel-Frankfurter inquiry. The brethren accepted Frankfurter's suggestion, and reargument in *Brown* was
placed on the Court's fall 1953 docket.

During the Court's deliberations in *Brown,* Frankfurter discussed
the issues and the split among the Justices with Philip Elman, his
former clerk and then a lawyer in the Justice Department. At the
time Elman was one of the government attorneys working on a
Justice Department brief supporting the NAACP's position. Since
the Justice Department was not a party to the suit, neither the
Justice nor Elman felt that their discussions compromised Frankfurter, although he would later be one of nine men to decide the
case.

Twenty-four years later Elman explained: "Today [in 1987] no
Justice should be talking about cases. But Felix was not discreet.
Everybody knew Felix talked too much. He told me about the split
on the Court in *Brown.* He didn't just talk to me—he talked to
Dean Acheson and Phil Graham [another former clerk] too. But I
was in the S.G.'s [solicitor general's] office, so I was always available. We weren't plotting strategy. Felix felt deeply about racial
discrimination. He saw this as a basic human rights issue and he
wanted to make a contribution."

Undisturbed about the propriety of their discussions, Frankfurter
and Elman concentrated on their overriding concern that even a
fragile majority achieved on the principle of desegregation would
shatter when the Justices confronted the enormous problems of
implementation. The two men concluded that the best hope for
success required separating the issue of constitutional principle
from proposed remedy. In the government brief, therefore, Elman
argued that the Court should strike down segregated school facilities as a violation of the equal protection clause but postpone
decision on implementation.

On September 8, 1953, Chief Justice Vinson died, Frankfurter's
first indication, he later said, that there was a God. In this instance,

Frankfurter's theology was dominated by his fear of a disastrous result in *Brown* with Vinson presiding. To fill the Vinson vacancy, President Eisenhower nominated California Governor Earl Warren. Frankfurter rejoiced in the appointment: "He brings to his work that largeness of experience and breadth of outlook which may well make him a very good Chief Justice provided he has some other qualities which, from what I have seen, I believe he has."

Josephine Black's death in December 1951 had temporarily destroyed Justice Black's ebullient spirit. And though the loss of his wife had dominated his depression in the early fifties, the Justice's dark mood spread to other concerns as well. A severely painful case of shingles cut down Black's mobility and forced an operation. The Court's work was a diversion but far from fulfilling. The Justice's resolute views on civil liberties did not go down well with the Court majority or most of his countrymen during the tyrannical reign of Joe McCarthy. "They [the Justices] will soon be back deciding all those cases wrong again," a fatalistic Justice Black told his law clerk one August afternoon in 1953.

Frankfurter was not always a comfort to Black on the Court in those days, particularly in First Amendment cases. Their personal relationship, however, became increasingly close. Frankfurter, the intrepid meddler, would not leave his friend alone. While Black suffered from shingles, Frankfurter insisted that Alexander Bickel drive Black to and from his Alexandria home. After Black's successful operation, Frankfurter added his advice to that of the doctors:

Dear Hugo:

  Marion is right, I'm sure, when she says that no one is more ignorant than I am about the human body. But I think I know a good deal concerning the consequences of inserting the surgical knife into the body. Over the years I have watched the effects of operations, and I care not how "simple" or "conventional" the operation was supposed to be. There is no "simple" operation, so far as need for going slow—and very slow—is concerned. A disequi-

librium results and it takes time to restore the old equilib-
rium.

So I say to you—go slow: indulge yourself and accept
the facts of physiology, more important than any controlling decision of the U.S.S.C.!

Good luck to you and love to Jo-Jo.

Yours, FF

Black assured Frankfurter that he was "going to take it slowly
enough to get the full advantage of the treatment." Neither patient
nor friend could have confidently taken the restless Black at his
word. Indeed, three months later, he had returned to the tennis
court, declaring that exercise was accelerating his recovery.

In the fall of 1953 both Black's tennis and his recuperation were
coming along nicely, just as he had predicted. The arrival of Chief
Justice Earl Warren provided additional tonic to his flattened spir-
its. The Chief, Black wrote his sons,

> is a very attractive, fine man. Just a short acquaintance
> with him explains why it was possible for him to get
> votes in both parties in California. He is a novice here, of
> course, but a man with his intelligence should be able to
> give good service. I am by no means sure that an intelli-
> gent man with practical, hard common sense and integrity
> like he has is not as good a type to select as could be found
> in the country.

Warren's skills as a superb politician were demonstrated almost
immediately upon arrival at the Court. In one of his first official
acts, he asked Hugo Black to preside at the early judicial conferences. This one gesture paid homage to the senior sitting Justice
and bought Warren important time to learn more about his new
job.

Black responded admirably, running the conferences fairly and
expeditiously, as Frankfurter was the first to acknowledge. Frankfurter wrote: "Dear Hugo: This is to say how admirably I thought
you conducted the proceedings. You stated, and stated well, the
cases that should have been put to the Conference for discussion
and guided the talk as talk should be guided—by a gentle but, or
firm but gentle rein. Yours, FF."

Meanwhile, Frankfurter happily prepared tutorials for his newest student, the Chief Justice, and Warren graciously accepted his steadily increasing visits, memos and reading lists. Warren's office soon became a thoroughfare with associates, including Frankfurter, eagerly stopping by to cultivate the friendship of the Chief.

Hugo Black waited in his chambers, secure in the knowledge that his and Earl Warren's political backgrounds would make a close personal and professional collaboration inevitable. Soon enough, the Chief paid an unannounced visit. Would Black be kind enough, Warren asked, to recommend a book on opinion writing? Black enthusiastically recommended Aristotle's *On Rhetoric,* a single ancient volume on the art of analyzing and making arguments. Earl Warren followed Black's advice that day and on many days to come.

But when the Court engaged in final deliberations in *Brown v. Board of Education,* the Chief Justice did not depend on either Black or Frankfurter for advice. With confidence built on a solid foundation of moral certainty, Warren urged the brethren to accept his conclusion that school segregation had been created and sustained for the single purpose of imposing conditions of inferiority on blacks. It was both unfair and unconstitutional, Warren said, and he worked among his colleagues with consummate skill to achieve unanimous support for his view.

On the morning of May 17, 1954, David Vann, Black's law clerk, drove the Justice to the Court in his old green Plymouth. Once inside the Court building, Vann noticed Robert Jackson, recently hospitalized and near death, being robed. The *Brown* decision, Vann knew, was imminent. After two and a half years of reading briefs, listening to oral argument and squabbling among themselves, the Justices' final decision was reduced by the Chief Justice to a simple, direct and unequivocal opinion. "Separate educational facilities," Warren wrote, "are inherently unequal."

Although *Brown* was not Frankfurter's opinion, he considered it in no small measure his triumph. He believed that his strategy of delay had enabled the Justices to postpone a final decision until Earl Warren could be appointed and a consensus molded. But Frankfurter also recognized Warren's achievement. "It was an agreeable term," Frankfurter wrote Black a month after *Brown.* He gave major credit for the success to the Chief, who showed the greatest qualities of leadership since Charles Evans Hughes had presided. Frankfurter took "deep satisfaction" in the entire term's work, but the segregation cases stood as the Court's transcendent achievement.

Still, there was work to be done, and Frankfurter, who had successfully argued that the implementation decree should be severed from the decision declaring the principle in *Brown,* knew exactly where to begin. From his summer retreat in Charlemont, Massachusetts, Frankfurter wrote Warren suggesting the direction that the Court should take in implementing *Brown.* A study of American politics, Frankfurter noted, underscored "the great fertility in gerrymandering devices." The Court must review successful administrative experiments in other sections of the country before making recommendations for the South, he advised. "The Southern States are fever patients," Frankfurter wrote the Chief. "Let us find out, if we can, what healthy bodies do about such things in order to guard against attributing to the fever conduct and consequences that are not fairly attributable to fever."

The second shoe dropped on the South in May 1955 when Chief Justice Warren, for a unanimous Court, announced the implementation decision, commonly referred to as Brown II. Frankfurter could justifiably be proud of his role in forging the implementation decree, for it reflected his thinking more than that of any other Justice, including Earl Warren. He had labored long and insistently among his colleagues advocating separation of Brown I from Brown II. Declare the principle first, Frankfurter counseled; announce the remedy later. The crucial phrasing of the order of school desegregation "with all deliberate speed" in Brown II belonged to Frankfurter, who had borrowed the phrase from an opinion by his idol, Oliver Wendell Holmes, Jr. The phrase signaled that the Court understood the South's trauma and would allow the region sufficient time to make a good faith adjustment to the judicial mandate.

Black had shunned a leadership role throughout the Court's deliberations in both Brown I and II. To be sure, his position—to outlaw school segregation—was clearly articulated and his vote never in doubt. But Black left it largely to Frankfurter and Warren to persuade reluctant colleagues to join the unanimous Court opinions, even though he believed as strongly as they that the Court must speak with one voice, "if humanly possible." He also supported the position that *Brown* should be limited to the named plaintiffs and the Court should "say and do as little as possible."

Black emerged from *Brown* with his Southern liberal credentials intact. He extended his impressive judicial record of opposition to official racial discrimination. At the same time, he sympathized with white Southerners who, in good faith, prepared to change their schools and their racial attitudes but needed time for their emotions and life's habits to keep pace. The "all deliberate speed" formula, he hoped, would provide valuable time to Southern moderates, whom Black did not want to put on the spot, to take a leadership role in the transition period.

But Hugo Black badly misread the mood of the South, as did the other members of the Court. And no Justice felt the cruel post-*Brown* lash of the old Confederacy more than Black. In letters to Black from his native Alabama, segregationists registered their disbelief and outrage. "How proud I used to be of our Hon. Hugo Black, and many times I have supported you with pride and admiration," wrote a former supporter from Oneonta. "I just could not believe you voted to do away with segregation without even a protest." A Huntsville resident was blunter: "YOU ARE A DISGRACE TO THE STATE OF ALABAMA."

Supportive letters, fewer, to be sure, also arrived at Black's Supreme Court chambers. A young man from Montgomery planning to attend the Emory University Medical School praised Black for "taking a positive attitude toward segregation." And Hugo Black, Jr., graduate of the Yale Law School and budding young labor lawyer in Birmingham, assured his father that the *Brown* decision was both courageous and correct.

But the wind of Southern hostility blew through Hugo, Jr.'s, Birmingham. Although no one told Hugo, Jr., to his face that his father had betrayed the South, the tension was there, and Hugo, Jr.'s, friends confided that there was much uninhibited discussion of *Brown* when he was not around. A concerned Hugo, Jr., wanted to talk to his father about his future the next time the Justice visited Alabama. But such a visit in that frenzied post-*Brown* atmosphere, the Justice wrote his son, was not advisable.

In the years following *Brown,* Hugo, Jr., and his wife, Graham, received fewer social invitations, and their young children stayed closer to home as well. Hugo, Jr.'s, law business also suffered. Word spread that Hugo, Jr., and his senior partner, Jerome "Buddy" Cooper [Justice Black's first law clerk], could not win many jury verdicts because of "this integration thing."

The situation was so bad, Hugo, Jr., told his father, that he was seriously considering moving his family out of the state of Alabama. Justice Black responded sympathetically to Hugo, Jr.'s, problems, indicating that he did not oppose a move. Indeed, the Justice recommended that Hugo, Jr., consider a new home in Florida or the West where the law business and climate might better suit his son and his family.

Brown II's "all deliberate speed" formula failed, and that failure was apparent almost immediately after the decision had been announced. The Southern moderates, whom both Black and Frankfurter had expected to lead, were shouted down by white supremacist politicians. Sadly the Justices realized that they had promoted a perverted, spirited competition among the South's political office seekers. In Alabama, for example, one gubernatorial candidate vowed to go to jail for the cause of segregation, a second promised to die for it and a third trumped both opponents by pledging to go to jail *and* die for the old South. Those in office, like Governor Orville Faubus of Arkansas, enjoyed unprecedented popularity by shaking their fists at the nine men on the U.S. Supreme Court.

For their part, the Justices said little publicly, content initially to issue terse unsigned orders reminding recalcitrant school districts in the South that there could be no retreat from *Brown.* And they waited for the President, Dwight D. Eisenhower, to use his extraordinary popularity and the prestige of his office to bolster the constitutional mandate. But Ike gave only grudging support to the Court, leaving the Justices isolated and furious. The times demanded the presidential leadership of a Lincoln or an Andrew Jackson, Frankfurter observed privately, and regrettably Dwight Eisenhower had neither the will nor the vision to meet the challenge.

Southern politicians sniffed the mood of their constituents and leaped ahead of the pack. The Arkansas legislature passed a constitutional amendment dedicating the state to oppose "the uncon-stitutional decision of *Brown v. Board of Education*" by every available method. In September 1957, Governor Faubus set a no-torious standard of defiance that eventually presented the U.S. Supreme Court with one of the greatest challenges to its authority in its history.

The events leading to the confrontation began on the first day of school that September when Faubus ordered units of the state National Guard to Little Rock's Central High School. The troops were instructed to keep the school "off limits" to the nine entering black students, even though the city's school board had included them in its desegregation plan. President Eisenhower countered by sending federal troops to Central High to escort the black students, creating an eerie American scene that dominated the front pages of newspapers from coast to coast.

Five months later the Little Rock School Board, under increasing pressure from segregationists led by the governor, petitioned the federal district court to delay public school desegregation until "tempers had cooled." U.S. District Judge Harry Lemley responded by granting a thirty-month delay, the first break by a lower federal court with *Brown.* But the Court of Appeals for the Eighth Circuit reversed Lemley's ruling only two weeks before the scheduled opening of the Little Rock schools on September 2, 1958, and, at the same time, stayed its order for thirty days so that the Little Rock School Board could petition the U.S. Supreme Court for re-view. Heightening the tension, Governor Faubus called a special session of the state legislature for the express purpose of preparing a series of bills giving the governor power to close public schools facing integration and to transfer public school funds to private segregated schools.

"There was but one event that greatly disturbed us during my tenure," Earl Warren wrote in his memoirs, "and that was the Little Rock case which gave Governor Faubus the national spot-light." *Cooper v. Aaron,* the case challenging the Court's authority to desegregate the Little Rock public schools, captured the nation's attention because it represented an open flouting of the *Brown* mandate. But a controversy among the Justices in the case may have disturbed the Chief Justice as much as the constitutional issue.

At the center of the internal dispute were the Chief and Felix Frankfurter. By the time the Court had delivered its final word in *Cooper v. Aaron,* the relationship between Warren and Frankfurter, warm and mutually supportive only four years earlier in *Brown,* was in tatters. The dispute, moreover, engaged every other member of the Court and provoked Justices Hugo Black and William J. Brennan, Jr., a recent Eisenhower appointee, to rally to the Chief's side.

There had been no hint of disagreement between Warren and Frankfurter when the Court first heard argument on August 28 by the Little Rock School Board attempting to justify a two-and-a-half-year delay in desegregation of the city's schools. The Justices listened intently to the Board's attorney, Richard C. Butler, who, only minutes into his argument, uncovered the raw anger of the Chief Justice. Warren's explosion from the bench followed a statement by Butler "that if the governor of any state says that a United States Supreme Court decision is not the law of the land, the people of that state . . . have a doubt in their mind and a right to have a doubt."

"I have never heard such an argument made in a court of justice before," Warren shouted, "and I have tried many a case through many a year. I never heard a lawyer say that the statement of a governor as to what was legal or illegal should control the action of any court."

The Arkansas attorney, known for his courtly, calm courtroom demeanor, was visibly shaken by the Chief's attack. His plea for time "to work in a period of peace and harmony rather than turmoil and strife" did not satisfy an impatient Chief Justice.

"Can we defer a program of this kind," asked Warren, "because elements in a community will commit violence to prevent it from going into effect?"

"Mr. Chief Justice," Butler said, "you have been governor of a great state."

Warren interrupted, "But I have never tried to resolve any legal problem of this kind as governor of my state. I thought that that was a matter for the courts, and I abided by the decision of the courts."

Shortly after the oral argument, the Arkansas legislature, as expected, passed the bills enabling Governor Faubus to close the

state's public schools and use public funds to operate private segregated schools. The Little Rock School Board, however, refused
to bow to the pressure of the governor and legislature and postponed the opening of the Little Rock schools for two weeks. The
Board "is placed between the millstones," its attorney later told
the Court, "in a conflict between the state and the federal government."

To Frankfurter, the Little Rock School Board, and particularly its
attorney, Richard Butler, represented the best hope for the South
to obey the rule of law laid down by the Court in *Brown*. With its
postponement of the opening of the Little Rock public schools, the
Board, it seemed to Frankfurter, "showed a good deal of enterprise
and courage to stand up against Faubus and Company." Frankfurter thought the Court could help the Board and the larger cause
of desegregation in the South by recognizing the efforts of moderates like Butler. With this in mind, Frankfurter suggested to Warren
that he acknowledge the Board's "courageous" action just before
attorney Butler addressed the Court for his second oral argument
on September 11. "My own view has long been that the ultimate
hope for the peaceful solution of the basic problem largely depends
on winning the support of lawyers of the South for the overriding
issue of obedience to the Court's decision," he wrote Warren.
"Therefore, I think we should encourage every manifestation of
fine conduct by a lawyer like Butler."

Warren flatly rejected Frankfurter's suggestion, causing Frankfurter to complain about the Chief Justice's lack of statesmanship.
"Of course Faubus has been guilty of trickery," Frankfurter wrote
Associate Justice John M. Harlan, "but the trickery was as much
against the School Board as against us. And in any event the fight
is not between the Supreme Court and Faubus, though apparently
this is the way it lay in the C.J.'s mind. I am afraid his attitude
towards the kind of problems that confront us is more like that of
a fighting politician than that of a judicial statesman."

Less than four years after *Brown*, Frankfurter's view of Warren
had been transformed. No longer did the Chief possess "the
breadth of outlook" that Frankfurter had found so appealing earlier. He had become, in Frankfurter's mind, a rather simple-
minded, moralistic politician who was incapable of understanding
the subtle nuances of constitutional decision making. Frankfurter

found disturbing reinforcement for his revised opinion of the Chief Justice in the fact that Warren had begun to vote regularly with Justices Black, Douglas and Brennan to expand constitutionally protected individual rights. For his part, Warren suspected Frankfurter of attempting to subvert his authority on the Court; the Chief Justice forbade his clerks to speak to Frankfurter's clerks or to Frankfurter.

At the oral argument on September 11, Warren resumed his attack on the state of Arkansas's attempts to obstruct the orderly process of desegregation laid down in *Brown*. Wasn't it a fact, asked an angry Chief Justice, that the state had passed a constitutional amendment and other laws to frustrate the rights of black students? And if Arkansas, whether represented by the governor or legislature or the Little Rock School Board, was frustrating the rights of these children, the Chief had no doubt that the state was violating the U.S. Constitution.

Following oral argument, Warren called the Justices into conference and declared that they should reaffirm the Court of Appeals ruling; there could be no delay by the state of Arkansas in implementing the mandate of *Brown*. No one disagreed with the Chief Justice. "We knew the kind of opinion we wanted," Justice Brennan recalled. "I remember Justice Harlan saying that this was the biggest crisis in Court history, since we were told that governors and other courts were not bound by our decision."

Warren asked Justices Frankfurter and Harlan to write a brief, unsigned order supporting the appellate court ruling, and Justice Brennan was given the more difficult assignment of drafting the opinion explaining the reasoning of the Court. Before Brennan could begin a first draft, Governor Faubus signed into law the bills passed at the special session of the state legislature opposing *Brown* and declared that he was closing the Little Rock public schools.

Aware of the importance of a prompt Court response, Brennan worked quickly, circulating an eighteen-page draft opinion only six days after the Chief had given him the assignment. In the draft Brennan first laid out in meticulous factual detail the background of the case. His conclusion, however, was never in doubt. On behalf of the Court, he reasserted the authority, first declared by the great Chief Justice John Marshall in 1803, that it was the duty of the judiciary, and ultimately the U.S. Supreme Court, to serve as the final interpreter of the Constitution. *Brown* must be obeyed.

At the conference in which the Justices discussed the Brennan draft, Frankfurter proposed that each Justice sign the opinion as a further sign of the Court's unanimity. The Chief later recalled that conference:

> Mr. Justice Frankfurter called our attention to the fact that there had been a number of changes in the membership of the Court since *Brown v. Board of Education.* He suggested that in order to show we were all in favor of that decision, we should also say so in the Little Rock case, not in a per curiam or in an opinion signed by only one Justice, but by an opinion signed by the entire Court. I do not recall this ever having been done before. However, in light of the intense controversy over the issue and the great notoriety given Governor Faubus' obstructive conduct in the case, we thought well of the suggestion, and it was done.

Brennan returned to his chambers to rework his draft, having received many suggestions for changes from the other Justices. Justice Harlan, in particular, was troubled by both the language and organization of portions of the opinion and offered several pages of revisions, much of which Brennan politely rejected. Six days and three drafts later, Brennan circulated his opinion to his colleagues, which, in analysis and organization, did not differ radically from earlier versions. The tone, however, had acquired a dramatic urgency, as the result of a new opening paragraph contributed by Justice Black. It began:

> As this case reaches us it involves questions of the highest importance to the maintenance of our federal system of government. It squarely presents a claim by the Governor and Legislature of a State that there is no duty on state officials to obey federal orders resting on this Court's deliberate and considered interpretation of the United States Constitution. . . . We have concluded that these contentions call for clear answers here and now.

Frankfurter responded to the final Brennan draft enthusiastically. "Dear Bill," he wrote in the margin of the draft. "You have now made me content. Yours FF."

His contentment was short-lived. Even as he agreed to sign the Court opinion, freshly redrafted by Brennan, Frankfurter shocked his colleagues by announcing in conference that he would file a concurring opinion. The brethren were incredulous. Frankfurter, after all, had introduced the idea of a unanimous opinion in *Cooper v. Aaron* signed individually by the Justices. In fact, he had been the primary force behind the drive for unanimity in the school-desegregation cases dating back to 1950! And now it was the same Felix Frankfurter who willingly was breaking the tradition of unanimity in the school-desegregation cases that he, more than any other Justice, had established.

Frankfurter's explanation of his puzzling course seemed feeble to all but the Justice himself. He wanted to send a special message to the lawyers and law professors of the South, he later wrote, because that was "an audience which I was in a peculiarly qualified position to address in view of my rather extensive association, by virtue of my twenty-five years at the Harvard Law School, with a good many Southern lawyers and law professors."

Chief Justice Warren recalled that Frankfurter's action "caused quite a sensation" among the brethren. Brennan remembered the episode more pointedly. "Felix was a pariah around here for days," he said.

Warren was outraged, as were Brennan and Black, who drafted an opinion disassociating themselves from the Frankfurter concurrence and reiterating their support for the Court's opinion. Only a last minute tongue-in-cheek admonishment by Justice Harlan "that it is always a mistake to make a mountain out of a molehill" diffused the volatile situation. Frankfurter filed his concurrence, but Black and Brennan withdrew their separate opinion.

Brennan's anger and frustration were vented in the margins of a circulated draft of Frankfurter's concurrence. Frankfurter had written that "only the constructive use of time will achieve what an advanced civilization demands and the Constitution confirms." Amid his own exclamation points and question marks, Brennan scribbled, "Isn't this bound to be confusing to judges faced for the first time with applications against school boards? As an interpretation by the [an] author of the basic *Aaron* opinion, won't it be read as allowing them to take hostility into account?"

Frankfurter's estrangement from most of his colleagues was temporary. But that was not the case with Chief Justice Warren. The close working relationship between Warren and Frankfurter, apparent early in the Chief's tenure, had gradually become tenuous as the overbearing Frankfurter personality began to grate on the proud Warren. The two men split irrevocably with Frankfurter's concurrence in *Cooper v. Aaron.*

Throughout his life, Warren had broken ties with those whom he felt had betrayed or humiliated him. Once on his personal enemy list, there could be no reprieve. In the Chief's mind, Frankfurter's concurrence was a blatant attempt to undermine Warren's authority on the Court. It was an act of treachery, and unforgivable.

The damage to Frankfurter as a result of his concurrence in *Cooper v. Aaron* was severe. The judicial track that he had supported and, in large part, designed for the Court in the school desegregation cases had progressed in an orderly, if not always predictable, fashion. But suddenly Frankfurter, who had taken a leadership role in the progression, found himself isolated from his colleagues, and permanently alienated from the Chief Justice.

In the wake of the devastation, Hugo Black, who had assumed a far more modest profile in the desegregation cases than Frankfurter, enjoyed greater respect and authority than ever. He had contributed the key introductory paragraph to the Brennan opinion in *Cooper v. Aaron,* a paragraph that in characteristically taut, commanding language had warned Governor Faubus and the country that the Supreme Court's word on the unconstitutionality of school segregation was final.

Frankfurter's remaining years, both on the Court and after his retirement in 1962, were not happy ones for him so far as the direction of constitutional law was concerned. He watched Warren and Brennan join Black and Douglas to form a solid bloc that consistently voted for the constitutional expansion of civil rights and liberties. And with increasing success, the four attracted a fifth vote to their position. Slowly but unmistakably, the Court majority held both the federal government and the states to the highest standards of protection of individual rights and liberties in the nation's history. The egalitarian revolution of the Warren Court was launched, with Hugo Black serving as a principal intellectual architect and Earl Warren as spiritual leader. And Felix Frankfurter was left behind.

CHAPTER VIII

"Not a Razor Edge's Difference"

FELIX FRANKFURTER HAD ALWAYS treated his colleagues on the Court as if they were his students. And so it was natural for him to seize the special opportunity of tutoring one of his brethren who, in fact, had been his student at Harvard. He admitted that the prospect of sitting in judicial conference with his former student, William J. Brennan, Jr., was disconcerting, and seemed, in his mind, to accelerate the ineluctable aging process. But the benefits were equally attractive and Felix did not protest too much.

The courtship began with a small dinner party for Brennan given by Frankfurter. The host "bagged" Dean Acheson for the occasion and, to make the guest list complete, urged Judge Learned Hand to attend. "It would give Brennan the greatest possible kick and me an even greater pleasure to have you present," Frankfurter wrote Hand (who politely declined the invitation).

The party was a success as, indeed, were all off-the-Court relations between Frankfurter and Brennan. Felix became good friends with Brennan's young daughter, as well as with his wife, Marjorie. The professional relationship began well enough too, with Brennan openly receptive to instruction from his former professor. "I looked to Felix to help a novice get his feet wet," Brennan remembered. "And Felix went out of his way, but he did that for everybody. After a while, I realized it was not just out of kindness." Subtlety had never been the most brilliant hue on Frankfurter's palette of persuasive arts, and it was not long before Felix's kindness toward Brennan was accompanied by urgent lessons on the Court's business.

Frankfurter had lost Chief Justice Warren to the Black-Douglas wing of the Court and the prospect of a fourth vote for what he perceived as unbridled judicial activism greatly disturbed him. But he repeated the mistake that had so antagonized Warren—by patronizing his newest colleague. And Brennan, like the Chief before him, did not respond well to such treatment. "After I came on the Court I was treated as one of Felix's students—and not a favorite one either," Brennan recalled. Brennan was only slightly reassured by his observation that Frankfurter treated everyone on the Court in exactly the same way, even Hugo Black.

Frankfurter saw it differently, of course, and what was viewed as his overbearing nature by his colleagues was nothing less than a desperate fight with Hugo Black for the soul and future of the U.S. Supreme Court. In the late 1950s Frankfurter's philosophy of judicial restraint still commanded a majority in almost all civil liberties cases. Even when a Court majority reasserted itself on behalf of individual liberties in the wake of the McCarthy era, Frankfurter remained dominant as the Justice who carefully weighed the individual liberty at stake against the legitimate claims of the government in combating subversion. And so, when the Court finally chastised the House Un-American Activities Committee for trampling on the constitutional rights of witnesses, Frankfurter offered the moderating concurring opinion assuring the nation that HUAC's transgression was a matter of intemperate zeal, not flawed purpose.

The first successful challenge to HUAC's power arose after labor organizer John Watkins willingly testified about himself but refused to answer questions about past associates whom he did not believe were then members of the Communist party. Watkins was cited for contempt of Congress and challenged the committee's action by charging that the investigation served no public purpose, but was designed to expose individuals solely for the sake of exposure.

Chief Justice Warren wrote the opinion for the Court, excoriating the excesses of HUAC and other investigative committees that wandered far from any prescribed legislative purpose. Such wild excursions, the Chief warned, seriously jeopardized the individual freedoms protected by the First Amendment. Following the expansive sermon on the dangers of legislative abuses of civil liberties, the Chief chose to base his specific decision on the finer constitutional point that HUAC had not informed Watkins of the purpose of the investigation and, therefore, had deprived him of his due process rights.

Frankfurter was displeased with the broad dicta in the Chief's lecture on civil liberties and felt it necessary, in his concurrence, to emphasize that the Court had rested its decision on the very narrow grounds of due process. He left out all references to the larger libertarian matters that had dominated Warren's opinion.

In the 1950s Frankfurter continued his habit of assigning his colleagues to one of two professional stations, either a state of judicial grace or damnation. In the first category he placed those, like himself, who conducted their professional affairs as judges, committed by principle and pragmatism to the Court's limited role in the constitutional structure. Those in Frankfurter's second category, like Hugo Black, were labeled "politicians," bent on doing JUSTICE, whatever that meant (and Frankfurter did not know),* regardless of the sober lessons of judicial history. After two years on the Court, Brennan was relegated to Frankfurter's subterranean world of misguided Justices.

Brennan recalled that his votes in two decisions in his early years on the Court proved pivotal in Frankfurter's ultimate assessment of him. In the first, a right to counsel claim in an arson case, Brennan had initially voted with a tenuous five-man majority denying the claim. Later, he changed his vote, and thereby the majority, in favor of the individual liberty protection.

Frankfurter's displeasure with Brennan in the second decision also followed a decisive fifth vote by Brennan in support of a civil libertarian argument. The dispute arose in the case of Albert Trop, who, as a twenty-year-old army private stationed with American

---

* Frankfurter wrote Brennan, for example, that "I do not conceive that it is my function to decide cases on my notions of justice and, if it were, I wouldn't be as confident as some others are that I knew exactly what justice required in a particular case." On the other hand, Black was not embarrassed to use the word "justice." Describing the newly appointed Brennan to his son Hugo, Jr., Black wrote that, though Brennan had been a labor lawyer for business, there was no indication "that such lawyers do not have as much desire to do justice as lawyers that represent the labor unions themselves."

troops in French Morocco in 1944, had twice been thrown in the
stockade for breaches of military regulations. After Trop was re-
captured for the second time, a court martial convicted him of
desertion and sentenced him to three years of hard labor, forfeiture
of all pay and a dishonorable discharge. But that was not the worst
of it. Eight years later, Trop discovered, when his application for a
U.S. passport was denied, that he had been deprived of his status
as a U.S. citizen.

Trop challenged that final punishment as a violation of his constitutional rights of citizenship. A five-man majority of the Court,
including Brennan, supported Trop's claim. In dissent, Frankfurter
contended that the majority had created a constitutional right to
travel that could not be justified by history, precedent, logic or the
wording of the Constitution. "We [Frankfurter and Brennan] really
had a parting of the ways after that," said Brennan.

"When Felix didn't get his way, he was like a child," Brennan
recalled. "In his letters to friends like [Learned] Hand and [Charles]
Burlingham he would unburden his soul about those who didn't
agree with him. But his views were distorted. And yet right afterward, when we saw eye to eye, he believed we saw the light of
day."

Frankfurter's disappointment in Brennan, when he didn't see
"the light of day," was accompanied by condescending private
commentary. "I wish he [Brennan] was less shallow and thereby
less cock-sure," he wrote Justice John M. Harlan, "but his honesty
cheers me much and gives me considerable hope. To me it is a
constant puzzle why men like him can't read or rather reflect on
what they read."

In a very short time, Hugo Black's passionate advocacy had
drawn Brennan to his side. The difference between Black's and
Frankfurter's advocacy, according to Brennan, was not in the intensity of the arguments, but in their styles. "Hugo would sneer,
'How can you think *that?*' But he was usually brief, except in 5–4
votes when he could make quite a stump speech. More often than
not the speech was brief and to the point. Felix, on the other hand,
argued at a higher decibel level, running around in conference,
grabbing books off the shelves. He would go to Volume 360 [of
the U.S. Reports] and quote page and paragraph ad nauseam.

When he felt strongly about something, he could be a pain in the neck."

Frankfurter was significantly more successful in his proselytizing efforts with another new Court appointee in the mid-1950s, John M. Harlan. A graduate of Princeton and New York Law School, and a Rhodes Scholar, Harlan had earned an impeccable reputation for integrity and competence as a New York corporate lawyer. President Eisenhower had appointed Harlan to the U.S. Court of Appeals for the Second Circuit in 1954 and elevated him to the Supreme Court a year later. Almost immediately upon his appointment to the Court, Harlan, whose view of the Court's limited function mirrored Frankfurter's, joined Frankfurter in virtually all civil liberties cases. Harlan's opinions in those cases characteristically were written with lawyerly caution, always alert and usually sympathetic to the government's defense against an individual-liberty claim.

Once Frankfurter initiated a philosophical ally like Harlan into his club, privileges of membership included wide-ranging intellectual discourse. In one spirited exchange of letters, the two Justices debated the issue of whether Harlan's grandfather, Justice John M. Harlan (who served on the Court from 1877 to 1911), would have voted to strike down public school segregation as unconstitutional. Their debate was made intellectually tantalizing by the fact that Harlan the Elder, alone, had dissented in *Plessy v. Ferguson,* writing the memorable line that "our Constitution is color-blind." Frankfurter, however, argued that Harlan's "color-blind" dissent was narrowly confined to transportation facilities, not education, and did not presume to outlaw public school segregation. He maintained that another Court decision, in which Harlan had written the opinion for the majority, strongly suggested that he did not favor a declaration of school segregation's unconstitutionality. But Harlan the Younger adamantly stood his ground on behalf of his grandfather's anti-segregation position, citing the *Plessy* dissent as definitive proof of the validity of his argument.

Frankfurter, unfortunately, could descend to a distinctly lower depth in nurturing his friendship with Harlan, indulging in vituperative gossip about his less-favored colleagues. Frankfurter's all-time low in scurrility may have been reached in a letter to Harlan in

1958, complaining about Hugo Black's plan to attend the annual American Bar Association meeting:

> For members [of the Court] and their wives to go out there as guests of the Association—except a Justice who had an active share in the program—strikes me as a bit shabby. And the excuse that their presence will generate good will for the Court strikes me as reliance on fatuous notions. ... I almost puked when I heard Hugo say that if it would be good for the Court, he'll go. Gosh! For nearly twenty years I have heard his uniform condemnation of the A.B.A. and his contempt for their views. And now he puts on that noble act. The truth of course is, I have not a particle of doubt, that this will afford a pleasant trip for his young wife.* He is not the only old Benedick I know who is more eager to please his new bride than ever he was his first wife (Josephine Black was an uncommonly lovely person). I have little doubt that Hugo now believes it will help the Court, for he has infinite capacity—beyond anyone I've known—for self deception.

It is highly unlikely that Harlan responded to Frankfurter's unseemly personal attack on Black, and no written response is on record. By temperament, the steady, genteel Harlan seemed incapable of participating in such back-fence gossiping. Moreover, his personal relationship with Black was extremely close, even though Harlan and Black rarely agreed on issues before the Court. The Harlan-Black relationship was described by their colleague, Justice Brennan:

> There was a 180-degree difference between them on many constitutional issues. Their arguments provided some of my most delightful days on the bench. Harlan, patrician and low-key, would make his arguments without emotion. Hugo would come out ranting and raving.

---

* Black married his secretary, Elizabeth DeMeritte, forty-six years old and a grandmother, six years after the death of Josephine Black. By all informed accounts, the marriage was extremely successful. For a loving reminiscence of the marriage, see *Mr. Justice and Mrs. Black: The Memoirs of Hugo L. Black and Elizabeth Black*, Random House, 1986.

> And yet they had the deepest respect and affection for each other.

Harlan's friendship with Frankfurter was built primarily on the very different foundation of philosophical agreement. Their partnership in support of judicial restraint was crucially displayed in the late fifties at a time when the Court came under political attack. Conservative Senator William Jenner of Indiana denounced civil libertarian decisions (for example, *Watkins v. United States*) handed down "Red Monday after Red Monday." Reacting to the Court's decisions, Jenner and other rabid anti-Communist Senators introduced legislation that would have seriously curtailed the Court's constitutional power. The bills were narrowly defeated, and the restraining influence on the Court of Justices Frankfurter and Harlan in decisions like *Barenblatt v. U.S.* were credited with avoiding a potential constitutional crisis.

Lloyd Barenblatt had enrolled at the University of Michigan as a graduate student and teaching fellow shortly after World War II and later joined the faculty at Vassar College in the psychology department. During a hearing before a subcommittee of HUAC in 1954, a witness who had first refused to name those he believed to have been members of the Communist party "voluntarily" (after threat of prosecution) named names, including Barenblatt's. After he was summoned to appear before HUAC but before his actual appearance, Barenblatt learned that his teaching contract at Vassar would not be renewed. At the HUAC hearing Barenblatt refused to answer the Committee's questions about whether he had been a member of the Communist party. In refusing to respond to the Committee's questions, Barenblatt did not rely on the Fifth Amendment privilege against self-incrimination, but instead claimed a First Amendment protection of his political and religious beliefs and freedom of association. Following his declaration of constitutional protection, Barenblatt was convicted of contempt, fined and sentenced to six months in jail.

A Court majority, which included both Frankfurter and Harlan, sustained Barenblatt's conviction. In his opinion for the Court, Justice Harlan first recounted the extensive congressional history which, he wrote, supported a broad mandate for HUAC's investigations to protect the national security. Harlan then asserted that Congress's need to protect the nation from subversion through HUAC's hearings outweighed Barenblatt's civil liberties claim. "The provisions of the First Amendment," he concluded, "have not been offended."

Besides contributing a dissenting vote, Hugo Black wrote an uncompromising twenty-eight-page opinion attacking the position of his good friend John Harlan. For Black, Harlan's majority opinion presented a fanciful picture of HUAC's high-mindedness. The purpose of HUAC, he charged, was to punish suspected Communist witnesses "by humiliation and public shame." But worse than the majority's determination to find a constitutionally acceptable purpose in HUAC's witch-hunts, Black accused Harlan of the more serious error of failing to understand the intention of the author of the First Amendment, James Madison. Black then turned history professor, reminding his brethren that the framers had inserted no qualifying phrases in protecting freedom of speech, religion and association. "This [balancing] is closely akin to the notion that neither the First Amendment nor any other provision of the Bill of Rights would be enforced unless the Court believes it is *reasonable* to do so," Black declared. "Not only does this violate the genius of our *written* Constitution but it runs expressly counter to the injunction to Court and Congress made by Madison when he introduced the Bill of Rights."

Frankfurter had long suspected that Black's First Amendment "absolute" argument had been inspired less by scholarly conviction than by rhetorical strategy. But in this assessment, as in many others, Frankfurter badly underestimated the depth of Black's constitutional creed. Shortly after he wrote his dissenting opinion in *Barenblatt,* Black accepted an invitation from the New York University School of Law to deliver the first James Madison Lecture, using the occasion to expound on his views of the Bill of Rights and pointedly to attack the "balancing" jurisprudence of Felix Frankfurter and John Harlan.

Black had first expressed an interest in speaking at NYU after he had heard that the Law School planned a course on the Bill of Rights. "For many years I have thought that law schools should emphasize courses in this field," Black wrote NYU Law Professor Edmund Cahn. "The fact that your school proposes to inaugurate such a course is, therefore, of great importance to me." Black's desire to speak publicly about the Bill of Rights intensified after *Barenblatt,* and the Madison Lecture provided the perfect forum.

The primary sources for Black's NYU lecture, appropriately enough, were the writings of James Madison. But he also wrote out in longhand on two pages of a yellow legal pad a list of quotations from the decisions of Justices Frankfurter and Harlan. And in his lecture, Black presented the "balancing" decision of hypothetical "Judge X," but did not make a great effort to disguise whom he had in mind.

What is a Bill of Rights? Black asked early in his Madison Lecture on February 17, 1960. It was, he answered, a document to protect the liberties of the people. "Some people regard the prohibitions of the Constitution, even its most unequivocal commands, as mere admonitions which Congress need not always observe," he said. Returning to the theme he had first articulated in *Bridges v. California* nineteen years earlier, Black emphatically rejected the Frankfurter-Harlan approach, which, he noted, was based on the English model of parliamentary supremacy. "The whole history and background of our Constitution and Bill of Rights, as I understand it, belies the assumption or conclusion that our ultimate constitutional freedoms are no more than our English ancestors had when they came to this new land to get new freedoms," he said.

To illustrate the threat to civil liberties posed by a judicial balancing approach, Justice Black offered a "practical demonstration." Suppose the United States were faced with a great national emergency, Black hypothesized, and that Congress passed a law allowing the government to seize land for the national defense without paying just compensation to the landowners, guaranteed by the Fifth Amendment to the Constitution. Black's Judge X balanced the two interests and had no difficulty finding in favor of the government. "Weighing as I must the loss the individual will suffer because he has to surrender his land to the nation without compensation against the great public interest in conducting war," Judge X concluded, "I hold the act valid."

In times of crisis, the government will always find it necessary to protect itself, Black warned, regardless of the rights of individuals. And if balancing proved an acceptable judicial test, Black had no doubt that even the most conscientious judge would reject the claim of individual liberty in a time of national emergency. For Black, the solution had been written in 1791: "Where conflicting values exist in the field of individual liberties protected by the Constitution, that document settles the conflict."

Felix Frankfurter never responded to the challenge in Black's Madison Lecture, but his former clerk and protégé, Yale Professor Alexander Bickel, willingly served as his surrogate. In an article in *The New Republic* written shortly after the lecture, Bickel attacked Black's "absolute" theory, suggesting that its author suffered from either ignorance, naïveté or a woeful misunderstanding of constitutional history.

Bickel's criticism provoked his fellow Yale Law professor, Fred Rodell, to dash off a savage rejoinder denouncing Bickel's failure to disclose his close association with Black's behind-the-scenes antagonist, Frankfurter, and his disparaging treatment of Black's position. "Yours [Bickel's] was a sniper's attack," wrote Rodell. "Yours was a small boy's yah-yah technique, aimed at picking out little flaws of logic or language to poke fun at—as though you could thus make Black's position untenable and rationally disreputable." *The New Republic* refused to publish the Rodell letter, which did not surprise either Rodell or Justice Black (who had been sent a copy of the letter by the author).

But if Rodell had hoped to receive praise from Black for his attack on Bickel (and Frankfurter), he was disappointed. Black thanked Rodell for sending him a copy of his letter to *The New Republic* but made no comment on its contents. "I must confess to you that Professor Bickel's article has not tended to give me apoplexy or anything like that," he wrote Rodell. "If my memory serves me correctly, I have previously been attacked by men of equal importance to the Professor."

Black's outward calm sometimes hid a private rage over what he considered to be dangerous views on the Constitution. After a book by legal historian Leonard Levy offering a new interpretation of the First Amendment was published in 1960, Black came very close to suffering the apoplexy that he had assured Rodell had not afflicted him in reading the Bickel article. In his book *Legacy of Suppression,* Levy argued that the framers, including Thomas Jefferson, had not intended to prohibit all government impingement on speech at the time of ratification of the Bill of Rights. To support his thesis, Levy wrote that suppression of political speech occurred at the time of the adoption of the Bill of Rights and for years afterward. He contended that Jefferson only slowly came to embrace a libertarian creed as his own and did so only after successful prosecutions under the Alien and Sedition Act punished members of his own Jeffersonian Republican party. Suppression and persecution were the precursors to liberty, Levy concluded, a historical thesis that did not thrill Justice Hugo Black.

Black's displeasure was heightened by a favorable review of the Levy book in the *New York Herald-Tribune* by his friend NYU Professor Edmund Cahn. Cahn, who admired Black and generally shared his libertarian views, praised the Levy book for "the sheer excellence and profundity of his research," though the reviewer did not agree with all of Levy's interpretations. That Cahn would give even a qualified endorsement to a book that questioned the commitment of the framers to the absolute protections of the First Amendment bordered on the subversive in Black's mind.

Three days after the Cahn review was published, Black drafted a heated letter to Cahn declaring that "my opinion is that this book strikes one of the most devastating blows ever directed against civil liberty in America." If an accepted history of the First Amendment concluded that the government could punish for seditious libel at the time the Bill of Rights was ratified, Black reasoned, then "martyrs to the cause of civil and religious liberty could be sent to jail in this country today precisely as they were in England." His basic disagreement with Levy, Black wrote, "is that I think the First Amendment was intended to give us a legacy of liberty and not, as he says, a legacy of suppression."

Black softened the tone of the letter to Cahn in a second draft but retained the original premise. "The book, I think, will give aid and comfort to every person in the country who desires to leave Congress and the states free to punish people under the old English seditious libel label," he wrote Cahn. He concluded that the First Amendment was adopted to bar such prosecutions "then and thereafter."

In a later exchange of letters, the two men drew closer to each other, with Cahn contending that Levy was a "sincere but mistaken" libertarian and Black expressing his regret that Levy did not have the good sense to seek Cahn's advice before he published his book. Black continued to insist that the acceptance of the Levy thesis supplied dangerous ammunition to those who searched for excuses to qualify the Bill of Rights protections. He meant what he said in *Barenblatt* and in his Madison Lecture, and those on the Court and off wasted their time in straining to discover a moderating thesis from Hugo Black.

One of the most astute observers of the modern U.S. Supreme Court, Professor Paul Freund of Harvard, credited Justice Hugo Black's ultimate success on the Court to "brains, rectitude, singleness of purpose and time." By the early 1960s there was ample evidence to support Freund's statement. For Justice Black had, in the quarter-century of his service on the Court, seen much of his original jurisprudence become a permanent part of our constitutional literature. Neither his "absolute" theory of the First Amendment protections nor his "incorporation" of the Bill of Rights making them applicable to the states under the Fourteenth Amendment was ever accepted whole by the brethren, but the intellectual force and vehemence of his argument moved the majority unmistakably in his direction. He was, indisputably, a seminal influence in the Warren Court Revolution, which expanded individual rights and liberties to unprecedented levels of protection.

Two Court decisions in the early sixties, *Mapp v. Ohio* and *Baker v. Carr*, demonstrated the powerful influence that Black maintained with his colleagues. Ironically, Black did not write the majority opinion in either case. The decisions could not have been written, however, without the intellectual contributions of Hugo Black, who had provided the theoretical underpinnings in two of his earlier dissents. In both of the earlier Court decisions in which Black dissented, Felix Frankfurter had furnished the majority with the scholarly foundation for their conclusions. The arguments came full circle by the early sixties, and Frankfurter found himself on the losing side in both cases.

Dolree Mapp seemed an unlikely champion for civil liberties. Police had confiscated obscene material in her Cleveland apartment in a raid that Mapp claimed violated her due process rights under the Fourteenth Amendment. The Supreme Court's majority opinion, written by Justice Tom Clark, reached beyond Mapp's specific claim and delivered a victory for the Cleveland woman that resonated with civil liberties consequences for law enforcement authorities in all fifty states. For the majority expressly declared that the states must uphold the guarantees of the Fourth Amendment of the Bill of Rights, as incorporated through the Fourteenth Amendment. With the announcement, the Court unceremoniously overruled Frankfurter's earlier majority opinion which had clung to the venerable constitutional theory that the Fourteenth Amendment's due process clause contained all the authority necessary to strike down state conduct that was fundamentally unfair.

The majority in *Mapp* did not exactly celebrate the triumph of Black's incorporation theory since the Justices refused to accept Black's premise, first fully articulated in his 1946 *Adamson* dissent, that all of the Bill of Rights applied to the states through the Fourteenth Amendment. But the decision added the explicit guarantees in another amendment—the Fourth—to the growing number in the first nine amendments to the Constitution that now applied to the states. In a concurrence, Black suggested that the express guarantees of the Fourth and Fifth Amendments should have been the basis for the Court's decision, but this protest was not registered with the stridency of his original *Adamson* dissent. He knew that time and *Mapp* were on his side in his marathon constitutional argument with Frankfurter.

An even more shattering defeat for Frankfurter followed quickly on the heels of *Mapp* in the reapportionment case of *Baker v. Carr.* In *Baker,* the Justices were confronted with the politically sensitive issue of whether or not the courts should intervene to correct the distortions in representation in Tennessee's malapportioned state legislature. No one seriously disputed the fact that Tennessee's rural voters had benefited at the expense of the state's urban residents in their representation in the state legislature. Dominated by representatives of those rural voters, the state legislature had not hurried to reapportion to reflect the increasingly urban population in the state, even though the state constitution required it. Should the judiciary do the job that the elected representatives refused to do?

The Court's first answer, given in *Colegrove v. Green* in 1946,[*] was an emphatic no. Six Justices, led by Frankfurter, declared that the political business of reapportionment was for the politicians. By entering the "political thicket," Frankfurter warned, the Court risked political reprisals that could ultimately undercut its institutional authority. In his *Colegrove* dissent, Justice Black had expressed dismay over the Court's preoccupation with political considerations rather than its paramount responsibility (in his view) of determining whether legislative reapportionment violated the Constitution of the United States.

When the Justices took another look at the issue fifteen years later in *Baker v. Carr,* Black's prospects for winning a majority for his position appeared considerably better. The four Justices commonly considered the activists on the Warren Court—Black, Douglas, Warren and Brennan—supported Black's view. Frankfurter led the opposition to that view, as he had in *Colegrove,* but this time could count only four tentative votes (Harlan and Clark were firmly behind Frankfurter, and Charles Whittaker was leaning his way) in conference for his position that Court intervention would have disastrous institutional consequences. Justice Potter Stewart alone appeared genuinely undecided on the merits and made the request, quickly acceded to by the other Justices, that the case be put over for reargument on the Court's 1961 fall docket.

When Stewart had been appointed to the Court in 1958, he seemed to be the perfect candidate for the Frankfurter School of Judicial Restraint. Although he had graduated with honors from the Yale Law School, not Harvard, Stewart's background and record exhibited a modest but pervasive conservatism in all matters political and judicial.

A descendant of William Howard Taft and an active Republican in his home city of Cincinnati, Stewart carried his cautious views of the role of government from the Cincinnati City Council to the Sixth Circuit Court of Appeals. As a federal appeals court judge,

---

[*] *Colegrove* challenged, in the federal context, the malapportionment in Illinois's system of electing representatives to the U.S. House of Representatives.

Stewart earned a reputation as a centrist on most civil liberties issues, rarely drifting far from established precedents.

Once on the Supreme Court, Stewart's friendship and vote were carefully cultivated by both Black and Frankfurter. Stewart recalled the competition and the competitors:

> I was courted by both of them. Felix was more obvious about it but Hugo also engaged in it with memos and conversations. Felix was so unsubtle and obvious that it was counterproductive. He was the scholar who knew everything about everything. Hugo didn't impress me that way. He was largely self-taught and an old-fashioned populist who acted like a young fellow just appointed to the Court—until the end of his life.

Frankfurter had favorably assessed the talents of the new recruit, Stewart, shortly after Stewart's appointment to the Court. "I shall only say about the new man Stewart that on the meager showing to date, I should be much surprised if he does not turn out to be a judge," he wrote Judge Learned Hand. "I entertain a further hope about him," Frankfurter added. "I do not believe that he will convince himself that the mere fact that he sits on this bench calls for arrogant confidence in his own wisdom and learning."

Two years later Frankfurter held to his original opinion of Stewart, though he was not prepared to offer his definitive judgment. "I have every expectation that he will turn out to be a judge, i.e., not 'result-oriented,' " he wrote Hand. "I also think, however, that he is concerned how he appears to the world outside and, more particularly, he doesn't want to appear to be hung up with John [Harlan] and me."

Frankfurter had good reason to approve of Stewart's early judicial record, since Stewart regularly chose Frankfurter's path of judicial restraint. Frankfurter could therefore be optimistic about his chances of persuading Stewart to join him in *Baker v. Carr* in resisting the temptation, dangled by the Court's activists, of imposing judicial solutions to untidy political problems. Frankfurter bluntly told Stewart (and Charles Whittaker) in a letter that their votes in the reapportionment case would decide the most important case to come to the Court during Frankfurter's entire twenty-two years as a Justice, and that included *Brown v. Board of Education.* To Frankfurter, only one responsible course of action was available: "I believe that what we are being asked to do in this case," he wrote, "threatens the preservation of the independence of the Court."

But, alas, Stewart was unmoved by Frankfurter's plea for restraint. After the second argument in *Baker,* he joined the four activists in support of the view that the reapportionment issue was open to judicial resolution. Mindful that Stewart's vote was essential to the majority and that his conviction was less resolute than the four others, Chief Justice Warren assigned the majority opinion to Brennan with the implicit understanding that he must make the opinion acceptable to Stewart.

Meanwhile, Frankfurter acted as if *Baker v. Carr* were his Armageddon. "Felix fought a rearguard action," Brennan recalled. "My, how he fought. He really felt this was going to be a self-inflicted wound.* I never could figure out why he felt so strongly on this issue."

In writing the majority opinion, Brennan did not spare Frankfurter's feelings or avoid the tough issues that Frankfurter had raised. When he circulated his draft opinion in *Baker v. Carr,* Brennan attached a memorandum for three of his colleagues in the majority (Black, Warren and Douglas), informing them that Stewart was "entirely satisfied" with the opinion. He added that his lengthy draft opinion was inspired, in part, by a desire to respond to Frankfurter's long-standing objections to the position the majority was taking. "I should say further that, after much thought, I believe that the full discussion of the 'political question,' and its bearing on apportionment suits, is required if we are effectively and finally to dispel the fog of another day produced by Felix's opinion in *Colegrove v. Green.*" True to his word, Brennan wrote an exhaustive, scholarly treatise on the "political question" doctrine in constitutional law, concluding that the Court possessed under the Fourteenth Amendment both the authority and responsibility to decide if a malapportioned state legislature violated the equal protection rights of disenfranchised voters.

---

* The phrase was first used by Charles Evans Hughes to describe Court decisions, like *Dred Scott,* that diminished the prestige and authority of the Court.

By the winter of 1962, Frankfurter was eighty-two years old, and his health was faltering. Consequently he relied heavily on the drafting skills of his law clerk, Anthony Amsterdam, for much of his opinion in *Baker v. Carr.* But the emotionally charged message was Frankfurter's own. "[T]here is not under our constitution a judicial remedy for every political mischief," he wrote. "In a democratic society like ours, relief must come through an aroused popular conscience of the people's representatives."

His dissent was the public wail of a judge who felt the heavy blow of collegial rejection. Expressing his despair in private to Harlan, he wrote:

> What power fully emerged for me this afternoon is that men who so readily impose their will on the nation and the 50 states by exultingly overruling their most distinguished predecessors behave like subservient children when lectured by a martinet with a papa-knows-best [illegible]. . . . At the core of the sad performance was—is— a failure to appreciate the intrinsic and acquired majesty of the Court's significance in the affairs of this country and of the correlative responsibility of every member of the Court to maintain and further this significance. Why do I bother you with this? I suppose to prove the truth of a German saying that when the heart is full, it spills over on you—who alone gives me comfort.

Later that month, Frankfurter suffered a severe stroke and never returned to active service on the Court.

An ailing Felix Frankfurter agreed to conduct his final tutorial for the benefit of the President of the United States, John F. Kennedy, who would be the fourth President Frankfurter had so advised during his lifetime. The meeting occurred at 5 P.M. on July 26, 1962, three months after the disabling stroke had ravaged the left side of Frankfurter's body and left him in a semi-invalid state. Accompanied by Dean Acheson, the President was received in the drawing room of Frankfurter's home.

Kennedy had requested the meeting, whose historical significance was not lost on the participants. Almost thirty years earlier, another Democratic President of the United States had been escorted into the home of another Harvard Law graduate who had completed a long and distinguished career on the U.S. Supreme Court. The earlier meeting had been arranged by Professor Felix Frankfurter so that his friend, President Franklin D. Roosevelt, could be introduced to his mentor, Justice Oliver Wendell Holmes, Jr. This time the former Secretary of State, Dean Acheson, assumed Frankfurter's earlier role as intermediary, but stepped unobtrusively into the background as Kennedy and Frankfurter engaged in intense conversation—did Frankfurter know any other?—about the responsibilities of leadership in the White House. Naturally, Frankfurter did most of the talking.

During his recent hospital stay, Frankfurter told the President, he had conducted a series of impromptu seminars on the presidency with nurses, orderlies, attendants and doctors. Regrettably, he reported to JFK, he was not reassured by the results. There seemed to be a breakdown in communication between the President and the people who had chosen him to lead. Like FDR, Frankfurter told the President, Kennedy faced the challenge of educating the electorate about the fundamental purposes of the American democracy. Roosevelt had understood his role as national teacher and Frankfurter urged Kennedy to follow his example.

The President gently raised an objection to Frankfurter's analogy. The nation's problems during the Depression of FDR's administration were immediately recognizable to the American people, and Roosevelt's solutions, whether the voters agreed with them or not, could be understood by them. His own challenge was greater, Kennedy told Frankfurter, because the federal government was far more complicated and less comprehensible to the American people in 1962 than it had been in 1932. The Kennedy administration's legislative initiatives in the field of agricultural policy, for example, were not as simple in conception or result as in Roosevelt's time. In other areas, such as trade and finance, Kennedy told Frankfurter, his challenge in communicating with the business community was even more formidable, since he had to deal with "powerful people willfully trying to add confusion to complexity."

Frankfurter listened intently as the President vented his frustrations. Then the man who had served Franklin Roosevelt loyally for the entire thirteen years of his presidency advised Kennedy to lower his expectations, at least as far as the business community was concerned. No Democratic President would ever win the support of the business community—if he was doing his job properly —Frankfurter declared. The Justice then provided his reasons for that startling statement. Nearly all of the purposes that a Democratic President was trying to achieve—taking funds, goods and people and directing them to productive ends—transcended economic values, and those larger goals fell outside the experience of most American businessmen. A strong Democratic President was likely to mold American life in ways which seemed alien, if not frightening, to businessmen, Frankfurter concluded. As Frankfurter spoke, Kennedy listened very attentively and sympathetically to his observations.

After tea was served, Frankfurter offered Kennedy a few thoughts on great Presidents. He named Jefferson, Jackson, Lincoln and the two Roosevelts, Theodore and Franklin—and urged the President to emulate them in conceiving the broad nature of his office. Just as it appeared that the conversation might extend far into the evening, a presidential aide reminded Kennedy that his extended meeting with Frankfurter had put him far behind in his appointments schedule. As Kennedy rose, Frankfurter told him that the visit had not only been a great honor but also a great pleasure. Equally pleased with the meeting, Kennedy replied that he hoped to return to the Frankfurter residence for another visit later in the summer.

In early August, only two months before the start of the 1962 Court term, Frankfurter still nurtured hopes of returning to the bench. With this purpose in mind, he began reading petitions of certiorari addressed to the Court. For pleasure he sometimes was driven to friends' houses for short visits. One August day Frankfurter's driver pulled to the curb in front of the two-story red brick house at 200 South Lee Street in Alexandria, Virginia, the residence of Justice and Mrs. Hugo Black. Aware that Frankfurter was physically incapable of leaving the automobile, Black greeted his old colleague at the curb, then squeezed next to him in the back seat of the automobile.

The conversation flowed easily for more than half an hour, although Black found it painful to see the once vibrant and buoyant Frankfurter in his semi-helpless condition. The two Justices covered a wide range of subjects, ending with Frankfurter's inquiries about the three Black children, now grown. Tell Hugo, Jr., Sterling and Jo-Jo that I think of them often, Frankfurter said, and that I continue to have a great interest in them. "I am certain," Black wrote Hugo, Jr., after the visit, "from what he said when he was here and what he has told me many times before that he does have an affection for all three of you." (During Frankfurter's final illness, Black took his daughter, Jo-Jo, to the hospital for what Jo-Jo described as a "very moving" experience.)

On August 28, 1962, Frankfurter sent a letter to the President formally retiring from the Court that he had served for twenty-three years and seven months. The will to remain on the Court was still there, but, Frankfurter acknowledged, the hazards of therapy made a full judicial work schedule impossible. "To retain my seat on the basis of a diminished work schedule would not comport with my own philosophy or with the demands of the business of the Court," he wrote President Kennedy. "I need hardly tell you, Mr. President, of the reluctance with which I leave the institution whose concerns have been the absorbing interest of my life."

Frankfurter had begun thinking about suitable new appointees to the Court long before his own retirement. After Kennedy's victories in the 1960 Democratic primaries, Frankfurter had apparently entertained high hopes that the man who would be President would look to his alma mater for the next appointment to the U.S. Supreme Court. According to Justice Douglas, word had spread that there was a strong push for Harvard Law Professor Paul Freund: "The scuttlebutt is that Harvard Law School was and is all-out for Kennedy. Their propaganda machine is lead [sic] by Lewis [Anthony Lewis, who had been a Nieman Fellow at the Harvard Law School, then covered the Court for *The New York Times*]. They apparently think they have a deal that Paul Freund will be named to the first Court vacancy!"

But when Associate Justice Charles Whittaker resigned after five exhausting years on the Court, the President and his brother, Attorney General Robert Kennedy, showed that they did not share Frankfurter's overriding interest that the nominee be schooled, preferably at Harvard, in the philosophy of judicial restraint. The nomination went to Deputy Attorney General Byron White, a Yale

Law graduate who had rendered outstanding service to Kennedy in the 1960 election campaign and later as an important civil rights strategist in Kennedy's Justice Department.

In the fall of 1962, when his own replacement was contemplated, Frankfurter more than ever wanted the President to name a proponent of judicial restraint as his successor to the so-called scholar's seat. But Frankfurter was disappointed a second time, when Kennedy appointed his Secretary of Labor, Arthur Goldberg.

Frankfurter never expressed his disappointment in the two Kennedy Court appointments publicly but he did not hide his displeasure with White and Goldberg in the privacy of his correspondence with Alexander Bickel. Neither White nor Goldberg, he complained, possessed the requisite professional background as practitioner, scholar or judge to understand his proper role on the Court. He termed the work product of the new majority "shoddy" and urged Bickel and other law professors to criticize the Court's decisions. "I can assure you that explicit analysis and criticism of the way the Court is doing business really gets under their skins," Frankfurter wrote Bickel, "just as praise by their constituencies, the so-called liberal journals and well-known liberal approvers only fortifies them in their present result-oriented jurisprudence. . . ."

Bickel needed no urging from his mentor, having already begun to pepper his commentaries in *The New Republic* with acerbic attacks on the judicial product of the new Court majority. The Court's decisions expanding individual rights were criticized by Bickel as ill-conceived, poorly reasoned and result-oriented breaks with the constitutional past.

Praise from Frankfurter quickly followed. "Your piece in the N.R.," he wrote Bickel, "goes to the core of the merits of the reprehensible decisions of the Court and yet it is only another way of expounding the central mischief, namely, if you begin with a conclusion it most probably will come out a conclusion." It was the old story, retold another time by Frankfurter, that no one on the Court seemed to measure up to his standards.

Oddly enough, the Justice most responsible for the accelerated libertarian direction of the Court, Hugo Black, was largely spared Frankfurter's vitriolic pen. The opprobrium, instead, was primarily focused on Douglas, Warren and Brennan—with an added dash of disdain for Goldberg, who had joined the new majority with unmitigated enthusiasm and was labeled by a disgusted Frankfurter as "Goldberg, the scholar."

Frankfurter appeared to have entered a new era of exceptionally good feeling toward Black, documented in his last years with highly complimentary letters to his former nemesis. He praised Black's work and character and assured him that the two had never had serious disagreements. Black accepted Frankfurter's insistence on their eternal harmony good-naturedly. "He really believes *that*," Black told his wife, Elizabeth.

Frankfurter began one letter with an effusive (even for him) paean to Black. "So perceptive a person as you," he wrote, "need not be told in words of the attitude and feelings of another man who enjoyed the intimacy which you and I formed in our joint labors, particularly during the happy years during which I sat next to you on the bench, and it is needless I am sure for me to assure you that the impulse which makes me feel free to write to you as I am about to do, is my regard and esteem for you." That personal tribute was followed, predictably, by some serious judicial advice on how Black might better do his job.

With increasing apprehension, Frankfurter told Black, he had been reading about the "sit-down" civil rights demonstrations in the South and knew that Black and his colleagues would ultimately decide their constitutionality. No one could question his or Black's record on civil rights and, he assured Black, that he would not retreat "one millimeter" from *Brown* and *Cooper v. Aaron*. There was not, he asserted, a "razor edge's difference between the way you feel and the way I feel" on civil liberties, most particularly in the field of racial discrimination. Black would agree with him, Frankfurter was certain, that the Court should always strike down acts of official racism that were covered by the due process and equal protection clauses of the Constitution.

But civil rights demonstrations on private property presented an entirely different issue for the Court, Frankfurter contended, than had been raised in the school segregation cases. Black himself, he remembered, had on two occasions in judicial conference told the brethren that he would never consent to any Court decision compelling a person to do private business with someone he did not want to, unless state or federal funds had been used in the business or violations of procedural due process rights were involved.

"Even a few words of moderation along the lines I have tried to recall would have a powerful educative effect not only on the Negroes but also on Whites," Frankfurter wrote. "You could of course include an expression of your credo on the subject of racism, but were you also to add a moderating note it would be one of the greatest services you could render the Nation and the Court."

Frankfurter had to wait a year and a half for Black's formal response but, when it came, he was entirely satisfied. For Black, while continuing to support every Court decision enforcing *Brown* as well as others upholding black protesters' procedural rights, balked at extending the Constitution's protection to civil rights protesters' demonstrations on private property. In a memorable— and to many Black admirers, shocking—departure from the Court majority, Black spoke in dissent for the exact proposition that Frankfurter had urged upon him. The trespass convictions of civil rights demonstrators attempting to coerce a private restaurant to serve them should have been sustained, Black wrote in dissent. He contended that "none of our prior cases has held that a person's right to freedom of expression carries with it a right to force a private property owner to furnish his property as a platform to criticize the property owner's use of that property."

Frankfurter could not have been prouder of Black's dissent if it had been the work of one of his brightest Harvard Law students. "I am not even surprised, my dear Hugo," he wrote, "for while I was still active around the table, my ear was active, and I took in every word you said the first time the 'sit-in' problem came before the Conference." Frankfurter, nonetheless, wanted to express to Black his "great respect" for the dissent "and the powerful way in which you said it."

After Frankfurter's retirement, Black had graciously indulged him in his rosy, and selective, memories of their Court relations. Black had long ago learned the value of muting acrimony toward colleagues and former colleagues, and accentuating their good qualities. It had made for more effective advocacy in the conference room and would later make for more agreeable judicial history. His sensitivity also reflected his strong character and basic decency.

His letter responding to Frankfurter's praise of his trespass dissent matched Felix's in felicitous goodwill:

> Dear Felix,
>
> It was good to get your letter of December 15th which my office forwarded to me here [in Coral Gables, Florida]. Your agreement with the dissenting views I expressed in the "sit-in" cases was not surprising. More than a quarter of century's close association between us in the Supreme Court's exacting intellectual activities has enabled both of us, I suspect, to anticipate with reasonable accuracy the basic position both are likely to take on questions that importantly involve the public welfare and tranquility. Our differences, which have been many, have rarely been over the ultimate end desired, but rather have related to the means that were most likely to achieve the end we both envisioned. Our years together, and these differences, have but added to the respect and admiration that I had for *Professor* Frankfurter even before I knew him— his love of country, steadfast devotion to what he believed to be right, and to his wisdom. Feeling this way you can understand what I mean by saying to you it "was good to get your letter." Elizabeth joins me in sending our affectionate good wishes to you and Marion for a happy Christmas and New Year. You and she are the kind of people with the kind of wisdom who can be happy despite age and its infirmities.
>
> Sincerely your friend,
> Hugo

Shortly after Frankfurter's health had forced his retirement from the Court, Black made it a point to tell him that "we're going to miss you on the Court because we need you." He had added, "When some of my friends say to me, 'things will be easier on the Court now,' I tell them they couldn't be more wrong." With that statement, Black had paid Frankfurter the highest compliment. But there was more to the statement than sympathetic flattery of an old colleague in failing health. Black's core message was, in fact, true. The Court and the nation were stronger because Black and Frankfurter had served *together*.

Black's and Frankfurter's open challenges to each other often pushed them to their best and most impassioned advocacy. Black's first comprehensive opinion on the preferred place of First Amendment freedoms in the Constitution, for example, came after Frankfurter had insisted that the Court should look to Great Britain for its free speech model. Absolutely not, said Black in his *Bridges* opinion, claiming that the First Amendment was an essential made-in-America doctrine. Later, after Frankfurter had tried for several years to dissuade him, Black produced his ambitious *Adamson* opinion, arguing that the Bill of Rights applied, jot for jot, to the states under his reading of the Fourteenth Amendment. Frankfurter vigorously argued the negative side of that proposition and continued to dispute Black's historical interpretation for his remaining years on the Court.

Their vociferous disagreements sometimes diverted attention (even their own) from the many issues on which they agreed. For most of their professional lives both Black and Frankfurter were forceful advocates for individual rights; they disagreed, as members of the Court, on how these rights were to be protected. As attorneys, both Black and Frankfurter took strong public stands on behalf of the lowliest defendants within our justice system; their differences on the Court focused on the correct interpretation of the Constitution that would preserve those defendants' rights. Each man embraced Jefferson's doctrine of a wall of separation between church and state. Both were repulsed by the political repressions during the McCarthy era, though each offered his own opinions on what should have been done—and by whom. And both Black and Frankfurter believed that black Americans must, finally, be given first-class citizenship, each accepting the equal protection clause of the Fourteenth Amendment as the judicial instrument of change.

There was considerably more than "a razor edge's difference" between the two Justices, and volumes of Supreme Court opinions and Frankfurter's many private agitations are testimony to those differences. In conference Frankfurter could be infuriating, but he was rarely irrelevant. His judicial contribution, like Black's, was vitally important to the development of the jurisprudence of individual rights on the modern Supreme Court. The expansion of civil liberties and, particularly, First Amendment rights was firmly established in our constitutional literature because of Hugo Black.

But the limits of judicial authority were better understood and more fully appreciated because of the opinions of Felix Frankfurter. In the end, both Black and Frankfurter served as the nation's constitutional guardians, bound together by the recognition that they shared an absolute faith in America's democratic institutions and the individual freedoms those institutions protect.

Frankfurter's personal bitterness toward Black during their tumultuous times together on the Court spilled out in page after page of his diaries and correspondence. But even as he wrote vituperatively about Black's motives and conduct, Frankfurter functioned on a second, higher level. He invited Black to private luncheons for visiting dignitaries and showed kindly attention to Josephine Black and the three Black children. After Josephine's death, Frankfurter sensed Hugo's vulnerability and tried to comfort him. In Frankfurter's last, painful years, Black responded with equal warmth and sensitivity, treating Frankfurter with the affection reserved for an intimate friend.

During the Court's winter break in February 1965, Hugo and Elizabeth Black visited Hugo Black, Jr., and his family in Miami. Afterward, Justice Black and his wife began the drive north toward Washington, D.C., stopping for breakfast in St. Augustine, Florida. At the breakfast table Hugo opened the morning's newspaper and gasped at the headline: "Ohhh, Felix is dead!" And then he wept.

Source Notes

The source notes are, for the most part, self-explanatory. I have used acronyms to identify frequently used sources. Felix Frankfurter's papers at the Library of Congress are cited as FFPLC. U.S. Supreme Court decisions and law review articles follow legal methods of citation: *West Virginia Bd. of Education v. Barnette*, 319 U.S. 624 (1943), means that the Supreme Court decided the case in 1943 and that the opinions begin at page 624 of volume 319 of the *United States Reports*, the official volumes of the Court's decisions. A law review article cited as 47 *Harvard L. Rev.* 565 (1934), means that the article was published in 1934 and can be found on page 565 of volume 47 of the *Harvard Law Review*.

INTRODUCTION

page 9
Judicial questions, see A. de Tocqueville, *Democracy in America* (New York, 1946, first edition, 1835); R. McCloskey, *The American Supreme Court* (Chicago, 1960).

PROLOGUE

page 13
Frankfurter hearings, see R. Mersky and J. Jacobstein, eds., *The Supreme Court of the United States: Hearings and Reports on Successful and Unsuccessful Nominations of the Supreme Court Justices by the Senate Judiciary Committee, 1916–1975*, Vol. 4 (Buffalo, N.Y., 1977); background on hearings, *Baltimore Sun, New York Herald-Tribune, New York Times*, 1-12-39, 1-13-39; see also M. Josephson, "Profile: Jurist," *New Yorker*, 12-7-40.

page 13
"I suppose . . ." *Baltimore Sun*, 1-13-39.

page 13
Frankfurter's views on hearings, R. Mersky and J. Jacobstein, eds., *op. cit.,* pp. 107, 108.

page 14
"correspond to . . ." *ibid.,* p. 6.

page 14
"Christian government," *ibid.,* p. 100.

page 15
"I should think . . ." *ibid.,* p. 107.

page 15
Frankfurter's testimony before subcommittee, *ibid.,* pp. 107–128.

page 15
"somewhat droll interest," *ibid.,* p. 112.

page 15
"What has been . . ." *ibid.*

page 16
Stone on Black, P. Anderson, "Marquis Childs and Justice Black," *Nation,* 5-21-38; M. Childs, "The Supreme Court Today," *Harper's Magazine,* May 1938; M. Childs, *St. Louis Post-Dispatch,* 1-22-38; W. Hamilton, "Mr. Justice Black's First Year," *New Republic,* 6-8-38; A. Mason, *Harlan Fiske Stone: Pillar of the Law* (New York, 1956) pp. 468–476.

page 17
Frankfurter appointment's popularity, *New York Times,* 1-6-39.

page 17
"abhorrence of the second rate . . ." *New Republic,* 1-18-39.

page 17
"Frankfurter's whole life . . ." *Nation,* 1-14-39.

page 17
Gallup poll, *New York Times,* 9-23-38.

page 17
Lawrence opinion, *Washington Star,* 1-6-39.

page 18
"From every point . . ." *New York Herald-Tribune,* 1-6-39.

page 18
Frankfurter's joining "liberal" wing, *New York Times,* 1-6-39.

page 19
Hitler's address, *New York Herald-Tribune,* 1-31-39.

page 20
Frankfurter's swearing-in, *New York Times,* 1-31-39.

CHAPTER I

page 21
Frankfurter meeting with Feisal, J. Lash, *From the Diaries of Felix Frankfurter* (New York, 1975), p. 26; M. Parrish, *Felix Frankfurter and His Times: The Reform Years* (New York, 1982), p. 143; H. Phillips, ed., *Felix Frankfurter Reminisces* (New York, 1960), pp. 155, 156.

page 22
"I've done . . ." FF to Marion Denman, 5-9-19, Felix Frankfurter Papers, Library of Congress (FFPLC).

page 23
"the personal instrument . . ." H. Phillips, *op. cit.,* p. 161.

page 23
"In no time . . ." *ibid.*

page 23
"We Arabs . . ." J. Lash, *op. cit.,* p. 26.

page 24
General background on Frankfurter, L. Baker, *Felix Frankfurter* (New York, 1969); F. Frankfurter, *Law and Politics: Occasional Papers of Felix Frankfurter, 1913–1938,* ed. A. MacLeish and E. Prichard, Jr. (New York, 1939); H. Hirsch, *The Enigma of Felix Frankfurter* (New York, 1981); J. Lash, *op. cit.;* W. Mendelson, ed., *Felix Frankfurter: A Tribute* (New York, 1964); M. Parrish, *op. cit.;* H. Phillips, *op. cit.*

page 24
"This man . . ." H. Phillips, *op. cit.,* p. 4.

page 25
"There are two . . ." FF to MD, 4-29-19, FFPLC.

page 26
" . . . in me there . . ." H. Phillips, *op. cit.,* p. 5.

page 26
"Bryan was . . ." *ibid.,* p. 6.

page 27
Frankfurter's recitation and patriotism, M. Parrish, *op. cit.,* p. 14; R. Burt, *Two Jewish Justices: Outcasts in the Promised Land* (Berkeley, Calif., 1988); R. Danzig, "How Questions Begot Answers in Felix Frankfurter's First Flag Salute Opinion," in *Supreme Court Review* (Chicago, 1978).

page 28
"I shall never . . ." M. Parrish, *op. cit.,* p. 14.

page 28
"everything under . . ." H. Phillips, *op. cit.,* p. 11.

page 28
"speculative Russian intellectuals," M. Parrish, *op. cit.,* p. 15.

page 28
"I have always . . ." H. Phillips, *op. cit.,* p. 34.

page 29
"I don't agonize . . ." *ibid.,* p. 16.

page 29
"You go off . . ." *ibid.,* p. 32.

page 30
"The first day . . ." *ibid.,* p. 18.

page 30
"My god . . ." *ibid.*

page 30
Frankfurter's examination paper, W. Mendelson, *op. cit.,* p. 124.

page 30
"like a race horse . . ." H. Phillips, *op. cit.,* p. 18.

page 31
"In my day . . ." *ibid.,* p. 27.

page 31
"Giants they were . . ." *ibid.,* p. 24.

page 31
Ames in class, *ibid.,* p. 20.

page 31
Frankfurter "on clouds," *ibid.*

page 31
"What he left . . ." *ibid.*

page 32
"He was a theologian . . ." *ibid.,* p. 21.

page 32
"instilled in one . . ." *ibid.,* p. 22.

page 34
"a quasi-religious" feeling, *ibid.,* p. 19.

page 34
"If you believe . . ." *ibid.,* p. 24.

page 34
"Hold yourself dear . . ." M. Parrish, *op. cit.,* p. 12.

page 35
Frankfurter and Stimson, H. Phillips, *op. cit.,* pp. 38–49.

page 35
"the other fellow's . . ." *ibid.,* p. 42.

page 36
"a campaign speech . . ." *ibid.,* p. 50.

page 36
"Oh, if only . . ." *ibid.,* p. 55.

page 36
Frankfurter in Washington, *ibid.,* pp. 56–66; J. Lash, *op. cit.,* pp. 101–123; M. Parrish, *op. cit.,* pp. 39–61.

page 37
"Wickersham has . . ." J. Lash, *op. cit.,* p. 108.

page 37
House of Truth, H. Phillips, *op. cit.,* pp. 105–112; J. O'Connell and N. Dart, "The House of Truth: Home of the Young Frankfurter and Lippmann," 35 *Catholic University Law Review,* 79 (1985).

page 38
"patience, his magnanimity . . ." J. Lash, *op. cit.,* p. 104.

page 38
Frankfurter letter to Holmes, FF to OWH, 2-10-12, in H. Hirsch, *op. cit.,* pp. 32, 33.

page 39
Frankfurter's anxiety, H. Hirsch, *op. cit.,* p. 49.

page 39
"If facts are changing . . ." F. Frankfurter, *Law and Politics: Occasional Papers of Felix Frankfurter, 1913–1938,* eds. A. MacLeish and E. Prichard, *op. cit.,* pp. 3–9.

page 40
"The air I breathe . . ." FF to E. Buckner, 8-2-12, FFPLC.

page 40
"You have the greatest . . ." HS to FF, 6-28-13, FFPLC.

page 41
"in other people's . . ." FF to P. Miller, 3-11-13, FFPLC.

page 41
"I can't quite . . ." FF to E. Buckner, 1-6-12, FFPLC.

page 41
"I have decided . . ." FF to OWH, 9-6-13, in H. Hirsch, *op. cit.,* p. 41.

page 42
"intellectual hand-to-mouth," H. Phillips, *op. cit.,* p. 82.

page 42
"I like it lots," FF to MD, 10-14-14, FFPLC.

page 42
"You learn . . ." L. Baker, *op. cit.,* p. 13.

page 43
"I don't find . . ." HL to OWH, 11-17-16, in J. Lash, *op. cit.,* p. 16.

page 43
"We make of them . . ." *ibid.*

page 44
Frankfurter telegram to Chief Justice White, H. Phillips, *op. cit.,* p. 99.

page 44
Frankfurter meeting with White, *ibid.,* pp. 99–101.

page 45
Frankfurter and McReynolds, *ibid.,* pp. 101–103.

page 45
"Good for you!" *ibid.,* p. 102.

page 45
"He [Frankfurter] lectured . . ." *Nation,* 3-15-17.

page 46
"We were products . . ." H. Phillips, *op. cit.,* p. 123.

page 46
"Every time . . ." J. Lash, *op. cit.,* p. 174.

page 47
"War is fought . . ." M. Parrish, *op. cit.,* p. 99.

page 47
"Trotsky and . . ." TR to FF, 12-19-17, FFPLC.

page 47
"My knowledge . . ." H. Phillips, *op. cit.,* p. 147.

page 48
"little boy," FF to MD, 12-11-18, FFPLC.

page 49
"You are dearer . . ." FF to MD, 12-7-18, FFPLC.

page 49
"I shall never . . ." MD to FF, 2-15-19, FFPLC.

page 49
"Mother loved . . ." FF to MD, 6-21-17, FFPLC.

page 49
"You hit him . . ." FF to MD, 6-26-17, FFPLC.

page 50
"Do you know . . ." J. Lash, *op. cit.,* p. 30.

page 50
"Evidently . . ." FF to W. Lippmann, 1-13-19, FFPLC.

page 51
"What's this . . ." M. Parrish, *op. cit.,* p. 121.

page 51
"Why do . . ." H. Phillips, *op. cit.,* p. 175.

page 52
"You know . . ." M. Parrish, *op. cit.,* p. 122.

page 52
"the worst practices . . ." H. Phillips, *op. cit.,* p. 174.

page 52
FF advises Hillman, M. Parrish, *op. cit.,* pp. 124, 125.

page 53
FF endorsement of La Follette, F. Frankfurter, *Law and Politics, op. cit.,* p. 314.

page 54
Frankfurter on Sacco and Vanzetti case, F. Frankfurter, "The Case of Sacco and Vanzetti," *Atlantic Monthly,* March 1927; F. Frankfurter, *The Case of Sacco and Vanzetti* (Boston, 1927).

page 55
"that long-haired . . ." *M. Parrish, op. cit.,* p. 179.

page 55
"Did you see . . ." *ibid.*

page 57
"By systematic . . ." F. Frankfurter, *The Case of Sacco and Vanzetti, op. cit.,* p. 59.

page 57
"His 25,000-word . . ." *ibid.,* p. 104.

page 57
"Perfection may not . . ." *ibid.,* p. 108.

page 58
"incapable of seeing . . ." H. Phillips, *op. cit.,* p. 202.

page 58
"pulverized . . ." *ibid.,* p. 217.

page 58
"Wigmore is a fool . . ." *ibid.*

page 58
"Sacco gone . . ." *ibid.,* p. 39.

page 59
"Dear Franklin . . ." FF to FDR, 11-8-28, in M. Freedman, ed., *Roosevelt and Frankfurter: Their Correspondence, 1928–1945* (Boston, 1967), p. 39.

page 60
"Felix has more . . ." G. Tully, *FDR: My Boss* (New York, 1949), p. 140.

page 60
"You have vindicated . . ." FF to FDR, 1-17-30, in M. Freedman, *op. cit.,* p. 44.

page 60
"mobilize the will . . ." FF to FDR, 11-7-32, in M. Freedman, *op. cit.,* pp. 93, 94.

page 60
FDR's Cabinet, FF to FDR, 2-23-33, in M. Freedman, *op. cit.,* p. 108.

page 61
"some felicitous way . . ." *ibid.*

page 61
"You are . . ." FDR to FF, 4-5-33, in M. Freedman, *op. cit.,* p. 124.

page 61
"the most influential . . ." *ibid.,* p. 303.

page 62
"It was the most . . ." H. Phillips, *op. cit.,* p. 249.

page 63
"shock," FDR to FF, 1-15-37, in M. Freedman, *op. cit.,* p. 377.

page 63
"Dramatically and artistically . . ." FF to FDR, 2-7-37, in M. Freedman, *op. cit.,* pp. 380, 381.

page 64
"All I can say . . ." H. Phillips, *op. cit.,* p. 283.

page 64
"We were all . . ." H. Ickes, *The Secret Diary of Harold L. Ickes, 1936–1939* (New York, 1954), p. 559.

CHAPTER II

page 66
Kolb campaigns, V. Hamilton, *Hugo Black: The Alabama Years* (Baton Rouge, 1972), pp. 11–14.

page 66
General background on Black, H. Black and E. Black, *Mr. Justice and Mrs. Black: The Memoirs of Hugo L. Black and Elizabeth Black* (New York, 1986); H. Black, Jr., *My Father* (New York, 1975); H. Davis, *Uncle Hugo* (Amarillo, Tex., 1965); G. Dunne, *Hugo Black and the Judicial Revolution* (New York, 1977); J. Frank, *Mr. Justice Black* (Westport, Conn., 1948); V. Hamilton, *op. cit.;* C. Williams, *Hugo Black: A Study in the Judicial Process* (Baltimore, 1950); speeches and Alabama newspaper clippings in Hugo Black Papers, Library of Congress (HBP).

page 67
"who cherished . . ." Black speech, 3-20-26, HBP.

page 68
"Shall we return . . ." *ibid.*

page 68
Martha's marriage, H. Black, Jr., *op. cit.,* p. 4.

page 69
"moneylender," H. Davis, *op. cit.,* p. 34.

page 72
"Well, they didn't . . ." *Birmingham Age-Herald,* 1-31-37; for a slightly different version, H. Black and E. Black, *op. cit.,* p. 35.

page 72
"to the responsible . . ." undated newpaper clipping, HBP.

page 72
Mandy's stories, newspaper clippings, HBP.

page 72
"I am inclined . . ." *Birmingham Age-Herald,* 8-27-12.

page 74
Black's teaser ads, HBP.

page 75
"the man of the hour," *Birmingham News,* 8-12-16, 8-13-16.

page 76
"the most uncivilized . . ." *Birmingham Age-Herald,* 9-23-15.

page 76
"There are ways . . ." *ibid.*

page 77
"Hugo Black has left . . ." *Birmingham Ledger,* 3-1-17.

page 78
"the spirit and patriotism . . ." *Birmingham Age-Herald,* 12-18-18.

page 78
"in the little frame . . ." *Birmingham Age-Herald,* 5-14-22.

page 78
"The Dramatic Life . . ." V. Hamilton, *op. cit.,* p. 77.

page 78
Black's jury awards, J. Frank, *op. cit.,* p. 35; V. Hamilton, *op. cit.,* p. 76.

page 78
"Old Ego," H. Black, Jr., *op. cit.,* pp. 46, 47.

page 79
"Hugo could get . . ." *ibid.,* p. 48.

page 79
"That's not funny . . ." *ibid.,* p. 50.

page 80
Black's individuality and conformity, see S. Hackney, "The Clay County Origins of Mr. Justice Black," 36 *Alabama Law Review* 835 (1985).

page 80
Josephine's background, H. Black, Jr., *op. cit.,* pp. 37–43; scrapbooks, HBP.

page 80
"She just seemed . . ." H. Black, Jr., *op. cit.,* pp. 39, 40.

page 81
"I had never . . ." *ibid.,* p. 40.

page 81
"If I have . . ." *ibid.*

page 81
Stephenson case, *ibid.,* p. 52; V. Hamilton, *op. cit.,* pp. 92, 111, 112.

page 82
U.S. Supreme Court case, V. Hamilton, *op. cit.,* p. 111; Mobile case, *ibid.,* pp. 98–100, 109, 110.

page 82
"engaged in bona fide bootlegging," *ibid.,* p. 109.

page 83
Black and KKK, *ibid.,* pp. 89–100; J. M. Thornton III, "Hugo Black and the Golden Age," 36 *Alabama Law Review* 899 (1985).

page 84
"I would introduce . . ." H. Black, Jr., *op. cit.,* p. 59.

page 84
Black campaign materials, HBP.

page 84
"I am personally . . ." HB to M. Pittman, 12-30-25, HBP.

page 85
Black campaign schedule, HBP.

page 85
"I ask . . ." *Cleburne* (Alabama) *News,* 3-25-26.

page 85
"there is not . . ." *Anniston* (Alabama) *Star,* 7-30-26.

page 85
"you have those Bankheads," T. Goodwin to HB, 7-3-26, HBP.

page 85
"I agree . . ." HB to T. Goodwin, 7-9-26, HBP.

page 85
"a line of royal succession," *Birmingham News,* 7-8-26.

page 86
"the closing . . ." *Birmingham Post,* 7-31-26.

page 86
Criticism of A. Smith, *New York Times,* 8-9-26.

page 86
"There are times . . ." *Birmingham News Age-Herald,* 1-31-37

page 86
Black before Klan, V. Hamilton, *op. cit.,* pp. 136–139.

page 87
Josephine in Washington, *Newsweek,* 3-14-36; V. Hamilton, *op. cit.,* p. 158.

page 87
New Senators, *New York Times,* 12-12-26.

page 87
Black's early Senate days, Alabama newspaper clippings, HBP; *New York Times,* 7-10-30.

page 88
"Let the Senator . . ." *Congressional Record,* 70th Congress, pp. 8687–91.

page 88
"When the farmer . . ." *Congressional Record,* 70th Congress, pp. 4189–90.

page 90
Black's thinking on maximum workweek, J. Frank, *op. cit.,* p. 89.

page 90
FDR's assurance, FDR to HB, 6-24-33, Franklin D. Roosevelt Papers, Hyde Park, N.Y. (FDRP).

page 90
Black's Senate investigations, G. Dunne, *op. cit.,* pp. 51–62; J. Frank, *op. cit.,* pp. 63–94; V. Hamilton, *op. cit.,* pp. 222–259; C. Williams, *op. cit.,* pp. 52–67.

page 92
"If you had not . . ." *New Republic,* 4-11-34.

page 92
"The chairman . . ." V. Hamilton, *op cit.,* p. 230.

page 94
"We intend . . ." *New York Times,* 8-16-35.

page 95
"gasping and indignant," *ibid.*

page 95
"My impression . . ." confidential source.

page 95
"there is no . . ." *Vital Speeches,* 9-1-37.

page 96
"Millions of people . . ." HB to FDR, 10-18-36, FDRP.

page 96
"You are the unquestioned . . ." HB to FDR, August (undated) 1932, FDRP.

page 96
"It was the French King . . ." *New York Herald-Tribune,* 2-6-37.

page 97
"Neither the people . . ." 2-23-37, in *Vital Speeches,* 9-1-37, pp. 674–677.

page 97
Sprigle articles, *Pittsburgh Post-Gazette,* 9-15-37 through 9-18-37.

page 98
Black radio address, *New York Times,* 10-2-37.

page 98
"The effort . . ." *New York Herald-Tribune,* 10-2-37.

page 98
"It was a grand . . ." J. Farley, *Jim Farley's Story* (New York, 1948), p. 108.

page 98
"and the humility . . ." FF to C. Burlingham, 9-9-37, FFPLC.

page 99
"Do you know . . ." HFS to FF, 2-8-38, in A. Mason, *op. cit.,* p. 469.

page 99
"I used to say . . ." *ibid.,* p. 470.

page 99
"She is altogether . . ." FF to FDR, 5-18-38, in M. Freedman, *op. cit.,* p. 457.

page 99
"Various experiences . . ." *ibid.*

page 99
"I took the bull . . ." *ibid.*

page 100
"I have high hopes . . ." *ibid.*

CHAPTER III

page 101
Background on Childs, Stone and Black episode, P. Anderson, *op. cit.;* M. Childs, "The Supreme Court Today," *op. cit.;* M. Childs, *St. Louis Post-Dispatch, op. cit.;* W. Hamilton, *op. cit.;* A. Mason, *op. cit.,* pp. 468–476.

page 102
Indianapolis Water Company decision, *McCart v. Indianapolis Water Co.,* 302 U.S. 419 (1938).

page 102
"Wherever the question . . ." *McCart* at p. 428.

page 103
Stone's speculation on Black opinion, A. Mason, *op. cit.,* p. 468.

page 103
Black's dissent in *Connecticut General Life Insurance Co. v. Johnson,* 303 U.S. 77 (1938) at p. 87.

page 104
"The *Post-Dispatch* . . ." *St. Louis Post-Dispatch,* 1-22-38.

page 104
"Just what is needed . . ." A. Mason, *op. cit.,* pp. 472, 473.

page 105
"I am calling . . ." *ibid.,* p. 474.

page 105
"did not remotely . . ." IB to HB, 5-10-38, in A. Mason, *op. cit.,* p. 475.

page 105
"I can assure . . ." HB to IB, 5-20-38, in A. Mason, *op. cit.,* p. 476.

page 105
Stone visit at White House, in A. Mason, *op. cit.,* p. 482.

page 106
Alpaca coat story, J. Lash, *op. cit.,* p. 66.

page 106
Minersville School District v. Gobitis, 310 U.S. 586 (1940); background on case, A. Barth, *Prophets with Honor* (New York, 1974); J. Garraty, ed., *Quarrels That Have Shaped the Constitution* (New York, 1962); J. Simon, *Independent Journey: The Life of William O. Douglas* (New York, 1980).

page 107
"Our beloved flag . . ." *Gobitis v. Minersville School District,* 21 F. Supp. 581, 585 (1937).

page 109
"I can express . . ." J. Lash, *op. cit.,* p. 68.

page 109
Frankfurter whistling, author's interview with P. Elman, 10-9-86, Washington, D.C.

page 109
"how much . . ." M. Freedman, *op. cit.,* p. 744.

page 109
Frankfurter's patriotism, R. Burt, *op. cit.,* R. Danzig, *op. cit.*

page 109
"I come . . ." J. Howard, Jr., *Mr. Justice Murphy: A Political Biography* (Princeton, N.J., 1968), p. 287.

page 110
"because of Frankfurter's moving . . ." J. Lash, *op. cit.,* p. 69.

page 110
"I am not happy . . ." FF to HFS, 5-27-40, Felix Frankfurter Papers, Harvard Law School (FFPHLS).

page 111
"I am truly . . ." HFS to FF, undated, FFPHLS.

page 111
"You have accomplished . . ." CEH to FF, handwritten note on Frankfurter draft opinion, FFPHLS.

page 111
"This is a powerful . . ." WOD to FF, undated, FFPHLS.

page 111
"this has been . . ." FM to FF, 6-3-40, FFPHLS.

page 111
Prichard story, author's interview with J. Rauh, Jr., 5-16-86, Washington, D.C.

page 112
"History teaches . . ." 310 U.S. 586 at 604.

page 112
"This seems . . ." 310 U.S. 586 at 606.

page 112
Frankfurter opinion, 310 U.S. 586 at 591.

page 112
"When a liberal . . ." J. Garraty, *op. cit.,* p. 235.

page 113
"I want to tell . . ." A. Mason, *op. cit.,* p. 531.

page 113
Frankfurters at Hyde Park, J. Lash, *op. cit.,* p. 70.

page 113
Attacks on Witnesses, J. Garraty, *op. cit.*

page 113
"We think . . ." *St. Louis Post-Dispatch,* 6-4-40.

page 114
"didn't like . . ." FF notes referring to HB visit to FF's chambers, 6-1-40, undated, FFPHLS.

page 115
"Hugo thinks . . ." H. Hirsch, *op. cit.,* p. 152.

page 115
Jones v. Opelika, 316 U.S. 584 (1942) at 623.

page 116
"the Axis," J. Lash, *op. cit.,* pp. 76, 197.

page 116
"a solid phalanx," *ibid.,* p. 176.

page 116
"hunting in packs," *ibid.*

page 116
"ominous situation . . ." *ibid.*

page 116
"a harangue . . ." *ibid.,* p. 174.

page 116
"the most systematic . . ." *ibid.,* p. 175.

page 116
"My dear Rutledge . . ." FF to WR, 1-10-43, FFPHLS.

page 117
Rutledge's view of Black, author's interview with P. Freund, 7-20-83, Cambridge, Mass.

page 117
Leva view, author's interview with M. Leva, 5-15-86, Washington, D.C.

page 117
"I thought that . . ." author's interview with M. Isenbergh, 5-14-86, Washington, D.C.

page 117
W. Virginia Bd. of Education v. Barnette, 319 U.S. 624 (1943).

page 118
"I have to . . ." author's interview with P. Elman; see also Frankfurter's notes for *Barnette* opinion, 5-25-43, FFPLC; Black's notes for *Barnette,* 5-25-43, FFPLC.

page 118
"Phil," author's interview with P. Elman.

page 118
"One who belongs . . ." 319 U.S. 624 at 646.

page 119
"unfit foreigners," *Congressional Record,* 71st Congress, pp. 4678–80.

page 119
"I am so firmly . . ." Black speech, 10-11-29, *ibid.*

page 120
Black's reading, author's interview with P. Freund.

page 120
Cox v. New Hampshire, 312 U.S. 569 (1941); see also M. Silverstein, *Constitutional Faiths: Felix Frankfurter, Hugo Black, and the Process of Judicial Decision Making* (Ithaca, N.Y., 1984), pp. 174–206.

page 120
Hughes's suggested modifier, CEH to FF, 3-28-41, FFPHLS.

page 121
"Why, of course . . ." FF to CEH, 3-28-41, FFPHLS.

page 121
Bridges v. California, 314 U.S. 252 (1941); background on *Bridges* case, A. Lewis, "Justice Black and the First Amendment," 38 Alabama Law Review 289 (1987); M. Silverstein, *op. cit.;* J. Simon, *op. cit.; Bridges* drafts and notes in HBP.

page 122
"Probation for . . ." 314 U.S. 252 at 271.

page 122
Frankfurter draft majority opinion, undated, HBP.

page 123
Black draft dissent, 7-17-41, HBP.

page 123
"He [Frankfurter] says first . . ." Black notes, HBP.

page 124
"The still-new robe . . ." J. Howard, Jr., *op. cit.,* p. 263.

page 124
"That's a very . . ." H. Hirsch, *op. cit.,* p. 158.

page 125
Black discussion with Isenbergh, author's interview with M. Isenbergh.

page 125
"No purpose . . ." 314 U.S. 252 at 265.

page 125
Frankfurter's criticism of Black's use of Holmes's test, FF to O. Roberts, 5-26-43, FFPHLS.

page 126
"Our whole history . . ." 314 U.S. 252 at 279.

page 126
"What you have . . ." JB to FF, undated, 1941, FFPHLS.

page 126
"beautifully done . . ." SR to FF, undated, 1941, FFPHLS.

page 128
Frankfurter's 1938 lecture, F. Frankfurter, *Mr. Justice Holmes and the Supreme Court* (Cambridge, Mass., 1938), pp. 74–87.

CHAPTER IV

page 130
Frankfurter-Murphy conversation, J. Lash, *op. cit.,* pp. 154, 155.

page 131
Background on Frankfurter's behind-the-scenes activities, M. Freedman, *op. cit.;* J. Lash, *op. cit.;* B. Murphy, *The Brandeis/Frankfurter Connection* (New York, 1982); M. Parrish, *op. cit.;* author's interview with J. Rauh, Jr.

page 132
"click," FF to FDR, 6-4-40, in M. Freedman, *op. cit.,* pp. 524, 525.

page 132
"his mind . . ." *ibid.*

page 132
"favors the forces . . ." *ibid.,* p. 500.

page 133
"Everything . . ." author's interview with P. Elman.

page 134
"Dear Frank . . ." FF to FDR, 12-7-41, in M. Freedman, *op. cit.,* p. 625.

page 135
"Marion has given . . ." FF to FDR, 9-12-41, in M. Freedman, *op. cit.,* p. 617.

page 135
"Dearest," FF to MDF, 1-16-40, FFPLC.

page 136
"It's awful . . ." FF to MDF, 11-27-44, FFPLC.

page 136
"This is another . . ." FF to MDF, 12-20-44, FFPLC.

page 136
Hugo on Josephine's qualities, H. Black, Jr., *op. cit.,* p. 40.

page 136
Background on Marion and Felix, J. Lash, *op. cit.;* H. Hirsch, *op. cit.;* M. Parrish, *op. cit.;* author's interviews with P. Elman, P. Freund, M. Isenbergh and J. Rauh, Jr.

page 136
Background on Josephine's unhappiness, H. Black, Jr., *op. cit.;* Josephine's correspondence and notes in HBP; author's interview with M. Leva.

page 137
"I am . . ." author's interview with M. Isenbergh.

page 137
"a mental invalid," *ibid.*

page 138
"She was . . ." *ibid.*

page 138
"Never have . . ." J. Black to A. Foster, undated, 1929, HBP.

page 138
"I hope . . ." H. Black to J. Cooper, 6-11-52, in J. Cooper, *"Sincerely Your Friend . . .": Letters of Mr. Justice Hugo Black to Jerome A. Cooper* (Tuscaloosa, Ala., 1973).

page 139
Josephine's pleas, scrapbooks, HBP.

page 139
"loved her much . . ." HB to JB, 11-12-41, HBP.

page 139
"All you have . . ." H. Black, Jr., *op. cit.,* p. 170.

page 139
"You will be . . ." HB to JB, 10-23-41, HBP.

page 140
"He was . . ." author's interview with J. Black Pesaresi, 6-28-83, New York.

page 140
"My father . . ." H. Black, Jr.'s, remarks at Conference on Justice Hugo L. Black and the Constitution, 1937–1971, Tuscaloosa, Ala., 3-18-86.

page 141
"I caused him . . ." H. Black, Jr., *op. cit.,* p. 92.

page 141
"Why do you . . ." *ibid.*

page 141
"This story," *ibid.,* p. 91.

page 142
"I hope . . ." HB, Jr., to JB, 2-21-38, HBP.

page 142
"In the first . . ." *ibid.*

page 143
"Mom said . . ." HB, Jr., to HB, undated, HBP.

page 143
"Daddy, do not . . ." HB, Jr., to HB, 7-12-42, HBP.

page 143
"She simply . . ." *ibid.*

page 143
"mastered the . . ." HB, Jr., to HB, undated, HBP.

page 144
Martin v. Struthers, 319 U.S. 141 (1943).

page 144
"I thought . . ." HB, Jr., to HB, 5-10-43, HBP.

page 144
"Ringing doorbells . . ." *ibid.*

page 144
"Also I did not . . ." *ibid.*

page 145
"The best way . . ." HB to HB, Jr., 8-4-43, HBP.

page 145
"However bad . . ." HB to HB, Jr., 8-10-43, HBP.

page 145
"Daddy, today . . ." HB, Jr., to HB, undated, HBP.

page 145
"I stammered . . ." *ibid.*

page 146
"You at least . . ." HB to HB, Jr., 12-23-43, HBP.

page 146
"So long . . ." *ibid.*

page 147
"We have gone . . ." HB to JB, 12-8-41, HBP.

page 147
"I think . . ." HB to HB, Jr., 11-30-43, HBP.

page 147
"a hardboiled . . ." HB to SB, 11-6-43, HBP.

page 148
Hirabayashi case, *Hirabayashi v. U.S.,* 320 U.S. 81 (1943); *Korematsu v. U.S.,* 323 U.S. 214 (1944); background on the cases, *Hirabayashi* and *Korematsu* folders in FFPHLS and HBP; W. O. Douglas conference notes, William O. Douglas Papers, Library of Congress (WODP); J. Howard, *op cit.;* P. Irons, *Justice at War* (New York, 1983); A. Mason, *op. cit.;* J. Simon, *op. cit.*

page 149
Stone in conference, P. Irons, *op. cit.,* pp. 227–234.

page 149
"grave damage," *ibid.,* p. 234.

page 149
"evils that attend . . ." *ibid.,* p. 235.

page 150
"encouraged their . . ." *ibid.,* p. 237.

page 150
"Is it not . . ." *ibid.*

page 150
"cheap oratory," J. Lash, *op. cit.,* p. 251.

page 151
"This is so . . ." P. Irons, *op. cit.,* p. 244.

page 151
Frankfurter's memo to F. Murphy, *ibid.,* p. 246.

page 153
"I stop . . ." *ibid.,* p. 322.

page 153
"I am ready . . ." FF to HB, 11-9-44, FFPHLS.

page 154
"approximate Lenin's . . ." P. Irons, *op. cit.,* p. 332.

page 154
"The Court . . ." *ibid.,* p. 332.

page 154
"because we are . . ." *Korematsu* at p. 223.

page 155
Commentary on Court decisions, see, for example, E. Rostow, "The Japanese-American Cases—A Disaster," 54 *Yale L. J.* 489 (1945).

page 155
"There's a difference . . ." G. Dunne, *op. cit.,* p. 213.

CHAPTER V

page 157
Background on Nuremberg, *Trial of the Major War Criminals Before the International Military Tribunal,* Volumes 2 and 9 (Nuremberg, 1947); W. Maser, *Nuremberg, A Nation on Trial* (New York, 1977); H. and J. Tusa, *The Nuremberg Trial* (New York, 1983); R. Jackson, *Report to the President on the International Conference on Military Trials,* Document LXIII.

page 158
"flushed with victory . . ." *Trial of the Major War Criminals Before the International Military Tribunal,* Volume 2, p. 99.

page 158
"Jackson is away . . ." A. Mason, *op. cit.,* p. 716.

page 158
Roberts's views of colleagues, OR to FF, 2-21-45 and 7-16-45, FFPHLS.

page 159
"vehemence" and "ruthlessness," OR to FF, 10-12-44, FFPHLS.

page 159
"fidelity to principle," HFS to Brethren, undated, FFPHLS; HFS to FF, 7-15-45, FFPHLS; FF to HFS, 8-25-45, FFPHLS; FF to Brethren, 8-30-45, FFPHLS; FF notes on Stone draft, FFPHLS; FF to HFS, 8-31-45, FFPHLS; RJ to HFS, 9-8-45, FFPHLS.

page 159
Background on Court division, G. Dunne, *op. cit.;* J. Howard, Jr., *op. cit.;* A. Mason, *op. cit.;* Frankfurter correspondence, FFPHLS.

page 159
"Attended Mary Acheson's . . ." J. Lash, *op. cit.,* pp. 173, 174.

page 160
Background on *Jewell Ridge* case, *Jewell Ridge Coal Corp. v. Local No. 6167,* 325 U.S. 897 (1945); G. Dunne, *op. cit.;* J. Frank, *op. cit.;* E. Gerhart, *America's Advocate: Robert H. Jackson* (Indianapolis, 1958); J. Howard, *op. cit.;* A. Mason, *op. cit.;* Frankfurter correspondence, FFPHLS.

page 160
"If the dissent . . ." A. Mason, *op. cit.,* p. 642.

page 161
"a declaration of war," E. Gerhart, *op. cit.,* pp. 262, 263.

page 161
"had no share . . ." FF to HB, 6-9-45, FFPHLS; see also Frankfurter's support for RJ, FF to RJ, 6-8-45, 6-9-45, FFPHLS.

page 162
"slowly," A. and J. Tusa, *op. cit.,* p. 150.

page 162
Jackson examination of Goering, *Trial of the Major War Criminals Before the International Military Tribunal,* Volume 9, pp. 418–571.

page 165
"There was . . ." J. Simon, *op. cit.,* p. 279.

page 165
"by the gong," A. and J. Tusa, *op. cit.,* p. 280.

page 165
Frankfurter-Jackson correspondence, RJ to FF, 1-25-46, FF to RJ, 2-6-46, RJ to FF, 4-28-46, FF to RJ, 5-11-46, FFPHLS.

page 166
Frankfurter's support for Stone, A. Mason, *op. cit.,* pp. 566, 567.

page 166
Fleeson article, *Washington Star,* 5-16-46; background on Vinson nomination and Jackson outburst, A. Mason, *op. cit.;* J. Howard, *op. cit.,* J. Frank, *op. cit.;* G. Dunne, *op. cit.*

page 167
Jackson's statement, *Stars and Stripes,* 6-13-46, in FFPHLS.

page 167
Newspaper reaction to Jackson attack, *U.S. News,* 6-21-46.

page 168
"I suppose . . ." FF to RJ, 6-12-46, FFPHLS.

page 168
"whether this is . . ." RJ to FF, 6-19-46, FFPHLS.

page 169
"Don't get . . ." author's interview with Judge Louis Oberdorfer, 5-13-86, Washington, D.C.; confirmed in author's interview with John Frank, 5-20-87, Washington, D.C.

page 169
Black's denial, author's interview with Justice William J. Brennan, Jr., 9-23-83, Washington, D.C.

page 169
Black's response to attack, *Newsweek,* 6-24-46.

page 169
"Four years later . . ." R. Allen and W. Shannon, *The Truman Merry-Go-Round* (New York, 1950). Frankfurter's denial, FF to HB, 9-30-50, FFPHLS.

page 169
Black's response, HB to FF, 10-2-50, HBP.

page 169
Black's remark to his son, author's interview with Hugo Black, Jr., 7-30-83, Atlanta, Ga.; Black's view confirmed in author's interview with Justice Brennan.

page 170
"Having been endowed . . ." FF to FM, 6-10-46, FFPHLS.

page 170
"Good morning . . ." G. Dunne, *op. cit.,* p. 241.

page 170
"The way Vinson . . ." Lash, *op. cit.,* p. 274.

page 171
"has appeared . . ." *ibid.,* p. 283.

page 171
"let loose . . ." *ibid.*

page 171
Hamilton's phrase, *The Federalist,* No. 78.

page 172
"No one has . . ." Black speech, Congressional Record, 83rd Congress, p. 1294.

page 172
Frankfurter's position on due process, FF to HB, 10-31-39, FF to HB, 11-13-43, FFPHLS.

page 172
Black's position on due process, Black's notes on due process, HBP.

page 173
Palko v. Connecticut, 302 U.S. 319 (1937).

page 173
"James Madison . . ." *Adamson v. California,* 332 U.S. 46 (1946) at p. 74.

page 174
"Once you go . . ." FF to HB, 11-13-43, FFPHLS.

page 175
"I am truly . . ." *ibid.*

page 175
Frankfurter concurring opinion in *Malinski v. New York,* 324 U.S. 401 (1945) at 414.

page 175
"This [Frankfurter's opinion] seems to me . . ." HB to Conference, 3-23-45, FFPHLS.

page 176
Adamson case, *Adamson;* see also P. Kurland and G. Casper, eds., *Landmark Briefs and Arguments of the Supreme Court of the United States,* Vol. 45 (Arlington, Va., 1975).

page 177
"twenty or fifty horses," P. Kurland and G. Casper, *op. cit.,* p. 543.

page 177
Frankfurter's views in *Adamson,* notes in WODP and FFPHLS, see also M. Silverstein, *op. cit.,* pp. 165, 166.

page 177
Twining v. New Jersey, 211 U.S. 78 (1908).

page 178
Black's preparation, Black's notes and drafts, in *Adamson* folder, HBP.

page 178
"I cannot consider . . ." *Adamson* at p. 89.

page 179
"shocked the conscience," *Rochin v. California,* 342 U.S. 165 (1952) at p. 172.

page 179
Frankfurter on Fourth Amendment, J. Rauh, Jr., "Felix Frankfurter: Civil Libertarian," 11 *Harvard Civil Rights–Civil Liberties Law Review* 496 (1976).

page 179
Black on the Fourth Amendment, G. Dunne, *op. cit.,* pp. 270–273; S. Strickland, ed., *Hugo Black and the Supreme Court* (Indianapolis, 1967), pp. 106–109.

page 180
Everson v. Board of Education, 330 U.S. 1 (1947); background on *Everson,* J. Howard, Jr., *op. cit.;* J. Lash, *op cit.;* Frankfurter correspondence in FFPHLS; Black correspondence in HBP.

page 181
"Dear Frank," FF to FM, 2-10-47, FFPHLS.

page 181
Black's drafts, *Everson* folder, HBP.

page 181
"must be kept . . ." *Everson* at p. 18.

page 181
"to utter noble . . ." J. Lash, *op. cit.,* p. 343.

page 182
" 'I will ne'er . . .' " *Everson* at p. 19.

page 182
"I cannot . . ." *Everson* at p. 29.

page 182
McCollum v. Board of Education, 333 U.S. 203 (1947).

page 182
Frankfurter's strategy, FF to R. Jackson, 1-6-48, FFPHLS; H. Burton to FF and HB, 2-7-48, HBP.

page 182
"I have just . . ." HB to Conference, 2-11-48, HBP; see also HB to W. Rutledge and H. Burton, 2-12-48, HBP.

page 183
Frankfurter's reaction, FF to H. Burton, 2-11-48, FF to R. Jackson, 2-12-48, FFPHLS.

page 183
"Burton is one . . ." J. Lash, *op. cit.,* p. 343.

CHAPTER VI

page 184
Background on Douglas, W. Douglas, *Go East, Young Man* (New York, 1974); J. Simon, *op. cit.*

page 184
"We never felt . . ." J. Simon, *op. cit.,* p. 27.

page 185
"Treasure," *ibid.,* p. 20.

page 185
"Others may have . . ." *ibid.,* p. 68.

page 186
"I was hardly . . ." *ibid.,* p. 7.

page 188
"I am bound . . ." FF to WOD, 12-2-41, FFPLC.

page 188
"what you are . . ." FF to WOD, 12-20-40, FFPLC.

page 188
"the two . . ." J. Simon, *op. cit.,* p. 218.

page 189
"I am sorry . . ." WOD to HB, 6-22-41, HBP.

page 189
"I said . . ." *ibid.*

page 189
"He [FDR] wants . . ." WOD to HB, 9-8-41, HBP.

page 190
"I am quite . . ." *ibid.*

page 190
"The prospect . . ." HB to WOD, 9-15-41, WODP.

page 190
"I have not seen . . ." WOD to HB, 9-20-41, HBP.

page 191
"more active," WOD to HB, 7-23-49, HBP.

page 192
"I myself . . ." JB to HB, Jr., undated but probably January 1945, HBP.

page 192
"your mother is . . ." HB to HB, Jr., 9-9-51, HBP.

page 192
"She ought to . . ." H. Black, Jr., *op. cit.,* p. 179.

page 193
"My thoughts . . ." HT to HB, 12-8-51, HBP.

page 193
"Dear Hugo . . ." FF to HB, 12-11-51, HBP.

page 194
" . . . he has . . ." draft of Frank review, HBP.

page 194
"I am compelled . . ." HB to JF, 2-28-50, HBP.

page 195
"Number One . . ." FBI memo to Director, 6-6-50, FBI files.

page 195
MacArthur's opinion of Frankfurter, J. Kelly to J. Hoover, 4-9-54, FBI files.

page 195
"It is felt . . ." FBI memo to Director, 3-23-50, FBI files.

page 195
"involved a serious . . ." D. Ladd to A. Belmont, 8-19-52, FBI files.

page 196
"go thoroughly . . ." *ibid.*

page 197
"If Communists . . ." M. Jahoda and S. Cook, "Security Measures and Freedom of Thought," 61 *Yale L.J.* 295, 307 (1952).

page 197
"It is hard . . ." FF to RJ, 10-8-51, FFPHLS.

page 197
Sacher et al. v. U.S., 343 U.S. 1 (1952).

page 198
"I repeat . . ." FF to RJ, 10-8-51, FFPHLS.

page 198
"There is . . ." FF to RJ, 11-13-53, FFPHLS.

page 198
"radiate examples . . ." FF to RJ, 2-27-52, FFPHLS.

page 198
Dennis v. U.S., 341 U.S. 494 (1951).

page 199
FF was appalled, FF Memorandum for Conference, 2-27-51, WODP.

page 199
"Those wanting . . ." WOD Conference notes, 12-9-50, WODP.

page 200
"History teaches," *Dennis* at p. 525.

page 200
"armed internal attack," Black comments on Vinson draft opinion, HBP.

page 200
"Now puts . . ." *ibid.*

page 200
"The goblin'll . . ." *ibid.*

page 201
"miserable merchants . . ." *Dennis* at p. 589.

page 201
"Public opinion . . ." *Dennis* at p. 581.

page 201
Feinberg Law challenge, *Adler v. Bd. of Education,* 342 U.S. 485 (1952); see also W. O. Douglas Conference notes, WODP.

page 201
"retain their beliefs . . ." *Adler* at p. 492.

page 201
"considerable satisfaction," FF to HB, 6-16-52, HBP.

page 202
Zorach v. Clauson, 343 U.S. 306 (1952).

page 202
"obtuse reasoning," FF to HB, 3-5-52, FFPHLS.

page 202
"As you probably . . ." HB to JF, 11-26-52, HBP.

page 202
"rest on our oars," FF to HB, 6-16-52, HBP.

page 203
Background on Court review of Rosenberg case, see M. Parrish, "Cold War Justice: The Supreme Court and the Rosenbergs," 82 *American Historical Review* 805 (Oct. 1977); J. Simon, *op. cit.,* pp. 299–313; for a different view, W. Cohen, "Justice Douglas and the Rosenberg Case: Setting the Record Straight," 70 *Cornell L.R.* 211 (1985).

page 204
Frankfurter's notes on Court deliberations in Rosenberg case, Rosenberg Memorandum, FFPHLS; Rosenberg Memorandum Addendum, 6-19-53, FFPHLS.

page 205
"My brethren . . ." Frankfurter memorandum for Conference, 5-20-53, HBP.

page 205
"who are as . . ." *ibid.*

page 205
"open hearing," *ibid.*

page 206
"Let it take . . ." Burton Conference notes, Harold Burton Papers, Library of Congress.

page 207
"The fact is that . . ." page proofs in *Rosenberg v. U.S.,* 346 U.S. 273 (1953), FFPHLS.

page 207
"We think . . ." *Rosenberg* at p. 289.

page 207
"It is not amiss . . ." *Rosenberg* at p. 301.

page 207
"To be writing . . ." *ibid.*

CHAPTER VII

page 209
Myrdal on Southern liberals, G. Myrdal, *An American Dilemma: The Negro Problem and Modern Democracy* (New York, 1944), pp. 466–473.

page 209
"really influential . . ." *ibid.,* p. 469.

page 209
Black's ambivalence, author's telephone interview with Jerome "Buddy" Cooper, 3-21-88.

page 209
"Anglo-Saxon courage," S. Strickland, *op. cit.,* p. 76.

page 210
Black's advice to women students, V. Hamilton, *op. cit.,* p. 212.

page 210
Chambers v. Florida, 309 U.S. 227 (1940).

page 210
"From virtually . . ." *Chambers* at p. 240.

page 211
Japanese-American exclusion case, *Korematsu v. U.S.,* 323 U.S. 214 (1944).

page 211
White primary case, *Smith v. Allwright,* 321 U.S. 649 (1944).

page 211
Restrictive covenant case, *Shelley v. Kraemer,* 334 U.S. 1 (1948).

page 211
Graduate education case, *Sipuel v. Oklahoma State Board of Regents,* 332 U.S. 631 (1948).

page 212
"our Moses," J. Garraty, *op. cit.,* p. 251.

page 213
Frankfurter article, "Can the Supreme Court Guarantee Toleration?" *New Republic,* 6-17-25.

page 213
Plessy v. Ferguson, 163 U.S. 537 (1896).

page 214
"Thank God . . ." J. Garraty, *op. cit.,* p. 248.

page 214
"The treatment . . ." G. Myrdal, *op. cit.,* p. 1020.

page 214
"They [Americans] stand . . ." *ibid.,* p. 1021.

page 215
"Those racial . . ." J. Garraty, *op. cit.,* p. 254.

page 215
Background on NAACP litigation culminating in *Brown v. Bd. of Education,* R. Kluger, *Simple Justice* (New York, 1976); see also J. Garraty, *op. cit.,* pp. 243–268.

page 215
McLaurin v. Oklahoma, 339 U.S. 637 (1950).

page 216
Sweatt v. Painter, 339 U.S. 629 (1950).

page 216
"You may find . . ." FF to HB, 4-11-(undated, probably 1950), HBP.

page 216
Frankfurter and Black in conference, D. Hutchinson, "Unanimity and Desegregation: Decision making in the Supreme Court, 1948–1958," 68 *Georgetown L.J.* 1 (1979).

page 217
"should not go . . ." H. Burton Conference notes, 4-8-50, Harold Burton Papers, Library of Congress.

page 217
"This is written . . ." HB to FV, 5-18-50, in D. Hutchinson, *op. cit.,* p. 27.

page 218
Vinson in *Brown, ibid.,* pp. 36, 37.

page 218
"If the 'great . . .' " FF to LH, in R. Kluger, *op. cit.,* p. 603.

page 219
Briggs v. Elliott, 347 U.S. 497 (1954); background on *Briggs,* R. Kluger, *op. cit.*

page 219
Frankfurter and Bickel in *Brown, ibid.,* pp. 614, 615.

page 220
"Today [in 1987] no Justice . . ." author's interview with P. Elman, 11-19-87, Washington, D.C.; see also P. Elman, "The Solicitor General's Office, Justice Frankfurter, and Civil Rights Litigation, 1946–1960: An Oral History," 100 *Harvard L.R.* 817 (1987).

page 220
Frankfurter on Vinson's death, R. Kluger, *op. cit.,* p. 656.

page 221
"He brings to . . ." FF to O. Gates, 10-29-53, FFPLC.

page 221
"They [the Justices] will soon . . ." D. Vann at Black Conference, 3-17-86, Tuscaloosa, Ala.

page 221
"Dear Hugo: Marion . . ." FF to HB, 7-10-53, HBP.

page 222
"going to take . . ." HB to FF, 7-16-53, HBP.

page 222
"is a very attractive . . ." HB to HB, Jr., and SB, 10-15-53, HBP.

page 222
"Dear Hugo: This . . ." FF to HB, 10-8-53, HBP.

page 223
Background on Black's and Frankfurter's relationship with Earl Warren, B. Schwartz, *Super Chief: Earl Warren and His Supreme Court—A Judicial Biography* (New York, 1983); E. Warren, *The Memoirs of Earl Warren* (New York, 1977); G. White, *Earl Warren: A Public Life* (New York, 1982).

page 223
Black's recommendation to Warren, D. Vann, "Confessions of the Law Clerks," 2-27-66 (celebrating Black's eightieth birthday).

page 223
Brown v. Board of Education, 347 U.S. 483 (1954).

page 223
"Separate educational . . ." *Brown* at p. 495.

page 223
"It was an . . ." FF to HB, 6-12-54, HBP.

page 224
"the great fertility . . ." FF to EW, 7-5-54, FFPHLS.

page 224
"with all deliberate . . ." *Brown v. Board of Education,* 249 U.S. 394 (1955) at p. 301.

page 225
"if humanly possible," Frankfurter Conference notes, 4-16-55, FFPLC.

page 225
"How proud . . ." J. Patterson to HB, 5-18-54, HBP.

page 225
"YOU ARE . . ." H. Turner, Jr., to HB, 5-20-54, HBP.

page 225
"taking a positive . . ." J. Shelbourne to HB, 5-23-54, HBP.

page 225
HB–HB, Jr., correspondence after *Brown,* HB, Jr., to HB, 5-23-54, HB, Jr., to HB, 11-28-54, HB to HB, Jr., 12-1-54, HBP.

page 226
"this integration thing," HB, Jr., to HB, 8-18-57, HBP.

page 226
Black's response, HB to HB, Jr., 8-21-57, HBP.

page 226
Alabama gubernatorial candidate, HB, Jr., to HB, 8-18-57, HBP.

page 226
Frankfurter on Eisenhower, FF to Dean Acheson, undated, 1958, Dean Acheson Papers, Yale University, New Haven, Conn. (DAP).

page 227
"the unconstitutional decision . . ." B. Schwartz, *op. cit.,* p. 289.

page 227
"There was . . ." E. Warren, *op. cit.,* p. 298.

page 227
Cooper v. Aaron, 358 U.S. 1 (1958); background on *Cooper,* P. Kurland and G. Casper, eds., *Landmark Briefs and Arguments of the Supreme Court of the United States:* Vol. 54 (Arlington, Va., 1975); see also B. Schwartz, *op. cit.,* pp. 289–303; D. Hutchinson, *op. cit.,* pp. 73–86.

page 228
Oral argument, P. Kurland and G. Casper, *op. cit.*

page 229
"is placed between . . ." *ibid.,* p. 685.

page 229
"showed a good deal . . ." FF to EW, 9-11-58, FFPLC.

page 229
"My own view . . ." *ibid.*

page 229
"Of course . . ." FF to JH, 9-2-58, FFPHLS.

page 230
Warren suspected Frankfurter, author's telephone interview with Prof. Harry Wellington, 10-17-88.

page 230
"We knew . . ." author's interview with Justice Brennan, 11-17-87, Washington, D.C.*

page 230
Brennan drafts, W. J. Brennan, Jr., Papers, Library of Congress (WJBP).

page 231
"Mr. Justice Frankfurter . . ." E. Warren, *op. cit.,* p. 298.

page 231
"As this case . . ." Brennan draft, WJBP.

page 232
"Dear Bill . . ." *ibid.*

page 232
Justices' shock, author's interview with Justice Brennan.

page 232
"an audience . . ." FF to C. Burlingham, 11-12-58, FFPLC.

page 232
"caused quite . . ." E. Warren, *op. cit.*

page 232
"Felix was . . ." author's interview with Justice Brennan.

page 232
"that it is . . ." J. Harlan concurrence, 10-6-58, WJBP.

page 232
Brennan's comments on Frankfurter draft, WJBP.

page 233
Frankfurter as Warren's enemy, G. White, *op. cit.,* p. 183.

CHAPTER VIII

page 235
Frankfurter on aging, FF to LH, 10-25-56, FFPLC.

page 235
"bagged," *ibid.*

page 235
"It would . . ." *ibid.*

---

* This was the second of two interviews with Justice Brennan. The first occurred on 9-23-83.

page 235
"I looked . . ." author's interview with Justice Brennan, 9-23-83, Washington, D.C.

page 236
"After I came . . ." *ibid.*

page 236
Watkins case, *Watkins v. U.S.,* 354 U.S. 178 (1957).

page 237
"I do not . . ." FF to WB, 4-10-57, FFPHLS; "that such lawyers . . ." HB to HB, Jr., 10-26-56, HBP.

page 237
arson case, *In re Groban,* 352 U.S. 330 (1956).

page 237
Trop case, *Trop v. Dulles,* 356 U.S. 86 (1958).

page 238
"We [Frankfurter and Brennan] really . . ." author's interview with Justice Brennan.

page 238
"When Felix . . ." *ibid.*

page 238
"I wish he . . ." FF to JH, undated, 1957, John M. Harlan Papers, Princeton University, Princeton, N.J. (JMHP).

page 238
"Hugo would sneer . . ." author's interview with Justice Brennan.

page 239
Frankfurter's debate with Harlan, FF to JMH, 7-6-56, JMH to FF, 7-12-56, FF to JMH, 7-18-56, JMH to FF, 7-28-56, FF to JMH, 7-31-56, FFPHLS.

page 240
"For members . . ." FF to JMH, undated, probably 1958, JMHP.

page 240
"There was . . ." author's interview with Justice Brennan.

page 241
"Red Monday . . ." J. Simon, *In His Own Image: The Supreme Court in Richard Nixon's America* (New York, 1973), p. 34.

page 241
Barenblatt v. U.S., 360 U.S. 109 (1959).

page 242
"The provisions . . ." *Barenblatt* at p. 134.

page 242
"by humiliation . . ." *Barenblatt* at p. 153.

page 242
"This [balancing] is . . ." *Barenblatt* at p. 143.

page 242
"For many years . . ." HB to EC, 7-8-59, HBP.

page 243
Drafts of Black's Madison Lecture, HBP.

page 243
"Some people . . ." Madison Lecture, HBP, reprinted in 35 *NYULR* 865 (1960).

page 244
Bickel's attack on Black, "Mr. Justice Black: The Unobvious Meaning of Plain Words," *New Republic,* 3-14-60.

page 244
"Yours [Bickel's] was . . ." Rodell letter to *New Republic,* undated, HBP.

page 244
"I must confess . . ." HB to FR, 3-29-60, HBP.

page 244
L. Levy, *Legacy of Suppression: Freedom of Speech and Press in Early American History* (New York, 1960).

page 245
E. Cahn review of Levy book, *New York Herald-Tribune,* 10-16-60.

page 245
"my opinion is . . ." draft of Black letter, HB to EC, 10-19-60, HBP.

page 245
"The book . . ." HB to EC, 10-24-60, HBP.

page 245
"sincere but . . ." EC to HB, 10-25-60, HBP.

page 245
Black response, HB to EC, 10-26-60, HBP.

page 246
"brains, rectitude . . ." J. Simon, *In His Own Image, op. cit.,* p. 216.

page 246
Mapp v. Ohio, 367 U.S. 643 (1961).

page 246
Baker v. Carr, 369 U.S. 186 (1962).

page 246
Earlier dissents, *Adamson; Colegrove v. Green,* 328 U.S. 549 (1946).

page 248
"political thicket," *Colegrove* at p. 556.

page 248
Background on Justices in *Baker,* W. O. Douglas Conference notes, WODP.

page 249
"I was courted . . ." author's interview with Justice Stewart, 9-23-83, Washington, D.C.

page 249
"I shall . . ." FF to LH, 10-29-58, FFPLC.

page 249
"I have every . . ." FF to LH, 7-10-60, FFPLC.

page 250
"I believe . . ." FF to PS and CW, 10-11-61, JMHP.

page 250
"Felix fought . . ." author's interview with Justice Brennan.

page 250
Brennan's draft opinion, WJBP.

page 250
Brennan's memorandum to HB, EW and WD, 1-27-62, WJBP.

page 251
"[T]here is not . . ." *Baker* at p. 270.

page 251
"What power . . ." FF to JMH, 3-5-62, JMHP.

page 251
Frankfurter meeting with Kennedy, 7-26-62, reported by Dean Acheson, DAP.

page 254
"I am certain . . ." HB to HB, Jr., 8-10-62, HBP.

page 254
"very moving," author's interview with J. Black Pesaresi.

page 254
"To retain . . ." FF to JFK, 8-28-62, HBP.

page 254
"The scuttlebutt . . ." WOD to HB, 7-27-(undated, probably 1960), HBP.

page 255
"I can assure . . ." FF to AB, 3-18-63, FFPLC.

page 255
"Your piece . . ." *ibid.*

page 256
"Goldberg, the scholar," FF to AB, 11-14-62, FFPLC.

page 256
"He really . . ." G. Dunne, *op. cit.,* p. 372.

page 256
"So perceptive . . ." FF to HB, 5-7-63, HBP.

page 257
Trespass decision, *Bell v. Maryland,* 378 U.S. 226 (1964).

page 257
"none of our . . ." *Bell* at p. 325.

page 257
"I am not . . ." FF to HB, 12-15-64, HBP.

page 258
"Dear Felix . . ." HB to FF, 12-22-64, HBP.

page 258
"we're going . . ." confirmed in Black letter to F. Friendly, 2-7-63, HBP.

page 260
"Ohhh, Felix is . . ." H. and E. Black, *op. cit.,* p. 102.

Index

Photo Credits

About the Author

JAMES F. SIMON received a B.A. from Yale College and a law degree from the Yale Law School. He has served as correspondent and contributing editor of *Time* magazine, specializing in legal affairs. He is the author of *The Judge; In His Own Image: The Supreme Court in Richard Nixon's America;* and *Independent Journey: The Life of William O. Douglas. In His Own Image* won the American Bar Association's Silver Gavel Award in 1974. *Independent Journey* won the Scribes Award of the American Society of Writers on Legal Subjects in 1981. Simon has been a Visiting Lecturer in American Studies at Yale University and a Harvard Fellow in Law and the Humanities at Harvard University. He is Dean and Professor of Law at New York Law School.